Under Fire and Fury

CW01426111

Under Fire and Fury

This is a work of historical fiction. While it draws on real events, locations, and figures from the Second World War, the story, characters, and dialogue have been fictionalised for dramatic effect. Any resemblance to actual persons, living or dead, other than clearly referenced historical individuals, is purely coincidental.

ISBN: 978-1-0681502-0-3

Interior formatting by the author & Sage Proofreading and Copyediting Services

Copyediting and proofreading by Lorraine Sage

Sage Proofreading and Copyediting Services – info@sageproof.co.uk

First Edition

© Richard A. Basquill 2025

richardabasquill.com

Published by Basquill Books

BASQUILL
BOOKS

Acknowledgments

Writing books has been a lifelong dream of mine, and after completing my first novel, *Under Fire, Under Command*, I discovered that it's far from a solitary endeavour. This second book would not have been possible without the support and encouragement of many people.

To my friends and family, thank you for your unwavering support throughout this journey. Your interest, insights, and encouragement have been a constant source of motivation, especially as I set out to write this second novel.

To Sue, my wonderful wife, your endless love and understanding, your patience with my late-night writing sessions, and your unshakable belief in me have kept me going when I needed it most. I also must thank you for being my first ever sale, even if it was made with my own bank card. Love you!

To my editor, Lorraine Sage of Sage Proofreading and Copyediting Services, thank you for your sharp eye, honest critique, and genuine passion for the story. Your expertise and dedication helped shape this book into something far stronger than I could have achieved alone.

And finally, to the readers — thank you for choosing to spend time with these pages. It's your imagination and curiosity that bring these words to life, and I'm truly grateful for every moment you spend in this world I've created.

Maps

The following maps are artistic interpretations intended to support the reader's understanding of the story. While based on contemporary geography and wartime records, they have been deliberately simplified to emphasise narrative clarity over cartographic precision.

Dunkerque and Western Flanders

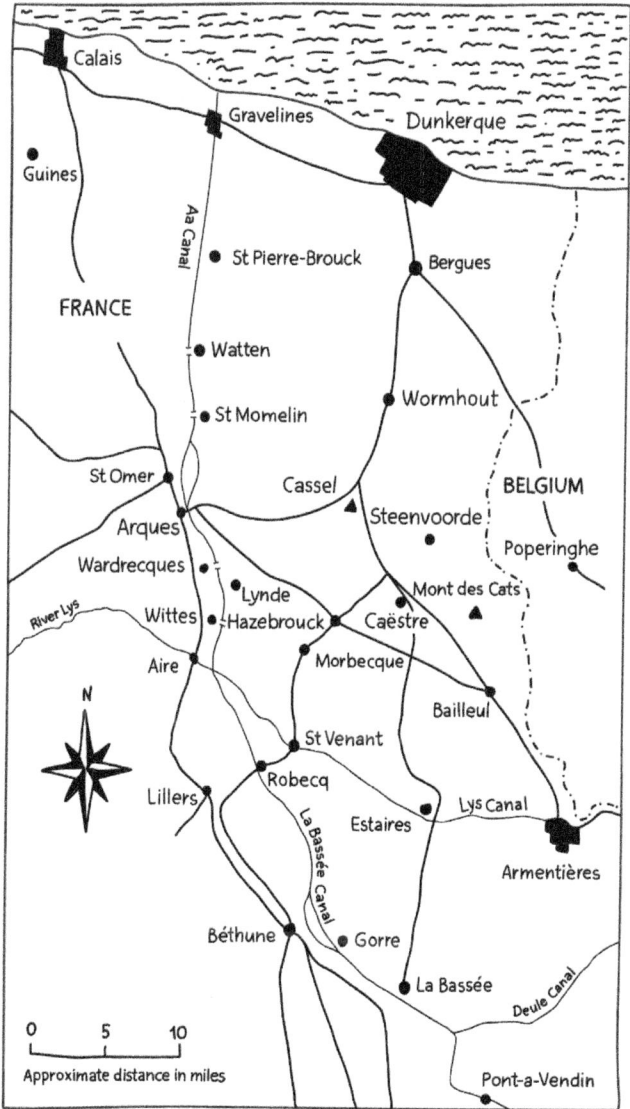

Calais

Gravelines

Dunkerque

Guines

Aa Canal

St Pierre-Brouck

Bergues

FRANCE

Watten

Wormhout

St Momelin

St Omer

Cassel

BELGIUM

Arques

Steenvoorde

Poperinghe

Wardrecques

Lynde

Mont des Cats

Wittes

Hazebrouck

Caëstre

River Lys

Aire

Morbecque

Bailleul

N

St Venant

Robecq

Lillers

Estaires

Lys Canal

La Bassée Canal

Armentières

Béthune

Gorre

La Bassée

Deule Canal

0   5   10

Approximate distance in miles

Pont-a-Vendin

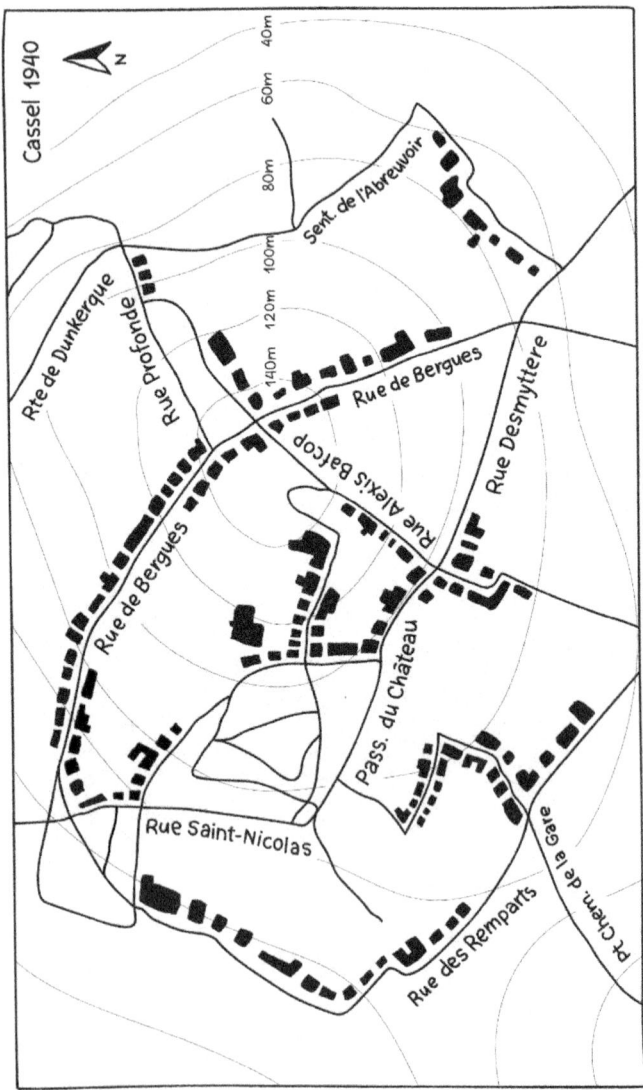

Cassel 1940

N

Rte de Dunkerque

Rue Profonde

Sent. de l'Abreuvoir

40m
60m
80m
100m
120m
140m

Rue de Bergues

Rue de Bergues

Rue Alexis Balcop

Rue Desmyttere

Pass. du Château

Rue Saint-Nicolas

Rue des Remparts

Pt Chem. de la Gare

Foreword

By late May 1940, the British Expeditionary Force (BEF) found itself in a desperate struggle for survival. Less than three weeks earlier, on May 10, Germany had launched Fall Gelb: the invasion of France and the Low Countries. Utilising a bold and unanticipated thrust through the Ardennes, the Wehrmacht bypassed the heavily fortified Maginot Line and shattered French defences at Sedan. The German Blitzkrieg, a devastating combination of rapid armoured advances and concentrated air support, tore through Belgium and northern France, leaving the BEF, along with their French and Belgian allies, in a perilous position.

By May 20, German Panzers had reached the Channel coast at Abbeville, cutting off the bulk of the BEF from the rest of the French Army. General Lord Gort, commander of the BEF, recognised the impending disaster and, despite French pleas for a counterattack, began shifting his forces towards the coast for evacuation. The only option for escape was the small port of Dunkirk.

Retreating across northern France, the BEF's condition deteriorated. Many units had been fighting continuously for over a week, forced into a chaotic withdrawal under the constant attack from German aircraft, artillery and advancing infantry. Supply lines collapsed, food and ammunition dwindled, and some battalions had been reduced to a fraction of their original strength. Yet, despite these conditions, the BEF continued to fight, attempting to slow the German advance and buy precious time for the evacuation.

As part of this delaying action, British forces—including elements of Somerforce which was a composite unit hastily formed from remnants of different battalions—were ordered to hold key towns along the retreat corridor. Cassel, Wormhoudt, and Hazebrouck became crucial defensive positions, with British units fighting to the last round in an effort to stall the German onslaught.

By May 25, the BEF was in full retreat. Units that had once been part of a well-coordinated army were now disjointed, scattered and improvising their movements. Stragglers from shattered battalions banded together in the countryside, some trying to reach Dunkirk, others simply trying to survive. Officers found themselves commanding men they had never met before, forming ad hoc groups to navigate the rapidly shrinking corridor to the coast. The situation was desperate: roads were choked with abandoned vehicles, bridges had been destroyed, and German patrols roamed unchecked, hunting down isolated British troops.

It is in this world—one of crumbling defences, exhausted men, and last stands—that 2nd Lieutenant Archer and the remnants of 6th Platoon find themselves. They are not merely retreating; they are fighting for every mile, every hour, in a battle against overwhelming odds. Their mission is simple yet impossible: hold the line just long enough for those who could still escape to reach Dunkirk.

Chapter 1

Archer ducked under the low doorway of the old schoolhouse, the air inside stale with sweat and smoke. The room was dimly lit, a single oil lamp casting flickering shadows over the maps and field orders strewn across a battered desk. Captain Pembroke looked up from his notes, his face drawn but breaking into a faint smile when he saw Archer. "Tom," Pembroke said, waving him closer. "You're looking better than I expected after what you've been through."

"Morning, Sir," Archer replied, his voice heavy with exhaustion. "Six hours of rest will do that. What's the situation?"

Pembroke gestured for him to sit on a rickety chair near the desk. He leaned forwards, his tone softening. "First things first. Hargroves is gone. Artillery strike yesterday morning. Ellis has taken over the battalion. It's...been a rough 24 hours."

Archer absorbed the news with a tightening in his chest. Hargroves had been a steady hand, and his loss left a hole that felt larger than just the chain of command. He let out a slow breath. "How's Ellis holding up?"

Pembroke rubbed a hand over his stubble, his eyes briefly dropping to the map on the desk. "He's doing his best, but you know how it is. Taking over in the middle of all this—it's a thankless job. He's steady though, and he's doing what he can, same as the rest of us."

Pembroke continued, "but the battalion's taken a beating. We're spread thin, morale's shaky, and Jerry's massing for another push." He tapped a hand on a hand sketched map, drawing Archer's attention to a cluster of markings.

Archer reached into his battledress pocket, feeling the familiar weight of the flask Pembroke had given him back in Armentières some three weeks ago. He pulled it out, unscrewed the cap, and offered it across the desk. "Here, and how you holding up?"

Pembroke's eyes lit up briefly with a glimmer of humour.

"I'm good. You still carrying this thing around?" Pembroke hesitated for only a moment before taking the flask and raising it slightly in a quiet toast.

"To Hargroves," he said, his voice softening. He took a measured sip, letting the warmth spread through him before handing it back.

"And to the poor bastards holding the line," Archer raised the flask and returned the flask to his pocket. The gesture was small, but it seemed to lift a fraction of the weight hanging over the room.

Archer leaning towards the desk, his jaw tightening. "What's the latest?"

Pembroke leaned back, his voice dropping lower. "Situation's dire. Ellis has us stretched across these positions, but if Jerry breaks through here, it's a clear road to Cassel's centre. The chapel's one of the last defensible spots on this flank. They'll hit it hard—and soon."

He paused, running a hand over the map.

"The orders from brigade are clear, Tom. We're to hold the line—last man, last round. There's no fallback, no reinforcement. We're buying time for the lads heading to Dunkirk, and that means every minute we hold, matters."

Archer exhaled slowly, the weight of the words pressing on him. He already knew the stakes, but hearing them spoken aloud, made them feel heavier—more real. Hold the line to the last man, the last round. The words weren't new to him, but their finality settled on his shoulders like a stone. He thought of his men—Mallory, Jacks, Matthews, and the others—men who had trusted him through hell and back. How many of them would be standing when the last round was spent?

Pembroke, his face grim, turned back to the map, tapping a thick, smudged pencil against the marked positions. "Right, listen up. You're moving into the chapel and cottages here," he said, tracing the defensive line with the pencil. "That flank is critical, and if Jerry gets through it, we'll lose the whole eastern side of the town. Battalion's thin as it is—this position's got to hold.

"You're taking 6th Platoon in to reinforce the position. You'll also take on what's left of 8th Platoon—they've been chewed up, down to about twenty men. Their officer didn't make it, and Sergeant Wilkins has been holding things together." Pembroke paused, his sharp eyes settling on Archer. "What about your lot? How's 6th Platoon holding up?"

"Well, as of this morning, we're fourteen, including myself, Sir," Archer replied, his tone grim but steady. "We lost six during the mission. One wounded—he's been evacuated."

Pembroke frowned, his jaw tightening as he processed the numbers. "Bloody hell, Tom. Six. That's a hell of a price." Archer held Pembroke's gaze; his voice was quiet but resolute. "We've had hard days, Sir. No different to anyone else." His expression hardened as he straightened. "But the men are ready. They'll do what's asked of them." Pembroke studied him for a moment longer, his expression unreadable, before nodding and turning back to the map. The weight of their conversation lingered for a beat, but when he spoke again, his tone had shifted—brisk, measured, and all business.

"Right. Artillery support is available, but there are restrictions." He tapped the map again, tracing the defensive positions. "We've got a battery of 25-pounders covering the area, but they're stretched. We can't waste shells—we're running low as it is. Priority targets only." He pointed to the chapel, his voice firm. "Ellis has the final say on all artillery requests. There's a field phone set up at the chapel—it connects directly to me here, and up to Battalion HQ. You need something, you call me first, and I'll push it up the chain. But don't expect miracles." Pembroke looked back at Archer with a sharp expression.

"What's your ammo situation?"

Archer hesitated, "Er, not great. We're running low, Sir. Maybe thirty rounds per rifle on average, two Bren magazines for each of the Brens. We scrounged what we could through the night, but it's not much."

Pembroke's lips pressed into a thin line, and he let out a heavy breath. "It's better than I expected, but it won't last if Jerry pushes hard. I'm pretty sure they will, Tom. That chapel is key, and they know it."

"We'll stretch it," Archer said simply, his voice was steady, trying to absorb the information as its being relayed. "What about Jerry's movements?"

Pembroke sighed, rolling the pencil between his fingers. "They've been probing us all night, feeling for weak spots. You can expect more of that today—machine-gun fire, mortars, and probably a heavier push during the day. If they bring armour, well..." He trailed off for a beat before continuing. "Let's just hope they don't." Pembroke gave a grim smile. "The bigger picture is survival, if we're lucky. Brigade's relying on Cassel to keep Jerry bottled up as long as we can. It's the linchpin of the withdrawal. Lose this, and we lose the corridor to Dunkirk. That's why we're stretched so thin—we're holding the bloody door open for everyone else to get through." Archer's gaze drifted to the map, his eyes tracing the thin lines marking their defensive positions. "And if we don't?"

"Then the Channel's full of Tommies who didn't make it," Pembroke replied bluntly. "But let's not think that far ahead, eh?" Archer nodded firmly.

"Understood, Sir." With that, Archer turned to leave. "Good luck, Tom!" Pembroke called out.

To which Archer responded. "Good luck to you too, Sir." He turned for the doorway, the shifting light playing over the maps and papers, making them ripple with a ghostly unease.

Outside, the night loomed, heavy and waiting. Archer

approached the platoon who were gathered along an old brick wall of the schoolhouse. He called Mallory, Jacks, and Wilson over. "Here's the situation," he began quietly, his voice low but firm. "We're reinforcing 8th Platoon at the chapel. They're chewed up, down to twenty or so men. Wilkins is holding them together, but morale's shaky, and Jerry's massing for a push. We're low on ammo, artillery's restricted, and there's no fallback."

Mallory's jaw tightened, his eyes narrowing as he processed the words. "Wilkins, you say?" he muttered, a faint note of familiarity breaking through. "Stubborn bastard—he'll be holding that lot together with spit and curses."

Archer gave a curt nod. "Then let's make sure he doesn't have to do it alone."

Jacks frowned. "No fallback? What?"

Archer cut him off, his voice firm but calm. "Last round. Last man." The words hung heavy in the air. All four men exchanged a look, the full weight of the order settling over them as they tried to digest what it meant. Archer left the NCOs and walked over to Matthews, pulling him aside. "Matthews," Archer began quietly, his tone firm but not unkind. "You've done a hell of a job so far, but there's no need for your...particular set of skills now. I want you to get out—make your way to Dunkirk."

Matthews' face darkened, and he shook his head sharply. "Not a chance, Sir. You think I'm leaving you lot here?"

Archer's gaze held steady, his voice dropping lower. "Corporal, we've had orders to stand to the last. This is no longer your fight. I want you to get out. Get home."

"Sir!" Matthews snapped, his voice rising slightly before he caught himself. "I've fought alongside you and these men more than once, and I'm not going to turn my back now. Not when it matters most."

For a moment, Archer just stared at him, the pride he felt

9

for the man surging through him like a charge of electricity. Words felt inadequate. Instead, he reached out and gripped Matthews' shoulder firmly. "Thank you," Archer said quietly, the two simple words carrying all he couldn't express.

The first hints of dawn crept over the horizon as Archer led 6th Platoon towards the chapel. The sky was a muted grey, streaks of pale light clawing through the lingering darkness. The air felt heavy, carrying the acrid tang of smoke and cordite, the remains of yesterday's bombardment. Each step brought them closer to the battered remains of the Norman chapel, its once-proud stone walls now pockmarked and fractured from shellfire.

The land around it bore the scars of war. Craters marred the earth like festering wounds, pools of stagnant water shimmering faintly in the dim light. The remnants of a stone cottage slumped to one side, its roof collapsed, and blackened beams still smouldering faintly as if reluctant to admit defeat. Scattered debris littered the ground—spent casings, torn uniforms, and the shattered, broken furniture that had been dragged from homes to fortify defences.

Archer's eyes flicked to the chapel itself as it came into view. Its bell tower, though still standing, had lost half its height, jagged edges reaching skyward like broken fingers. The stained-glass windows were gone, replaced by gaping holes that offered fleeting glimpses of movement inside—Wilkins' men preparing for whatever the morning might bring. Nearby, trenches had been hastily dug, their earthen sides sagging from rain and overuse, while makeshift barricades of sandbags and wooden carts formed a defensive perimeter around the stone buildings.

The air was unnaturally still, save for the distant crackle of small-arms fire and the occasional rumble of artillery far to the east. It was the kind of silence that hung like a shroud, unnatural and waiting to be broken. Archer tightened his grip on his rifle. "Steady now," he murmured, the men behind him moving like shadows among the ruins, bracing for the inevitable storm.

As they approached the battered perimeter, Archer scanned the trenches and barricades. Movement stirred from within the chapel—shapes of men, tired but determined, huddled behind the crumbling walls.

"Looks like Wilkins has been busy," Mallory murmured beside him, his eyes sweeping over the makeshift defences.

Archer nodded, his gaze hard. "Let's see what we're walking into."

As they reached the edge of the chapel's perimeter, Archer spotted a figure rising from one of the trenches—a broad-shouldered man with a stocky build, his uniform caked in dirt and sweat. Sergeant Wilkins. Wilkins climbed out of the trench with a tired grunt, helmet slanted to the back of his head. His face was lined with exhaustion, but his sharp gaze remained steady as it landed on Archer and Mallory.

"Lieutenant," he said simply, giving Archer a nod of acknowledgement. His voice was hoarse, worn thin by shouting orders and the dust of the trenches.

"Wilkins," Archer replied, matching his tone. Wilkins turned briefly to Mallory, a flicker of recognition breaking through his weariness.

"Mallory."

"Wilkins," Mallory returned with a curt nod, his expression tight but familiar. "Still holding the fort, then?"

"Still breathing, if that counts," Wilkins replied, a hint of dry humour creeping in before his face settled back into its hardened lines. "And you? I half expected to find you laid up by now."

Mallory snorted faintly. "You know me better than that."

Archer stepped into the conversation, "Sergeant, what's the situation?" Wilkins let out a quiet grunt before turning his attention back to Archer. "Last count this morning, we are twenty men. They're exhausted but who ain't." He gestured vaguely toward the chapel and surrounding defences. "We've been shoring up where we can, but Jerry's been probing us since last light. It won't hold much longer without help." Wilkins ran a hand over his stubbled jaw, his eyes flicking to the chapel and the rough perimeter beyond.

Mallory glanced at the trenches and makeshift barricades—sandbags sagging, craters gaping open in the earth, and the shattered fragments of a stone wall. "Looks like you've had a time of it," he said gruffly.

Wilkins shrugged, the movement stiff. "You can say that but we're still here, aren't we?"

Wilkins led the way, gesturing towards the stone wall as they moved along the perimeter. "This is the main line," he said, his voice hoarse but steady. "The wall runs most of the way around the chapel, but as you can see," he pointed to a gaping hole where jagged stones crumbled into the earth. "It's not what it used to be. That's where they've been testing us, probing for weaknesses. The lads have been doing their best to patch it, but we're stretched thin."

He paused at a section of the wall reinforced with sandbags and broken beams, gesturing towards the far edge of the position. "7th Platoon is dug in over there, about fifty yards along that line." He pointed towards a cluster of craters and rough barricades. "They're holding the western approach. Not much better off than us, but they've got decent sightlines across the fields. Lost the platoon sergeant yesterday."

Mallory responded obviously knowing the man "Campbell?" Wilkins said nothing but just nodded to confirm.

Wilkins moved further along, pointing towards a shallow trench that connected to the rear of the chapel. "Headquarters' platoon's just behind us, tucked into those trees near the old schoolhouse. They're the fallback point if things really go south, but we're not supposed to count on that."

"What about the other companies?" Archer asked, scanning the horizon as the faint light of dawn crept over the landscape.

"A Company's on the northern side of the town, near the main road. They've been taking the brunt of it—Jerry's been hitting them with everything they've got. If they hold, it'll be a bloody miracle." Wilkins' voice dipped slightly, a note of concern creeping in. "B Company's spread thin along the southern perimeter. Last I heard, they were holding, but they've had to pull back twice already. As for C Company, they're covering the western flank near the hill. It's quieter over there for now, but if Jerry tries to swing around, they'll be the first to know."

Wilkins stopped, turning back to Archer with a grim look. "It's a patchwork, Sir. Everyone's just holding on by their fingernails, but this chapel? It's the keystone. If we lose it, the whole eastern side collapses, and Jerry will roll straight into Cassel." The sergeant continued, leading Archer towards the rubble of a nearby cottage. "Like I said, we've got the Vickers on the left flank, covering the lane. The Brens are split between the gaps in the wall and the flanks. Ammo's thin, but we've made every shot count so far."

"And the barbed wire?" Archer asked, his eyes flicking to the faint glint of wire strung haphazardly across the front of their position. "It's not much, but it slows them down enough for us to get a shot off." Wilkins sighed, running a hand over his stubbled jaw. "That's the picture, Sir. A patchwork and prayers, but we're still standing."

Archer absorbed the information, his gaze drifting over the battered landscape. Trenches dotted randomly through the torn earth, craters yawned open between them, and here and there, helmets caught the rising light—faint markers of men dug in and running thin. He clenched his jaw.

Archer crouched near the wall, running a hand along the jagged edge of a shell-blasted section. His sharp eyes scanned the terrain beyond—churned earth, broken trees, and twisted strands of barbed wire strung irregularly in the distance. The rise leading to the chapel gave them the advantage of high ground, but it also made them a clear target.

"What's your ammunition status?" Archer asked, his tone steady but sharp.

Wilkins replied grimly, "Twenty rounds per man if we stretch it, three full belts—750 rounds—for the Vickers. The Brens are down to three mags each, maybe less. We've been stripping rounds off the lads who... won't need them anymore."

Archer turned to Mallory; his voice was low but firm. "Alright, here's how we set it up. This wall is our anchor—Wilkins' lads have done what they can, but we'll reinforce it. Get the boys digging shallow trenches along this line, about twenty feet apart. We'll need overlapping fields of fire."

Archer glanced towards the rubble of the cottages. "Drop one of the Brens. We don't have enough ammo for four. Put one here, covering this gap in the wall—it'll work with the Vickers to create a crossfire. If Jerry pushes straight up the rise, they'll be caught between the two." He continued, his tone decisive. "Get Pritchard up in what's left of the bell tower. Best shot we've got—he can pick off their officers and NCOs before they reach us." Wilkins, standing nearby, exchanged a brief glance with Mallory, a flicker of approval crossing his face. This officer knew what he was doing.

Archer straightened, his gaze sweeping over the rise again. "They'll hit us head-on, no question. The high ground makes it hard for them to manoeuvre, but it also means they'll throw everything at us to take it. Mortars, machine-guns, the lot. If we hold here though, we can bleed them dry before they get close. If we can get them in a bottleneck, we make life extremely unpleasant for them."

The lieutenant continued, his tone measured but firm. He pointed towards the left flank, where the remainder of a stone cottage sat crumbling against the edge of the line. "Position two riflemen and a Bren team there. They'll have a good line of sight to anything moving near those trees. That spot's exposed, so make sure they dig in properly and keep their heads down."

He turned his attention to the right, where the gaps in the wall created vulnerabilities. "Get a section to dig in along those gaps," Archer said firmly. "Use rubble, sandbags—whatever you can find to shore them up. Make sure the men stay low and keep their positions tight. If Jerry tries to force his way through, we'll need to make every shot count."

Wilkins gestured towards the Vickers. "The machine-gun's our strongest point, but if they hit us with a heavy push, it'll be the first thing they target."

Archer nodded, his gaze drifting to the well-dug emplacement where the Vickers rested, its barrel angled down the lane. "You're right—they'll try to take it out fast. But with the Bren covering the left and the riflemen dug in along the wall, we'll add layers of fire to that position. If they push hard, the crossfire will break their momentum before they can get close enough to overwhelm it."

Wilkins tilted his head, his brow furrowing slightly as he considered the adjustments. "And if they send armour?"

"We'll adapt," Archer replied, his tone steady, "and hope we can get the artillery in."

Archer continued. "The rise gives us the advantage. Their vehicles will be slower coming up, and the machine-gun will have time to focus its fire on any infantry support. If we hold the line long enough, Jerry will have to rethink their approach."

Wilkins grunted; his face still set with concern. "It's about buying time," Archer said firmly. "We don't need to stop them cold—just slow them enough to hold this flank." As the words left his mouth, Archer felt the weight of their reality pressing down on him. Buying time. It sounded simple, even logical, but he knew what it truly meant—holding this battered stretch of ground against a force far better equipped, and unrelenting in its advance. The rise gave them an edge, but it also made them a glaring target. The thought of mortars raining down, and of tanks grinding their way up the slope, filled his mind with images of men caught in the open, scrambling for cover that didn't exist.

He shifted his stance, his gaze sweeping over the battered landscape. The chapel's crumbling walls and the sagging trenches offered little reassurance. This wasn't a fortress—it was a patchwork defence held together by determination and desperation. His men were good, capable, but they were tired, low on ammo, and stretched thin. How long could they realistically hold?

Archer forced the thoughts aside, tightening his grip on his rifle. This wasn't the time for doubt. "We'll make them pay for every inch," he said quietly, almost to himself, before turning his attention back to Wilkins.

"Let's get everyone in place. We'll dig in, reinforce where we can, and be ready when they come," he added, his voice steady despite the storm building in his mind.

Wilkins' expression was tight as he absorbed the plan. Without a word, he adjusted his helmet and glanced once more at the battered rise beyond the wall "I'll get the lads sorted," he said, his tone resolute but low, almost under his breath. He shifted his rifle in his hand and strode towards the nearest group of men, his silhouette blending into the gritty haze of the morning light. The air hung heavy, the quiet unnerving, as Archer watched him go. Mallory stepped up beside him, his face set and unreadable. "He's a solid one," Mallory said. "Knows what's coming, though."

"So do we," Archer replied quietly, his gaze fixed on the jagged horizon. Mallory lingered a moment, his gaze fixed on the horizon where the first streaks of daylight painted the sky.

Archer scanned the rising ground, his jaw tightening as he took in the battered defences and the churned earth beyond. The silence felt unnatural, oppressive, as if the entire battlefield was holding its breath. His thoughts lingered on his men—Mallory, Jacks, Matthews—and the faces of those who wouldn't be standing with them today.

The faint breeze stirred the scorched grass, carrying the acrid scent of gunpowder and the promise of more to come. Archer adjusted his helmet, his grip tightening on the rifle slung over his shoulder.

"This is it," he thought, the weight of the fight ahead settling squarely on his shoulders. With a glance back towards the chapel, he straightened. "We hold here," he murmured under his breath. "No matter what." Archer knew it wouldn't be long now.

Chapter 2

The first light of dawn broke over the battlefield, a pale, hesitant glow that barely pierced the lingering haze of smoke from the previous day's shelling. The chapel stood as the heart of the defensive line, its weathered stone walls pocked with bullet scars and splintered by shrapnel. Fragments of stained glass still clung stubbornly to a few of the arched windows, catching the muted light and casting faint, fractured patterns on the crumbled floor within. The bell tower, jagged and incomplete, loomed over the scene like a sentinel. Inside, Pritchard's silhouette was barely visible against the sky as he crouched, rifle poised, watching the horizon.

Around the perimeter, trenches snaked through the earth, hastily reinforced with sandbags, wooden beams, and salvaged debris. Men were scattered at their posts: riflemen huddled low in shallow pits, a Bren gun team stationed in the rubble of a collapsed cottage, and the Vickers machine-gun at its commanding position on the left flank. Its barrel pointed unwaveringly towards the rise, where any assault would likely emerge. The barbed wire at the outer edges of the defence caught fragile rays of dawn: a thin and desperate barrier between the defenders and the coming storm.

The air was heavy with anticipation, every sound exaggerated in the quiet: boots shifting in the dirt, the metallic scrape of a rifle bolt, and the occasional murmur of low conversation. Beyond the rise, the land stretched out, deceptively peaceful, shrouded in a low mist that obscured the distant tree line. But everyone knew it was only a matter of time.

Jacks was hunched down low in his trench, his hands trembling slightly as he adjusted the strap of his helmet. He forced himself to focus on the rifle in his lap, meticulously checking the bolt and safety for the third time that morning. His mind raced with thoughts of home—images of his wife and son flashing unbidden in his mind's eye. "Just get through the day," he muttered to himself, a prayer and a plea wrapped into one. The sound of a distant birdcall jolted him back to the present, his eyes narrowing as he scanned the horizon.

Mallory, leaning against the jagged edge of the chapel's outer wall, took a long, steady breath. Each man's position and readiness registered at once, assessed with the precision of a seasoned soldier. His thoughts drifted briefly to Wilkins, appreciating the sergeant's efforts to keep the defence together despite the odds. But his focus quickly returned to the task at hand. "This isn't the first time, and it won't be the last," he muttered, gripping his Lee-Enfield with quiet determination. Yet, deep down, even Mallory couldn't entirely ignore the sinking feeling that this fight might be unlike any they'd faced before.

Archer stood behind the trench line, his gaze sweeping over the defensive position. The early morning light lent an almost surreal calm to the scene, but Archer knew better than to trust it. His hand rested lightly on the stock of his rifle, fingers drumming an unconscious rhythm as his thoughts churned. He had studied the ground they held—the jagged edges of the wall, the rise that gave them the high ground, and the weak points where Jerry would inevitably focus their attack. His eyes flicked across to the men scattered along the line. Mallory's steady presence by the wall, Jacks in his trench, hands tight around his rifle, and Pritchard poised in the bell tower, his rifle settled on the sill; its familiar shape was a quiet reassurance in the stillness. Each of them carried their own burdens, their own fears, but they stayed in place, ready to face whatever came. That was something Archer couldn't help but admire—and worry about.

The faces of the men they'd lost flashed unbidden in his mind: Mitchell and Bell amongst them. They hadn't come this far to let it all slip away now, but Archer couldn't ignore the feeling in his gut. The reality of their position was stark—they were outnumbered, outgunned, and running low on everything that mattered. Yet here they were, holding fast.

He exhaled slowly, letting the tension settle into something sharper: focus. "We hold here," he thought again, the Latin phrase from before echoing faintly in his mind. It wasn't just about this position; it was about every man standing with him, every individual life depending on them holding the line for as long as they could. For Archer, there was no alternative. He straightened his shoulders and set his jaw as determination cloaked him.

The first shells came with a distant, low whistle—a sound that grew into a piercing scream as they hurtled closer. Archer's heart clenched as he shouted, "Take cover!" The warning barely escaped his lips before the first shell hit. The explosion shook the ground like a giant's fist, dirt and rock erupting skywards. The chapel trembled under the barrage, its fractured bell tower groaning ominously. A section of the stone wall caved in, jagged chunks tumbling to the ground as defenders dove for cover. Dust and debris filled the air, choking and stifling, turning the faint morning light into an apocalyptic haze.

Archer ducked into the shallow trench, sharing the cramped space with Saunders. The young private hunkered down beside him, his face pale and streaked with grime. Though Saunders was likely the same age as Archer—nineteen—something about the weight of command made Archer feel years older. Saunders' wide, terrified eyes darted towards Archer, silently pleading for reassurance as the barrage shook the earth around them.

"Keep your head down!" Archer barked, his voice barely cutting through the deafening roar of explosions. Wreckage rained down on them, the concussive force of each blast threatening to pull the ground out from beneath their feet.

Archer pressed himself harder against the trench wall, his breath coming in sharp, uneven gasps. The earth around him trembled with each detonation, and loose dirt cascaded from above, stinging his face and filling his mouth with grit. The shells fell without rhythm or mercy—every thunderous crack was a reminder that survival here was a matter of chance, not skill. One moment a man was crouched beside you; the next, he was gone, replaced by a tangle of shattered flesh and smoking earth.

He clenched his fists around the rifle stock, his knuckles whitening against the strain. His heart hammered against his ribs, not just from fear but from the sickening knowledge of how random it all was. There was no pattern, no predictability. One shell landed close enough to blow his helmet off, another fell harmlessly in a patch of open ground. How could he protect his men against something so chaotic?

His ears rang with the echoes of explosions and the screams of the wounded, but his mind latched onto a single, stubborn thought. "You'll hold, damn it. You'll hold." The words came out low and fierce, more growl than whisper. He repeated them like a mantra, forcing the terror clawing at his whole body to back down. He didn't have the luxury of panic—not now. His men were counting on him, and if he faltered, they'd falter too.

He bit down hard, the coppery taste of blood filling his mouth as he suppressed a wave of nausea. His gaze darted towards Mallory, who was barking orders through the tumult, and to the men who crouched low in the trenches, their faces pale and eyes wide with the same fear that churned in him. This was a different kind of battle—one fought not just against the enemy, but also the sheer randomness of death itself. "They need you," he told himself, his voice sharp, cutting through the clamour in his head. "You stand, and they'll stand. You don't get to break."

Another blast shook the ground, showering him in dust. Archer straightened slightly, forcing his legs to obey, his grip on the rifle tightening. The barrage couldn't last forever. When it ended, they'd need him ready—focused. And no matter what came next, he'd face it standing. "Hold," he muttered again, this time with grim resolve. "No matter what."

Nearby, Mallory continued to bellow commands, his voice a raw lifeline amid the confusion.

"Keep low! Stay in cover!" he yelled, his words punctuated by the whine of an incoming shell. The ground shook violently as another explosion ripped through the line, scattering earth and stone.

Screams pierced the cacophony—some sharp and fleeting, others agonisingly drawn out. Archer risked a glance towards the left flank where the Vickers team had been positioned. One of the men lay crumpled, his body motionless, while the other clutched a bleeding arm, trying to drag his comrade to safety. The acrid stench of gunpowder and burning earth hung heavy in the air, searing Archer's throat with every stolen breath. His fingers dug into the dirt, gripping his rifle like a lifeline. Around him, the defenders huddled in the trenches, their expressions a mixture of fear and grim determination.

An explosion erupted near the chapel itself, the deafening roar drowning out the shouts of men below. The impact sent a cloud of dust and shards of stone cascading over the defenders. Archer's head snapped towards the bell tower just as it trembled violently, and chunks of its already fractured structure collapsed to the ground.

"Still here, Sir!" Pritchard's voice rang out faintly over the chaos, defiant but edged with strain. Archer caught a fleeting glimpse of the man's silhouette, knelt down precariously near the jagged edge of the tower. Relief mingled with dread in his chest— Pritchard was alive, but for how long? The tower swayed with each new blast, its integrity hanging by a thread.

Archer's throat tightened, his mind racing with guilt. He'd sent Pritchard up there, believing it was the best vantage point.

But now, watching the fragile structure teeter under the relentless shelling, he felt a knot of regret tightening in his chest. Yet, another blast shook the ground, dislodging more of the bell tower's stones. The faint glint of Pritchard's rifle was the only sign that the sharpshooter still held his post. Archer wanted to shout up, to tell him to come down, but the words stuck in his throat.

"Hold on, damn it," Archer muttered under his breath, his voice thick with frustration. He forced himself to turn away, focusing instead on the trenches and the men looking to him for direction. But the image of the swaying tower and the man inside it clung to his thoughts, a weight he couldn't shake.

The barrage seemed endless, each detonation blurring into the next, until finally, the thunder began to recede. The air remained thick with dust and the echoes of destruction, but the immediate threat abated. Archer rose cautiously, his ears ringing, and scanned the weakened defensive line. Men were stirring, coughing, and groaning as they emerged from their cover. The trenches were littered with debris, and the once-proud stone wall was little more than a jagged outline. Some soldiers scrambled to their feet, their faces etched with shock, while others stayed slumped, either wounded or dead.

From his trench, Mallory's voice provided the strength they needed to push down the rising panic. "Stand to! Stand to!"

Archer clenched his jaw as men scrambled into position, the faint metallic click of rifle bolts filling the air. He gripped his own weapon tightly, the weight of command settling like a leaden cloak on his shoulders. "This isn't over," he thought grimly. "Not by a long shot."

His gaze flicked to Saunders, still huddled beside him in the trench. The private's shoulders were taut, his hands gripping his rifle as though it might anchor him amidst the turmoil. Archer reached out and placed a firm hand on Saunders' shoulder, grounding him.

"You've got this, Saunders," he said, his voice steady despite his own fears. "Just keep your head and stay focused. We'll get through it." The young man swallowed hard, nodding without meeting Archer's eyes. Archer gave his shoulder a brief squeeze before letting go, his attention returning to the trench line. The weight of the moment pressed heavier, but he pushed it aside. Every man here was counting on him to hold the line.

From his trench, Mallory's voice steadily cut through the ringing aftermath of the bombardment. "Stand to! Stand to!" Around him, Archer heard the groans of wounded men rising with the smoke, some calling out for stretcher bearers. A strangled cry pierced the air, and his gut clenched, but he forced himself to focus. Jacks scrambled over, his face streaked with dirt and exhaustion.

"We've got two dead, Sir. Another three wounded. One of 'em's bad—won't make it without proper help." Archer clenched his jaw, his knuckles tightening on the edge of the trench. He glanced at the dark horizon. The enemy was gathering for their push. There was no time to dwell on the losses.

"Get the wounded seen to as best we can," he said firmly. "The dead...we'll deal with them later. Right now, prepare the men. This isn't over yet."

Jacks nodded, his expression grim, and moved off to relay the order. Around Archer, muted voices carried urgent instructions and blended with the scrape of metal against fabric as men adjusted their kit. The trench was alive with subdued movement—rifle barrels braced against shoulders, hands brushing away loose dirt, and the faint clatter of ammunition being secured.

A cold wind stirred the acrid dust, whipping it into the men's faces as they prepared for what was coming. His gaze shifted to what remained of the bell tower, its frame battered but still defiantly standing. Through the haze, he spotted Pritchard, composing himself for what was to come. He showed no sign of faltering. The bombardment had shaken them all, leaving their position even more precarious. The trenches were shallower now, walls collapsed in places where the earth had given way under the pounding. Smoke and dust still clung to the air, obscuring their view of the horizon. Archer squashed the wave of nausea down as it threatened to smother his composure. There was no time to dwell on it—the next assault would come soon enough.

Then the first mortar round thumped somewhere behind enemy lines, its trajectory was a low arc rather than the high-pitched whistle of artillery. Archer's stomach twisted. Mortars meant the enemy was getting closer—this wasn't the blunt force of distant guns. This was targeted, deliberate. The round landed with a sickening crump, spewing dirt and shrapnel through the air. Before the echoes faded, another followed, this one closer, the intervals tightening like a noose. Archer clenched his fists and watched as explosions edged towards the fractured wall and the shallowest points of their line.

A sharp explosion sent a spray of stone and dirt cascading down into the trench, forcing Mallory to duck instinctively. The fragmented edge of the wall crumbled further, each mortar blast eating away at their defences inch by inch. The air was thick with the groans of the wounded and the sharp crackle of debris ricocheting off the trench walls.

Mallory's eyes locked onto a young private huddled against the trench wall, shoulders hunched and trembling. The lad's rifle lay forgotten in the mud, and his hands clutched his helmet as though it might shield him from the havoc. Mallory clenched his jaw, his frustration flaring. He didn't have time for this—not now.

"Oi!" Mallory barked, striding through the choking dust and grabbing the lad by the collar. He hauled him upright with one sharp motion, ignoring the debris still raining down. "You don't get to fold now, son. Pick up that rifle, keep your head, and look sharp! You're still breathing! Act like it!"

The private's wild eyes darted to Mallory's face, his breaths shallow and erratic. For a moment, Mallory thought the lad might collapse entirely. But then he swallowed hard, his gaze steadying under Mallory's firm grip. His hands fumbled for the rifle, gripping it as if it were the only thing holding him together.

"Good," Mallory muttered, releasing him with a rough pat on the shoulder. He turned away, his attention snapping back to the defensive line. There was no room for hesitation here—only action.

A mortar struck just beyond the trench, and the explosion sent a tremor through the earth. Archer flinched as a shard of shrapnel sliced past his face with the precision of a scalpel. Pain flared across his right cheek, the inch-and-a-half long wound stinging sharply as blood trickled down towards his jaw. He swore under his breath, one hand briefly brushing the injury before he forced himself back into motion. Climbing out of the trench, he raised his arm, signalling to Saunders to hold his position.

Finally, the bombardment began to taper off, and the relentless crump of mortars was replaced by an eerie silence, broken only by the groans of the wounded and the rustle of boots in the dirt. Dust and smoke hung thick in the air, shrouding the horizon in a ghostly film.

Archer took a deep breath, ignoring the sting of his wound as he moved along the line. "Get ready!" he barked, his voice firm and commanding. "Check your front! They'll be on us any moment now!"

He paused near Mallory who was helping a young private steady his rifle. "Mallory, make sure the left flank's covered," Archer said, his tone clipped but steady.

"On it," Mallory replied, already moving.

"Pritchard," Archer called up. "Stay sharp and keep your eyes on the approach!"

"Aye, Sir," Pritchard replied, his voice calm despite the chaos.

Archer wiped a hand across his bloodied cheek, smearing the wet crimson. The sting was sharp, but he pushed the pain aside, his eyes sweeping over the men around him. They were stirring with renewed purpose, their movements quick and deliberate as they prepared for the next assault. The relentless pressure of the moment pressed down on him, but now wasn't the time to falter.

Removing his backpack, he reached inside and pulled out his field dressing, tearing it open with a sharp motion. He winced as he pressed the sterile pad against the cut. "Jacks!" he barked, his voice cutting through the din. Jacks appeared a moment later, his boots skidding slightly in the mud as he crouched beside Archer.

"Sir?"

"Here," Archer said, removing his helmet and holding the dressing against his cheek. "Finish it. Tight, but not too tight—I still need to talk!"

Jacks smirked faintly as he took over with steady hands. "Wouldn't want to silence you, Sir. Bad for morale." He worked quickly, wrapping the bandage around Archer's chin and head before securing it with firm but careful fingers. Archer barely flinched, his mind already on the next steps.

"Thank you," Archer said, pulling his helmet back on as Jacks tied off the bandage. "Now, listen carefully. Get a runner back to Battalion HQ—see if they can find stretcher bearers for the wounded. We can't afford anyone to deal with them and having them sitting here may be a distraction when Jerry comes back swinging." Jacks nodded, his expression tightening as he stood. "Understood, Sir."

"Make it fast," Archer added, his tone sharp but not unkind. He watched as Jacks jogged off, his figure quickly swallowed by the gritty haze The moment lingered, pressing at his nerves, but he knew better than to give it space. He turned back to the line. turning his attention back to the line.

The first shapes emerged through the smoke, shadows against the dull glow of the smouldering landscape. The Germans moved in co-ordinated waves, their figures growing sharper as they advanced with disciplined purpose.

Pritchard from his vantage point called out, "Jerry's coming!"

Archer's stomach clenched as he pulled out his binoculars-his little memento of his first kill. He scanned his immediate horizon and started to instinctively count the helmets cresting the rise—too many. What was he thinking? It was always going to be too many!

"Here they come!" Mallory's voice rang out, urgent but steady.

"Hold steady. Await my command!" Archer shouted, raising his hand to signal restraint. "Wait for my order!" Archer made his way back to his slit trench where Saunders stood, rifle pressed into his shoulder, resting on the sandbags which formed a slight parapet to the front of the trench. Two charge clips were placed on the sandbags, ready to be inserted into the Lee-Enfield when required.

The tension across the line was palpable. Fingers twitched on triggers, breaths came shallow, and eyes darted towards the looming threat. Archer could hear the pounding of boots as the enemy closed the distance. At last, when the first wave reached the marked range, he dropped his arm.

"Fire!" The roar of the Vickers was deafening as its heavy bursts ripped into the German line. Bren guns joined the cacophony, their chattering staccato sweeping across the slope. Rifle fire cracked sharply as the defenders aimed with deadly precision and picked off the advancing soldiers. The first wave faltered under the withering fire. Men fell in heaps: their cries were drowned out by the relentless noise of battle. A few managed to find cover in the craters and debris left by the bombardment, but the attack stalled. The survivors scattered.

For a brief moment, Archer allowed himself to hope. But then, the sharp rattle of German machine-guns echoed across the battlefield, peppering the line with suppressing fire. Archer ducked instinctively as dirt and debris once again showered down around him. The battle was fully joined now, both sides contesting the ground with relentless determination. The Germans, advancing across open land towards the prepared British position, were taking heavy casualties in the initial exchange. Yet the unyielding zip of their machine-guns began to exact a toll on the defenders, forcing them to keep their heads down. In the centre of the line, Jacks stood out as a force of energy. Hopping out of his trench, he fired a single shot from the knee before crouching low and sprinting along his positions, shouting words of encouragement.

"Win this fight!" he bellowed. "Increase your fire! O'Hara, good shot—keep it up! Webb, get stuck into them! Scouse, you can do better than that!" His voice rang out over the harshness of gunfire. "Come on, boys—let 'em have it! Win this fight!"

From his perch in the shattered bell tower, Pritchard was the sentinel of the battlefield. The vantage point gave him a clear view of the German advance, their co-ordinated waves surging forwards across the open ground. He steadied his breath, ignoring the sway of the crumbling structure beneath him and the relentless rattle of machine-gun fire all around. Through the open sights of his Lee-Enfield, he tracked a German officer barking orders, his arm gesturing wildly. Pritchard exhaled slowly, his finger poised on the trigger. The crack of his rifle was sharp and immediate, and the officer dropped mid-command, his body crumpling into the mud. Pritchard adjusted without hesitation, shifting his aim to a flash of a machine-gun relentlessly firing. Another shot rang out, and another followed, silencing the threat. He worked methodically, every shot deliberate, every movement precise. For Pritchard, there was no chaos—only targets and the calm, deadly rhythm of his craft.

On the left flank, Mallory crouched behind a jagged section of collapsed stone wall, his eyes locked on the rise ahead where the Germans were regrouping. The Vickers machine-gun roared beside him, its bursts of fire carving into the advancing enemy. A soldier from 8th Platoon knelt nearby and fed ammunition belts into the weapon with quick, practiced hands; his face was set in grim concentration.

"Keep it steady!" Mallory barked, his voice cutting through the discord. He raised his rifle, picking off a soldier who had broken from cover, then swung his gaze back to the team manning the Vickers. The gunner, a corporal from another platoon, shouted something unintelligible as German rounds thudded into their sandbagged position.

"They've got eyes on us!" Mallory snapped. "Stay down and keep feeding that gun—it's the only thing keeping them pinned!" He scanned the treeline, his jaw clenched, every nerve taut as he searched for the source of the fire. The pressure was immense, but Mallory held firm, knowing the line depended on this flank holding fast.

On the right flank, Lance Corporal Tug Wilson hunched down low behind the trench wall, his teeth clenched as German rounds chewed into the earth and sandbags around them. His section was holding steady, but the strain was beginning to show. Hawkins stood a few feet away, firing controlled bursts from his Bren gun, sweat dripping from his brow despite the cool morning air.

"Good work, Hawkins," Wilson called out, his voice steady despite the mayhem around him. "Short bursts! Don't cook the barrel."

Beside him, Carter was reloading his rifle when a sharp crack echoed above the din. Wilson turned just in time to see Carter jerk violently, and his rifle slipped from his grasp as he slumped into the dirt.

"Carter's hit!" someone shouted, panic creeping into their voice.

"Stay focused!" Wilson barked, dragging Carter further down into the trench, his hands quickly assessing the wound. Blood soaked the man's side. It was dark and spreading fast. "Hawkins, keep that Bren singing! Brewer, cover him!" He leaned closer to Carter, lowering his voice. "Hold on, mate. We'll get you patched up."

Carter's eyes fluttered, his face pale, but he gave a weak nod. Wilson's jaw tightened as he scanned the line, adrenaline sharpening every sound and movement.

"Keep it together, lads," he said, raising his voice for the rest of the section. "They're coming hard, but we've held worse! Hawkins, lay it on thick if they try the flank again. Brewer, keep an eye on that tree line. Let's give 'em hell!"

Archer crouched in his slit trench. The sharp staccato of rifle fire and the deeper roar of the Vickers machine-gun filled the air. Beside him, Saunders fired steadily, his face grim but determined, the barrel of his Lee-Enfield glowing faintly from the sustained heat. The young man muttered something under his breath—a prayer, perhaps, or a curse—but Archer couldn't hear it over the commotion. He stole a glance above the trench lip, taking in the terrifying scene. The Germans were pushing hard across the open ground, their grey uniforms blending with the churned-up mud and smoke. Bodies littered the field where the initial wave had been cut down, but the enemy kept coming, disciplined and relentless.

To Archer's left, the Vickers roared in defiance: its steady rhythm carved through the advancing lines. He saw Mallory's features behind the sandbagged position as he barked orders and directing fire with the calm authority of a veteran. Further up the line, Pritchard's shots rang out from the shattered bell tower, each one deliberate and precise. Archer watched as a German machine-gunner collapsed mid-charge, felled by Pritchard's unerring aim. The British line held firm, but Archer knew their position was precarious. Ammunition was running low, and the relentless pounding of German artillery had left parts of the line shallow and exposed. Every man knew the cost of failure, and yet they fought on, grim determination etched into every face.

Archer turned his attention back to Saunders whose hands trembled slightly as he reloaded. "Keep it steady," Archer said, his voice low but firm. "Pick your shots—make them count." He scanned the field again, noting the Germans shifting tactics.

Their machine-guns were focusing on the flanks now, trying to suppress the Vickers and Bren gunners. A mortar round exploded somewhere to his right, sending a shower of earth and stone cascading down. Archer flinched but stayed focused, his rifle prepared to act.

"This is what we trained for," he muttered to himself though the words rang hollow in his ears. Still, he straightened his back and set his jaw, his eyes scanning the battlefield for the next threat. For now, the line was holding, but something about the fire pattern tugged at him.

The relentless rattle of German machine-guns began to falter, their rhythm less co-ordinated, and the mortars now landed further back along the British lines. Archer narrowed his eyes, watching through the haze as the scattered shapes of enemy soldiers began to withdraw towards the rise. It wasn't a rout—they moved with practiced precision, laying down suppressing fire as they pulled back.

"They're covering a retreat," Archer murmured, his voice cutting through the noise. Saunders, still firing beside him, paused to glance over.

"A retreat?" the private asked, his voice tinged with both hope and disbelief.

"Looks like it," Archer replied, his tone cautious. He stood slightly taller, surveying the shifting battlefield. "But don't let your guard down. They might be regrouping, or worse, luring us into something." He gestured towards Saunders. "Keep your rifle ready. Hold fire unless you've got a clear target." Archer's gaze swept across the trench line, catching glimpses of other soldiers peering over their positions, the realisation of a possible reprieve beginning to spread. Still, the knot in his stomach tightened. The Germans were retreating, but Archer had seen enough to know this was far from the end.

The sporadic fire from the Germans dwindled further, and for a fleeting moment, Archer thought they might have seen the last of the assault. But then the mortar barrage began again—this time with renewed ferocity. The first round landed dangerously close, the explosion shaking the trench and sending clumps of dirt and rock hammering down. Archer instinctively threw himself against the wall, shielding Saunders as another round followed, even closer.

"Take cover!" Archer roared, his voice barely audible over the thunderous barrage. The air was choked with dust and the acrid stench of cordite. All along the line, men huddled in their trenches, shielding their heads as the relentless bombardment tore into their defences. A section of sandbags on the left flank erupted in a spray of earth and debris, exposing part of the Vickers crew. Screams cut through the blasts, and Archer clenched his jaw, helpless against the onslaught. Through the haze, Archer caught glimpses of the Germans retreating, their movements now unimpeded. The mortars weren't just suppressing fire: they were a deliberate screen, forcing the British to keep their heads down while the enemy escaped.

Archer felt a pang of frustration but knew better than to risk unnecessary lives chasing a retreating force. "Let them go!" he barked, his voice hoarse. "Focus on holding the line—this isn't over!"

When the barrage finally began to ease, Archer cautiously raised his head, scanning the battlefield through the swirling dust. The Germans were gone, disappearing over the rise and out of sight. He exhaled heavily, the tension in his shoulders easing slightly. Around him, the line was a mess of shattered sandbags, broken equipment, and men coughing through the lingering smoke. Saunders looked up at him, wide-eyed but steady, his rifle clutched tightly in his hands.

"Fuckin' 'ell, Sir! We won?"

Archer's gaze lingered on the empty battlefield; his expression was grim. "We held," he said finally, his voice flat. "For now, that's enough."

Archer's gaze lingered on the battered line; the men around him were slumped with exhaustion yet still gripped their rifles as if bracing for more. Survival was its own kind of victory, but the cost was etched into every face. "For now, that's enough," he murmured again though the knot in his chest said otherwise.

Chapter 3

The battleground lay in stunned silence, broken only by the distant crackle of flames and the low moans of the wounded. Smoke clogged the air, mingling with the sharp stench of cordite and burning earth. The once-firm line was a broken shadow of its former self—walls crumbled, sandbags ripped apart, and shallow craters pockmarked the ground where mortars had landed with merciless precision.

Archer crouched beside his slit trench as temporary relief ripped at his limbs. His hands trembled slightly, a combination of exhaustion and the fading adrenaline that had carried him through the last assault. Around him, the survivors moved like ghosts, their faces streaked with grime and blood. Some checked their rifles with mechanical efficiency; others slumped against the walls of their slit trenches with their heads bowed as if daring to snatch a moment of rest.

The chapel loomed behind them. Its bell tower leant precariously, casting long, jagged shadows in the pale morning light. Pritchard's silhouette was no longer visible in the shattered structure, and Archer hoped the sharpshooter had found safety amidst the anarchy. A section of the wall that had been their strongest point now lay in ruins, gaping like an open wound.

Somewhere along the line, a low voice muttered a prayer; the words blended with the soft thud of boots on dirt. Archer's gaze shifted to Saunders who was still clutching his rifle with white-knuckled determination, his face drawn but resolute. The battle might have paused, but its scars lingered in every breath, and every glance exchanged among the men.

Archer exhaled slowly, forcing his shoulders to straighten. There was to be no time to dwell. The war hadn't ended with the retreat of the Germans—it had only offered a brief, bitter reprieve.

Archer was wiping the grime from his rifle when the sound of boots crunching through the rubble reached him. He looked up to see Mallory and Jacks approaching, their faces as grim as the battlefield around them. Mallory's uniform was streaked with dirt, and Archer noticed his helmet was dented from a glancing blow. Jacks' usually sharp wit was nowhere to be seen—his jaw was tight, and his eyes carried the burden of bad news.

"Sir," Mallory said, stopping beside Archer's trench. He removed his helmet, running a hand through his matted hair. "It's not good."

Archer set his rifle aside and stood, brushing off the dirt clinging to his knees. "Go on."

Mallory nodded towards Jacks, who stepped forwards, his voice steady despite the strain. "Sergeant Wilkins of 8th Platoon, Sir. He didn't make it. Took a piece of shrapnel during the barrage." Jacks hesitated, his gaze flicking to the ground for a moment. "Carter's hit bad—it doesn't look good. Four others wounded too.

Mallory cleared his throat and added grimly, "Most of the casualties came from 8th Platoon, Sir. They took the brunt of it during the last push. So, it's six dead, including Wilkins, and the wounded leave them barely at half strength."

He braced himself, jaw stiff with resolve. "Corporal Mann is senior there now and is doing what he can to keep the lads together, but morale's shaken."

Archer exhaled slowly, letting the load of the news settle over him. "And the rest of the line?"

"We are total strength of twenty-three. They're shaken but holding," Mallory replied. "Pritchard's still up in that blasted tower, somehow. The Vickers crew's down a man, but they're operational. Ammo's running even lower across the board, though."

Archer nodded, his expression hardening. "Alright. Get the wounded seen to as best as we can. We'll deal with the dead later." He glanced towards the horizon where the haze still obscured the enemy's retreating movements. "Make sure Mann knows I'll be checking on him soon. For now, focus on keeping the line intact."

"Understood, Sir," Mallory said, replacing his helmet as he stepped back. Jacks lingered a moment longer, his mouth opening as if to say more. Then he sighed, pulled a crumpled packet of cigarettes from his pocket, and offered it to Archer. "You holding up, Sir?" he asked quietly, tapping out a cigarette for each of them. Archer accepted with a nod, the match flaring briefly between them as Jacks lit up.
They stood in silence for a moment, smoke curling in the still air—no words were needed.

Archer, his gaze still fixed on the hazy horizon, where smoke still clung to the earth like a stubborn veil Jacks knelt beside him, taking in a long drag from his glowing cigarette. A faint rustle of movement caught their attention, a soft disturbance against the eerie quiet, and Archer straightened, eyes narrowing as a group of figures emerged through the haze.

"Looks like stretcher bearers," Jacks murmured, as he slowly stood up. Leading the group was a tall man in a worn uniform, his clerical collar just visible above the dust-covered fabric. He moved with purpose, his calm demeanour standing in stark contrast to the chaos around him.

"That's a padre!" Jacks exclaimed, his tone a mix of curiosity and surprise. "Didn't know we had one." Archer watched as the man approached, his presence radiating a quiet authority.

As the group drew closer, the tall man at the front removed his helmet, revealing a face lined with both weariness and warmth. He came to a halt just in front of Archer before his gaze swept over the scene before settling on Archer.

With a small, respectful nod, he spoke. "Second Lieutenant Archer, I presume?" His voice was calm and steady, carrying just enough volume to be heard over the muted noise of the battlefield.

Archer stepped forwards, meeting the man's eyes. "That's me."

The man extended a gloved hand. "Reverend James Cartwright, chaplain attached to your battalion. Most just call me Padre." His Yorkshire accent was light but unmistakable, lending an air of quiet confidence to his words. "I've brought the stretcher bearers as requested. We'll do what we can for your wounded."

Archer shook his hand firmly. "Good to meet you, Padre. And thank you." Archer turned to Jacks. "Jacks show them to the wounded."

Archer moved along the line with Jacks at his side, their boots stirring the loose dirt beneath them. The line was battered but holding. The men crouched low or leant against the crumbling walls, some rested on the parapets of their slit trenches, their weapons close to hand.

Archer paused every few steps to offer a nod or a word of encouragement. "Keep sharp, lads. Jerry's not done yet," his tone firm but steady. One of the riflemen, his face streaked with grime, managed a faint smile.

Mallory chimed in, his voice carrying a gruffer humour. "You're still breathing—that's a good sign. Let's keep it that way."

As they passed the shattered remains of a sandbagged position, Archer's gaze fell on Reverend Cartwright. The padre knelt beside a wounded soldier, his hands working methodically to secure a bandage. His movements were precise but unhurried, and his expression was calm despite the disorder around him. A few quiet words passed between the two men, and Archer saw the faintest flicker of relief cross the soldier's face.

"He's a steady one," Mallory muttered, following Archer's gaze. "Not many can keep their head like that."

Archer nodded, watching as Cartwright gently patted the soldier's shoulder before rising to his feet. Making his way towards the padre, Archer felt an odd pang of guilt as his eyes strayed to the chapel ruins behind them.

"Padre," he called as he approached. Cartwright turned, offering a small smile. "Lieutenant."

Archer hesitated, glancing at the crumbling chapel. "I...I'm sorry about the chapel. It's not exactly being used as it was intended."

Cartwright's smile softened. "It's serving its purpose, Lieutenant. Walls or no walls, God's still here." He gestured to the wounded soldier. "And so are they. That's what matters."

Archer nodded, his respect for the man deepening. "Thank you, Padre.

As Archer spoke with Cartwright, the padre's eyes drifted briefly to the blood-stained dressing wrapped around Archer's head. His brow furrowed slightly, and his tone shifted, carrying quiet authority. "Lieutenant, I hope you don't mind me saying, but that dressing of yours doesn't look like it's doing much good. Let me have a look."

Archer started to wave him off. "It's fine, Padre. Just a nick."

Cartwright's hand rested lightly on Archer's arm, stopping him. "Humour me, Lieutenant. If it's not serious, I'll let you go on being a hero." Archer chuckled despite himself and sat down on the edge of a trench. "Alright, Padre. Let's get this over with."

Cartwright knelt beside him, untying the makeshift bandage with careful fingers. The dried blood cracked slightly as the fabric peeled away to reveal a shallow but jagged cut along Archer's temple. The padre examined it closely, his expression calm but focused.

"Well, you've got luck on your side, Lieutenant. Nothing too serious, but it's deep enough to warrant a few stitches. Let me clean it up first." He reached into his satchel and pulled out a small bottle of antiseptic and a clean cloth.

"This might sting," he warned, pouring the liquid onto the cloth before dabbing at the wound. Archer winced but said nothing and fixed his eyes on the horizon as Cartwright worked.

Cartwright threaded a needle with steady hands while he spoke, his tone conversational but probing. "You've got a good crew here. They look to you."

Archer's jaw tightened slightly. "They're good men. Better than I deserve some days."

Cartwright began stitching, his movements smooth and precise. "That's the burden of command, isn't it? Feeling responsible for every loss, even when it's beyond your control."

Archer glanced at him, his lips pressing into a thin line. "You've been talking to Mallory."

The padre chuckled softly. "No, just thinking of Kipling. 'If you can keep your head when all about you are losing theirs and blaming it on you.'"

Archer snorted, the shadow of a bitter smile crossing his face. "'If you can trust yourself when all men doubt you...but make allowance for their doubting too.'" He shook his head. "It sounds good on paper, doesn't it? But out here?" He gestured at the scarred horizon. "Out here, trusting yourself can get men killed."

Cartwright paused, needle hovering above the next stitch. "Perhaps. But doubting yourself could get even more killed." Archer stared at him for a long moment before looking away.

"Maybe. But it doesn't make it any easier when you're the one giving the orders." The padre's smile was faint but warm.

"No, but I've seen that look before. It stays with you, that weight. Long after the battles are over."

Archer shifted slightly, wincing as Cartwright secured the last stitch. "And what does your faith say about it, Padre? About sending men to their deaths?"

Cartwright met his gaze, his hands steady as he tied off the thread. "That no one man was ever meant to carry it alone." He leaned back, packing away his kit. "But out here, it's not just faith, is it? It's the men around you. The ones who look to you, follow you. They don't expect a saint, Tom. Just a leader who tries to bring them home."

Archer said nothing, his gaze sharpening as it shifted towards the trench line. The distant thud of artillery punctuated the stillness, and the low murmur of the men's voices drifted on the cold air. Cartwright inspected his work and leant back with a satisfied nod. "There. You're patched up, Lieutenant. Try not to let anything else hit you in the head today."

Archer smirked faintly, touching the stitches gingerly. "Thanks, Padre. I'll do my best."

As Cartwright stood, he placed a hand on Archer's shoulder. "For what it's worth, you're doing right by your men. Don't lose sight of that." Before Archer could respond, a lance corporal approached. "Padre, we're ready to move out."

Cartwright nodded, his reply immediate. "Good. Lieutenant, with your permission, I'll get the wounded out of here. And good luck." He held out his hand.

Archer took it in a firm shake. "Good luck to you too, Padre." With that, Cartwright turned and moved off, his confident stride carrying him back to his duty. Archer watched him go, the quiet settling over him once more, broken only by the distant echoes of war.

The faint sounds of movement around the line had dwindled to leave a brittle silence. Archer stood near the ruined edge of a wall, his gaze scanning the haze-covered battlefield. Mallory came over, crouching beside him.

"Too quiet," he muttered, his voice low but laden with unease. His hands anxiously gripped and released his rifle, his eyes darting towards the distant tree line. Archer nodded. An ache in his chest deepened. The battlefield was rarely silent without reason.

"How long's it been since they attacked? Thirty minutes?" The question hung in the air, more rhetorical than a genuine inquiry. "It's like they're waiting for something," he murmured. The thought hadn't even settled when it began—a faint hum in the far sky. Every man's head turned upwards instinctively, eyes scanning for the source of the sound. In the distance, black dots appeared against the grey sky.

The hum grew louder, and a low vibration seemed to press into their chests. The dots grew larger with each passing moment, their shapes sharpening into the unmistakable silhouettes of aircraft. Archer's throat tightened. These weren't the first planes the men had seen crossing the skies above Cassel, but there was something different about these.

A weight hung in the air, and an unspoken sense of foreboding gripped the line. The droning intensified, drowning out even the wind, and Mallory squinted and raised his arm to shield his eyes.

"Stukas," he said flatly, his voice cutting through the rising tension. The hypnotic stillness along the line broke as the planes, one by one, began their descent. Seven in total, their dark forms bearing down with menacing purpose. Then came the sound that turned their blood cold—the unmistakable, bone-chilling screech of dive bombers.

"Stukas!" someone shouted, his cry breaking through the stillness like a whipcrack.

Archer's blood ran cold as he instinctively ducked. The distant droning of engines swelled rapidly, a mechanical roar growing louder with every passing second. Then it came—the unmistakable scream of the dive. It wasn't just a sound; it was a visceral thing, a piercing wail that seemed to rip the air apart.

The Stukas' sirens, deliberately engineered to evoke terror, howled like banshees, their pitch rising higher and higher as the planes plummeted towards the earth.

The sound clawed at Archer's nerves, filling his chest with a primal dread he hadn't felt before. Around him, men pressed themselves into the ground, their faces pale and eyes wide, frozen by the sheer ferocity of the noise. The scream seemed to vibrate through the earth, shaking the already fragile defences of the line.

"Take cover!" Archer bellowed, but his voice was barely audible over the menacing screams. The wail of the Stukas was relentless. It was a sound that promised only destruction. Archer's heart pounded as he braced for the inevitable. The scream still echoed in his ears.

Men scrambled to the ground, pressing themselves into whatever shelter they could find. Archer hit the trench floor as the first bomb fell. A high-pitched whistle split the air before an earth-shaking explosion ripped through the line. The impact sent a cloud of dirt and shrapnel cascading down, strangling the air with smoke and debris.

The next wave came in quick succession, each detonation a deafening burst that felt like the world was being torn apart. Archer lifted his head just enough to see the carnage unfolding and witnessed a section of the line thrown into the air after a direct hit, swallowing two men in a spray of dirt and shattered timbers.

To his left, Mallory was shouting orders, his voice hoarse as he tried to keep the men focused. "Stay down! Keep your bloody heads down!"

Archer turned his head, coughing through the dust. He could just see Saunders a few feet away, his face pale but his grip steady on his rifle.

"You alright?" Archer shouted, though he wasn't sure the

younger man could hear him. Saunders nodded faintly, his lips moving in what looked like a prayer. Before Archer could say more, another bomb fell, and the shockwave hit the chapel with the fury of an unseen god. He felt the ground shift beneath him, and for a heart-stopping moment, he thought the entire chapel would collapse.

"Help!" someone screamed, their voice raw with panic. Archer twisted around to see a man dragging another soldier from a shallow crater, blood streaking the ground behind them. Through the swirling dust near the chapel, Pritchard emerged like a ghost, his rifle slung across his back as he hauled a wounded man towards safety.

Even as another bomb fell dangerously close, shaking the ground beneath them, Pritchard's voice remained calm and steady. "You're going to be alright, son. Keep breathing for me." His words came like an anchor to ground the terrified soldier. Kneeling beside the wounded man, Pritchard moved with practiced precision. His hands, steady despite the mayhem around him, quickly fashioned a tourniquet around the soldier's mangled leg. The wounded man moaned in pain, but Pritchard's quiet reassurance didn't falter. "Hold on. We'll get you through this."

The screech of another diving Stuka tore through the air, and Archer merged himself with the dirt, bracing for the impact. This one landed further back, shaking the ground but sparing their position. He stole a glance upwards to catch a fleeting glimpse of the black crosses on the wings as the planes pulled back into the sky, their assault momentarily halted. Archer pulled himself to his knees, his ears ringing as he assessed the damage. The line appeared to be in a shambles— craters now sat where walls and obstacles had previously been situated, and the air was thick with smoke and the cries of the wounded. He caught sight of Jacks helping a bloodied soldier to his feet, shouting something Archer couldn't hear.

"Sir!" Mallory appeared beside him, his face streaked with dirt and sweat. "The line's in bad shape. Six dead, maybe more wounded. It's not looking good." Archer forced himself to his feet, gripping Mallory's arm for support. His legs felt like lead, but he steadied himself. "Get the able-bodied men reorganised. Anyone who can still fire a rifle, get them to the front. We need to hold what's left of this line." Mallory nodded sharply, determination flickering through the weariness in his eyes. He moved off, shouting orders as he went, his voice hoarse but commanding. Archer turned his attention to Pritchard who was knelt beside a wounded soldier. Despite the pandemonium, Pritchard's hands were steady, and his expression was focused as he tied off a dressing around the soldier's leg.

Ahead, out of the swirling haze, Reverend Cartwright appeared, running with urgency but not panic. His clerical collar, which peeked above his dirt-smeared uniform, was a stark reminder of his role amid the carnage. Behind him, stretcher bearers followed in close pursuit with their kits rattling with every step as they closed in.

For a fleeting moment, Cartwright's gaze met Archer's. There was no hesitation, no fear—only calm resolve. Without breaking stride, the padre knelt beside Pritchard and gently took over, his hands moving with practiced precision.

"I'll take it from here," he murmured, already examining the wounded man. His voice was steady and reassuring as though the bombardment had never happened. Pritchard rose and moved to cover another soldier, leaving Cartwright to his craft.

Around them, the droning of engines began to fade as the Stukas retreated after their devastating assault. Yet the silence that followed was almost more oppressive than the noise. Archer knelt beside his slit trench, coughing against the settling dust. Around him, the men stirred slowly—some wiping blood from their faces, others too stunned to do more than blink.

Cartwright approached, his uniform smeared with blood and grime. His movements betrayed no exhaustion though Archer suspected it was there, buried beneath the padre's unwavering composure.

"Lieutenant," he said quietly, his voice cutting through the grim silence. "We've done what we can for the wounded. I'm getting them out now." Archer met his gaze, giving the padre a momentary insight into the weight of command that crushed Archer.

Archer nodded, his voice low. "Good work, Padre." Cartwright offered a brief, reassuring nod before turning back towards the stretcher bearers, already moving to help another injured man.

Archer exhaled and straightened, brushing more dirt from his uniform. He couldn't stay rooted in one spot any longer. With a quick glance around, he started to make his way along the line, needing to see the damage for himself. Each step felt heavier than the last as the destruction laid bare before him. The position was barely recognisable in places, sections cratered where the bombs had struck. Sandbags hung limply over the edges, spilling their contents into the muck below. Bodies of the dead lay where they'd fallen. One was half-buried in debris from the chapel. Archer forced himself not to linger on their faces. The living needed his focus now.

As he passed a rifleman reloading with shaking hands, Archer noticed it was Scouse Evans. He paused and placed a steadying grip on the man's shoulder.

"You're doing fine, Evans. Keep it up." Evans gave a faint wry smile, his expression a mix of exhaustion and resolve. Archer moved on, noting where the remaining Bren gunners were positioned, their weapons trained on the horizon. The left flank was in better shape with Mallory directing men to reinforce the battered wall with whatever materials they could salvage.

Mallory caught sight of Archer and gave a quick grimace, his expression hard but determined. "Sir, this side's holding, but ammo's scarce," Mallory said without preamble. "Might not hold another push if they come hard." Archer did not respond, just continued along the line.

His boots crunching through debris, and he found Jacks helping a bloodied soldier reload his weapon. The man's face was pale, and his uniform was streaked with dirt and blood, but he waved Archer off when he moved closer.

"Still got fight in me, Sir," O'Hara muttered with a steady voice despite the strain. Archer crouched briefly beside him, scanning O'Hara's injuries.

"Good to hear, O'Hara," Archer replied, his tone firm but not unkind. "Just keep yourself steady. We'll need every man standing."

O'Hara nodded faintly, his hands moving with determined purpose as he slid another clip into his rifle. "Won't let you down, Sir." Archer placed a hand on the soldier's shoulder for a moment before moving on, but the faint hint of resolve in O'Hara's voice lingering in his mind.

As Archer rose, Jacks straightened beside him, wiping sweat from his forehead. His words came quiet and measured, meant for the few who stood close enough to hear. "That's about the last of them who can still fight, Sir."

Archer glanced down the battered position, his jaw tense. "How many?"

Jacks hesitated, his eyes briefly meeting Archer's. "Seventeen still standing, Sir. Five from 8th Platoon, twelve from ours. 8th have taken the brunt on the left, Sir. As you saw, O'Hara's hanging in there, and so is Webb, but..." He trailed off, his voice dropping further. "We lost Tanner in the raid. And the ammo's run thin—Bren teams are down to their last mag, and most men've only got a handful of clips left."

Archer exhaled slowly, rubbing the back of his neck. The news settled over him like a shroud. "It's worse than I thought."

"Aye," Jacks replied, his steady tone edged with fatigue. "But the lads are holding together. They'll stand as long as you ask them to." Archer nodded, his gaze sweeping over the shattered line. "They're holding well." The harsh realities of their situation gnawed at him. Only seventeen men left—barely enough to cover the line. Two were manning the Vickers on the left flank which left him with fifteen others. Two Bren guns, eleven rifles, and little ammunition between them. It wasn't enough. He rubbed the back of his neck. The responsibility of command threatened to crush him.

"Jacks," he called, his voice low but firm. The corporal was beside him in moments, his expression grim.

"How much ammo does the Vickers team have?" Archer asked, his tone clipped.

Jacks hesitated before answering. "Last I checked, Sir, they've got two belts left. A few bursts but not much more." Archer nodded and took a deep breath. The Bren gunners wouldn't be much better off, and the riflemen? Ten rounds per man wouldn't hold against another determined push. They were hanging on by a thread, and he could feel it fraying.

He glanced at the haze-shrouded horizon at the faint shapes of the enemy just visible. They were regrouping. Archer had to make decisions, and quickly.

"Alright," he said, standing. "Here's what we're going to do. Jacks, tell the Vickers team to conserve their fire—short, controlled bursts only. Same goes for the Bren gunners. Riflemen don't shoot unless they've got a clear target."

Jacks nodded. "And if they come hard?"

"We hold as long as we can," Archer said, his voice steady despite the grasping knot in his stomach. "If the line's overwhelmed, we'll fall back to the second position behind the chapel. The Vickers will cover the retreat."

Jacks shifted, unease flickering in his eyes. "And if there's no retreat, Sir?"

"Then we hold here until the last round." There was an eerie pause before Archer finished. "Be sure to let Mallory know."

Jacks nodded slowly, his resolve firming. "Understood, Sir."

As Jacks moved off to relay the orders, Archer began the short walk towards what remained of the chapel. The bell tower was gone entirely, and its jagged remnants were scattered across the ground. Three of the chapel's walls stood no taller than a man, and the far wall, where a once-beautiful stained-glass window had been, was now little more than a shadow of its former self—a jagged outline framing the open sky.

Stepping into the ruins, Archer picked his way carefully through the debris, his boots crunching over shattered stone and glass. Near the corner where the field telephone had been, he spotted the remains of a splintered table now buried under a heap of timbers and rubble. With a grunt, he shifted the debris aside to reveal the telephone lying on its side, remarkably intact.

He crouched, picked it up and turned the crank. For a moment, he hesitated, half-expecting silence. But then, through the crackle of static, a voice came through, faint but unmistakable.

Archer exhaled in disbelief, pressing the receiver closer to his ear. "This is Second Lieutenant Archer," he said, steadying his voice. "Reporting from the chapel line. Here's our situation..." He began relaying the grim details, his words clipped and efficient as he outlined their casualties, dwindling ammunition, and the need for immediate support.

There was a pause on the other end, just long enough for Archer to wonder if the line had gone dead. Then came the unmistakable voice of Major Ellis, sharp and deliberate.

"Archer, it's Ellis. Understood. There are no reinforcements available. Any artillery support won't be immediate, and it'll be limited—we're stretched thin across the entire sector. Can your men hold?" Archer's grip on the receiver tightened. His face was taut as he looked up to the heavens, where God ought to be.

"We'll hold as long as we can, Sir, but if they hit us hard, I can't promise the line will hold without support."

"Noted," Ellis replied. His tone was firm but calm. "Lieutenant Archer, just so we are clear, no further fallback is authorised. We need every minute you can buy us. Do you understand?"

Archer's grip on the receiver tightened further, the significance of the words pressing on him like a vice. "Understood, Sir."

"Good man," Ellis replied, his voice carrying a faint edge of finality. "Godspeed, Archer. Out." The line went silent, leaving Archer staring at the battered phone in his hand. For a moment, the world felt crushingly still. Then, with a slow and deliberate motion, he replaced the receiver. Straightening his back, he turned towards the shattered line, the strain of Ellis's order heavy on his shoulders. But Archer hadn't moved away from the telephone. Ellis's final words echoed in his mind. "No further fallback." He exhaled heavily, forcing himself to move, when shouts rang out from the line.

"Stand to!" Mallory's voice cut through the haze. "Jerry's coming—and they've got tanks!"

Archer scrambled out of the ruins to the front of the line, jumping into his slit trench where Saunders was at the ready, his knuckles white on his rifle. Archer's stomach tightened as the ground began to tremble.

In the distance, three tanks emerged, their hulking forms

cutting a relentless path forwards. They were flanked by disciplined infantry advancing in formation. The tanks moved with deliberate menace, their treads grinding through the churned-up earth. The machine-guns mounted on their turrets began raking the battlefield ahead, forcing Archer and his men to duck as bullets zipped overhead and thudded into sandbags and the surrounding ruins.

"Focus on the infantry!" Archer shouted, his voice rising above the chaos. "Vickers team! Suppress their advance!" The Vickers gun roared to life, its steady bursts carving into the German ranks. The Bren teams opened as well, and their deadly fire ripped into the advancing infantry. Their momentum was stalled, but it did nothing to halt the tanks.

Mallory appeared at Archer's side, panting. "We can't stop those bloody things, Sir! What do we have left?" Before Archer could respond, Matthews scrambled out of his trench. His face was drenched in sweat and grime but lit with determination. He ran over to both Mallory and Archer.

"Can you give me covering fire? I've got something," he said, showing one last improvised bomb. "If you can cover me, I'll get close and lob this!"

Archer nodded sharply. "OK, but let's wait till they get closer. Take the one on the left, that way the Vickers can cover you." Matthews left with Mallory towards the Vickers machine-gun.

The first tank round—a German high-explosive— slammed into the earth near Archer's trench, detonating with a deafening crack that shook the ground. Dirt, shrapnel, and rubble erupted skywards before raining down on the defenders. Men ducked instinctively as another shell struck closer to collapse part of the chapel's ruined wall and send a soldier sprawling. The sickening stench of cordite was plastered to the air, and the concussive blasts left ears ringing and nerves frayed. One round struck a pile of sandbags and obliterated them in an instant, sending jagged fragments of debris slicing through the air like razor blades.

The next shell exploded perilously close to the Vickers position, hurling the gunner backwards with the force of the blast. His assistant scrambled forwards and dragged the weapon back into place even as another round whistled ominously overhead. The tanks were zeroing in on the last bastion of sustained fire. Relentless in their progress, they spewed fire and thunderous explosives directly at the British line.

Archer stared in disbelief—this was absurd. They were managing to thin out the supporting infantry, but the tanks kept coming, unstoppable juggernauts of steel. Before long, they were within 80 yards of his position. The explosions of high-explosive rounds were nearly constant, each detonation sending quivers through the earth and scattering debris. A sharp, piercing scream suddenly rang out—a soldier hit—but Archer couldn't see who. Hesitating only a moment, he forced himself into motion, sprinting back and forth along the trench, shouting words of encouragement to his men. He knew, deep down, this was futile—those tanks weren't stopping for anything.

Matthews, under the sporadic cover fire of the Vickers and with Mallory directing riflemen on the left flank, reached the thin line of barbed wire that lay 30 yards ahead of the British position. Keeping low, he crawled forwards, his movements deliberate and methodical to avoid detection. The onslaught of gunfire and shelling roared above and around him as he waited, barely breathing. Matthews felt his heartbeat threatening to drown out everything around him.

The tank rumbled closer, its grinding treads kicking up earth with every ominous step. When the nearest tank was within 15 yards, Matthews steeled himself. With steady hands, he struck the fuse on the bundle of TNT, and the small flame sputtering defiantly in the chaos. With a mighty throw, he hurled the explosive under the advancing vehicle. A split second later, an ear-splitting explosion tore through the battlefield. The tank shuddered violently, and its forwards momentum was halted as smoke poured from its undercarriage.

A cheer erupted from the British position, but it was fleeting as they helplessly watched another tank rotating its turret and zeroing in on where Matthews had risen. The high-explosive round struck with terrifying precision. It erupted in a plume of earth and grass that shot skywards to obscure the area in a haze of destruction. Archer's heart sank as he saw the blast, unsure of Matthews' fate.

Cautiously, Archer stumbled his way to Mallory's position near the Vickers, his heart pounding as the battle raged on. The tanks were still advancing with their machine-guns raking the British line while their infantry pressed forwards under the cover of the behemoth's relentless firepower. The high-explosive rounds had wreaked havoc on the defences—sections of the line were little more than craters. The sky pressed down, thick with the sting of gunpowder and the crude, metallic scent of upturned soil. He clenched his fists, scanning the devastation around him. Matthews' heroic act had bought them a moment, but it wasn't enough. The remaining tanks were closing in, and the line was barely holding. Archer knew what needed to be done.

He turned to Mallory who was barking orders at the riflemen. "Mallory!" Archer shouted, grabbing his attention. "Keep them firing! Don't let up!"

Mallory nodded, his face streaked with dirt and sweat. "We'll do what we can, Sir. But if those tanks get any closer—"

"I know!" Archer cut him off, already scrambling out of the trench. "I'll deal with it."

Dodging flying debris and bullets that kicked up dirt around him, Archer sprinted towards the chapel. His breath came in ragged gasps; his ears rang from the roar of the battlefield. The shattered pieces of the chapel loomed ahead, its walls barely standing. He ducked inside and found the relative quiet of the interior almost disorienting compared to the chaos outside.

The field telephone was still where he'd left it, miraculously intact despite the wreckage. He snatched up the receiver, turning the crank with trembling hands. Static crackled in his ear, but then a voice broke through.

"HQ, this is Archer!" he shouted, his voice raw with urgency. "We've got armour on our position—infantry and at least two tanks still operational. Our line won't hold much longer. We need artillery support immediately, or we're finished!" The seconds stretched unbearably as the operator on the other end relayed the message. Archer's grip on the receiver tightened; his knuckles were white. Again, Archer cranked the telephone, his voice sharp and urgent as the line crackled. "HQ, this is Archer! I need immediate artillery support on my position—armour and infantry are breaking through! We're at grid reference 042785—repeat, 042785! We can't hold without support!"

The reply came back after a moment's pause, clipped and calm. "Message received, Archer. Fire mission approved. Guns firing in two minutes." The line went dead, leaving Archer gripping the receiver as the gravity of the situation pressed down on him. He slammed the receiver back down, his mind in turmoil, and he darted back outside.

"Get down!" Archer bellowed, his voice cutting through the bellowing battle. Men threw themselves into the dirt as the first British shells screamed overhead. The ground convulsed violently with each impact. The deafening roar of explosions swallowed all other sounds. Plumes of dirt and debris shot skyward as the barrage tore into the advancing Germans.

The enemy infantry scattered under the relentless onslaught, their formation dissolving into disarray. One shell, which landed squarely among a group of soldiers, hurled bodies through the air like ragdolls. Another struck the lead tank. The explosion engulfed it in a fiery blast. Shuddering and grinding to a halt, black smoke billowed from the vehicle's ruptured hull. Matthews dove back into a trench, covered in dirt and coughing hard as yet another shell slammed into the battlefield to flip a second tank onto its side with a thunderous crash.

For a moment, the air seemed alive with fire and fury; the relentless bombardment showered destruction on the enemy's position. A ragged, relieved cheer erupted from the trench as the German assault faltered. The battlefield ahead had transformed into a smouldering wasteland, littered with twisted metal and the scattered remains of the once-relentless enemy force.

But Archer's gaze remained fixed on the horizon, his chest rising and falling heavily. He stared out at the smouldering remains of the battlefield—the jagged scars in the earth where shells had landed, the twisted wreckage of German armour, and the motionless forms of those caught in the barrage. The sight was both a grim testament to their resilience and a stark reminder of how close they had come to annihilation. Archer's grip tightened on his rifle as he fought to steady his thoughts. This is what victory looks like, he thought bitterly. Not triumph, but survival—barely hanging on, battered and bloodied, with too few men left to call it 'a line. Leadership clung to him like chainmail soaked in blood—unshakable, and heavier with every decision, every life lost, carving him hollow from the inside out.'

The silence that followed the barrage was almost more unnerving than the explosions. For a moment, Archer allowed himself to feel the exhaustion seeping into his bones. With the adrenaline fading, he was left with only the cold, heavy truth.

They had survived, but not because of strategy or skill—just luck and the raw power of the artillery that had answered his desperate call.

Mallory crouched beside him, his face streaked with dirt and sweat. He wiped his sleeve across his brow, glancing towards the broken line ahead.

"That bought us time, Sir," he said, his voice steady but grim. "But they'll be back." Archer didn't respond immediately. His eyes lingered on the devastation before them, replaying the destruction in his mind. How many more times could they hold? How many more lives could he ask these men to give before there was nothing left?

Finally, he nodded, his face taut as he pushed the thoughts aside. He couldn't afford doubt—not now, not here. "What's our status, Sergeant?" he said quietly.

Chapter 4

The command post was set in what remained of a once-cozy French café; its charm had been reduced to ruins by the chaos of war. The faint scent of scorched wood lingered in the air, mingling with the bitter tang of smoke and the dry, metallic bite of spent gunpowder which clung to every surface. A single lantern flickered on the scarred wooden table in the centre of the room, casting jagged shadows on the cracked plaster walls. The café's windows, once adorned with cheerful lace curtains, were shattered, their frames blackened by fire. Splintered wooden chairs and overturned tables were pushed against the walls to form crude barricades against any stray mortar fire.

The remnants of the 9th Greenmoors' officer cadre stood around the table. Their faces were etched with exhaustion and resolve. The faint glow of the lantern accentuated the grime ingrained on their uniforms and the tension that tightened their features. Behind them, the counter, where patrons had once sipped coffee and shared conversation, was now littered with maps, spent cartridges, and an empty water canteen. A chalkboard menu hung crookedly on the wall with its faded lettering advertising meals no one would ever serve again.

Outside, the rumble of artillery punctuated the uneasy quiet. The sound rolled over the shattered streets of Cassel like an ominous drumbeat. Occasional whistles of incoming rounds made the ground tremble, rattling loose debris from the sagging ceiling. Overhead, the moonlight filtered through a gaping hole in the roof, casting pale grey beams onto the ruined floor.

Major Ellis stood at the head of the table; his weathered face was lit by the uneven glow. His uniform, like those of the men around him, was streaked with dirt and soot, and the once-polished boots were scuffed and caked with mud.

Ellis' hands rested heavily on the table's surface, and his knuckles whitened from the pressure. Around him, the officers shifted uneasily. Their movements were slow, weighed down by fatigue and the unspoken realisation that they were likely making decisions for the last time together. The café, like the men, had been pushed to its limits. Its walls still stood, but its spirit had long since been gutted by war.

"Gentlemen," Ellis began, his voice low but firm, "I've called you all here because this is likely the last time we'll stand together as officers of the 9th Greenmoors." He paused, letting the weight of his words swallow the unease in the room. Outside, the rumble of artillery continued and punctuated the silence. "Our position here in Cassel is becoming untenable. Jerry's closing in from every direction, and there's no relief coming. The breakout to Dunkirk is our only option. But that doesn't mean we're all leaving together." Major Ellis's gaze swept across the faces before him, pausing briefly on each man.

Captain Pembroke, commanding D Company, stood calm and composed, his demeanour that of a man who had seen enough battle to know the odds but refused to let it show. Captain Thorne, leading A Company, sat rigidly in a chair, his face tight with suppressed frustration, and the magnitude of the situation pressed heavily on his disciplined frame. Captain Warren of B Company leant forwards slightly, his fingers digging into the back of a chair, and the strain evident in the taut lines of his hands. It was a reflection of the tension he carried but dared not voice. Beside them, the officer from C Company—a lieutenant, barely older than Archer—stood stiffly with his shoulders squared but his face pale. His eyes betrayed a determination to prove himself worthy of the role thrust upon him after Captain Norton's death.

Each man, in their own way, carried the burden of leadership: they were fully aware of the lives that depended on their decisions in the hours to come.

Ellis continued his stare at the officers who were gathered around the battered café table. His gaze was steady but heavy with the duty of command, he continued.

"Every company in this battalion has bled for Cassel. A, B, C, and D—you've all held when others would have broken, and under extreme examination you have all stood up to the burden we have had to carry." Ellis tapped the map with a blunt finger. "The breakout begins at first light. Our orders are simple: every man who can walk or fight is to head east towards Dunkirk."

He reached into his tunic pocket, producing four slips of paper. "Gentlemen, we need to cover the retreat. To do so, we will form a scratch force to hold the line during the withdrawal." Though his voice was calm, everyone felt the gravity of what came next settle over them

"This force will consist of two two-pounder anti-tank guns and their crews from the 53rd Anti-Tank Regiment, Royal Artillery. Sergeant Wallis has also volunteered to stay behind with two two-inch mortars though he's down to about ten rounds. And finally—" Ellis paused, his gaze sweeping the room, "—one rifle company."

The room was silent, the reality sinking in. "As I said, you have all done more than anyone could ask. To keep this decision as fair as possible, each company will draw lots to decide who stays. The other companies will break out with the battalion at first light."

The officers exchanged tense glances. The flickering lantern light continued to cast jagged shadows across their faces. The air felt suffocatingly heavy as each man silently reckoned with the possibility of being chosen to stay behind. Captain Thorne of A Company was the first to step forwards with a grim but composed expression. He reached for a slip, his hand steady, though a slight twitch at the corner of his mouth betrayed his anxiety. Warren of B Company followed with deliberate but hesitant movements as though the pressure of the moment had slowed him. The replacement lieutenant from C Company hesitated just a fraction too long before stepping forwards; his face was pale but determined as he took his slip with both hands; his fingers tightened around the paper. Finally, Pembroke of D Company stepped up with unhurried and deliberate movements; he was a man accustomed to carrying the burdens of his men.

The room fell eerily silent as the officers stood in a line, slips in hand. Every eye turned to Thorne as he unfolded his paper first. The faint rustle of the parchment was loud in the stillness. He held it aloft: the paper was blank. Thorne exhaled sharply, his shoulders dropping slightly as he nodded to the others.

"Next," he said evenly, though his relief was palpable. Warren followed and his jaw tightened as he unfolded his slip. Another blank. He let out a breath through his nose, loosening his grip on the paper.

"Two down," he muttered, stepping back. All eyes then turned to the replacement lieutenant who hesitated for the briefest moment, his hands trembling slightly as he unfolded the slip. When the paper revealed another blank, he visibly sagged with unmistakable relief.

The room seemed to hold its collective breath as Pembroke stepped forwards. He paused for a moment, rolling his shoulders as if loosening some unseen weight.

"Well bugger me," he said, a faint smile tugging at the corners of his mouth. "I always did have a soft spot for this old town." The dim lantern light caught the edge of his slip as he unfolded it, revealing the large X scrawled in bold, unforgiving strokes. Pembroke held it up for all to see: his expression was unreadable for a moment. Then, he glanced at Archer with a steady and unflinching glance.

"Tom, looks like we're up to bat," his tone was light, but it carried a weight that wasn't lost on anyone. "Let's hope I've got a few boundaries left in me." A murmur rippled through the room as some officers exchanged uneasy glances, and others bowed their heads in silent acknowledgement of the choice made for them.

Major Ellis nodded, his face grave. "Captain Pembroke, D Company will form the scratch force. Stay back when the others leave." He paused, letting the words settle. "The rest of you, prepare your men. Zero four hundred hours."

Ellis stood at the scarred table with his hand resting on a crumpled map. His gaze moved between Pembroke and Archer; his face was lined with fatigue and grief.

"Gents, you're all that's left of D Company's command," he said, his voice steady but tinged with sorrow. "I can't believe that in a matter of days, men I've led, and I've laughed with, I now don't have the time to mourn." He paused, his eyes dropping to the map for a moment before continuing. "D Company was my company not so long ago. I know what they're capable of. I know what you're capable of. You've already held when others would've broken."

Ellis forced a straightness in his spine as he met their eyes again. "Pembroke, you've got the experience. Archer, you've proven your mettle more times than I can count in the last few weeks. Now I ask that you go once again," he exhaled heavily, his tone softening. "I wish I could ask less of you. But the brigade—and every man heading to Dunkirk—is depending on you two.

"Now the withdrawal has already started with the first elements leaving around now, the Greenmoors are the last to leave at around zero four thirty." Ellis leaned over the scarred map, and his finger traced a jagged line leading through the town. "Here's the plan," he began, his voice steady but grim. "We've selected the Rue de Bergues and the northern entrance as your primary position. The Royal Artillery is already there, dug in and facing east. It's a natural bottleneck—Jerry will have to come through it, one way or another." He paused, glancing at Pembroke and Archer. "Your orders are simple: hold this position for as long as humanly possible. Make them bleed for every inch."

Ellis' scrutinised the men's response. "When you can't hold any longer—and make no mistake, that time will come—you'll execute a fighting withdrawal. Use this road here," he tapped a line running west towards Saint-Omer. "To break contact. From there, it's every man for himself. Make for Dunkirk by whatever means you can."

He exhaled, his tone softening slightly. "This isn't brilliant or elegant. It's as simple as it gets: hold, hold, and hold some more. Your stand here will buy time for the brigade, for the retreat, and for the thousands of men still making their way to the beaches. That's your mission."

Ellis's gaze lingered on Pembroke. "We go back a long way James, and I know D Company is in good hands." He extended a hand, and Pembroke grasped it firmly, responding with his usual good-natured smile.

"I won't let you down, Boomer."

Ellis, still smiling at the reference to his old school nickname, turned to Archer. "Tom, what can I say—green to old salt in two weeks." Archer hesitated for a moment, then took Ellis' outstretched hand.

His grip was firm as he replied, "Seems there's a lot of that going around."

"That there is," Ellis said, his tone carrying a rare note of warmth. But the moment of camaraderie was fleeting as the creak of the café door cut through the low murmur of the room.

All heads turned as a figure stepped inside; his uniform was crisp and starkly out of place among the battered men gathered around the table. His rank marked him as a colonel, and he was from brigade as he wore the telltale red gorget patch on each side of his collar. The man's posture had the undeniable stance of authority. He paused briefly, and his sharp gaze swept the room before he stepped forwards, his boots striking the floor with deliberate precision.

"Gentlemen," the officer began, silencing the room. "I'm Major Dawson from Brigade HQ. I've been sent by Brigadier Somersby to deliver reinforcements and his gratitude to the 9th Greenmoors." He stepped further into the room, setting a leather satchel on the table. "We've done what we could. A whip-round as it were... across the brigade. Engineers, gunners, even a few stragglers who refused to leave the line. You've got twelve volunteers to bolster your numbers."

Dawson motioned towards the doorway where a group of men hovered just outside. Their shadows spilt into the room like spectres.

"Captain Pembroke. They know what they've signed up for, and every one of them volunteered. I'm sure you can make use of them."

Pembroke rose slowly, his hands resting on the back of his chair as he regarded the doorway. His voice was calm but resolute. "Yes, Colonel."

Dawson nodded, his gaze shifting to Ellis. "Have you briefed them?"

Ellis inclined his head. "We've just finished, Sir."

Dawson turned to Pembroke and Archer, his eyes narrowing slightly. "You understand your orders?"

Both officers straightened instinctively, replying in unison, "Yes, Sir!"

Dawson's gaze stayed on each of them as he spoke again. "Every minute you keep Jerry occupied, buys time for this shambles to get to Dunkirk. There's no relief coming. No fallback beyond this position. You are the last line." The room fell silent, the weight of his words pressing heavily on the officers.

Dawson's expression softened slightly, and his tone dropped. "I know this may be of little comfort, but your actions—and those of the brigade—over the last days have made a difference. A real difference. And I know you'll continue to do so." He turned back to Ellis, his tone more formal but no less sincere. "I'll leave you to it, Major. Godspeed to you all." Dawson stepped back towards the doorway, his boots scraping faintly against the floor. He paused briefly, his gaze flicking to the volunteers waiting outside before disappearing into the night.

As Dawson disappeared into the night, the faint shuffle of his steps faded with him. Pembroke turned to Archer, his expression unreadable. "Well, Tom. Let's meet our reinforcements and get this show on the road." The two officers stepped outside into the cool night air.

Huddled together in an uneven line beneath the dim glow of a solitary lantern, the volunteers waited. Their uniforms were a patchwork of mismatched kit which was torn and stained with the grime of long days spent in retreat. The men stood silently. Their faces were a mixture of exhaustion and quiet determination.

Pembroke's eyes swept over them, and his gaze lingered on a few. One man, broad-shouldered and thickset, wore the insignia of an engineer. Another, younger and with a face barely touched by stubble, held a rifle awkwardly as though it were heavier than he'd imagined. A third, his boots scuffed and helmet slightly askew, gave a small nod when Pembroke's eyes met his.

Pembroke stepped forwards. His tone was steady and carried the authority of a seasoned officer. "I'm Captain Pembroke, and this is Lieutenant Archer. You've been assigned to a tough mission, and I won't sugarcoat it—it's only going to get harder. But you've done something most men haven't: you've stepped forwards when it counted, so thank you." He paused, letting his words settle, his gaze moving across the line.

"You'll be integrated with what's left of D Company. We've taken heavy losses, but we've held the line before, and we'll do it again. Stick together, trust the men beside you, and follow orders. We'll make it count."

A murmur passed through the group. Some nodded quietly while others shifted their weight as though trying to find some anchor in the moment.

Archer stepped forwards, his voice firm but approachable. "Get your gear sorted and ready. We're moving soon." His gaze settled on the engineer. "Corporal?"

A man stepped forwards, his voice steady. "Corporal Barrett, Sir." Archer met his eyes, a brief flicker of acknowledgement passing between them.

"Good. I'm counting on you to keep these men in line. You'll report to me as section commander. Now get them organised. We're heading to the Rue de Bergues in five minutes."

Pembroke adjusted the strap of his webbing, glancing towards the darkened horizon. "Right, Tom. I'll head to the Rue de Bergues now, see if I can get a sniff of the land before we move the whole lot into position." Archer closed the buckle on his webbing belt and slung his rifle over his shoulder. "Understood, Sir. I'll head back and round up the company. Shouldn't take long to get them moving." He glanced at his watch, the faint glow of its dial illuminating the time. "It's just gone 2200. We'll be in position before midnight if we keep things tight."

Pembroke gave a faint hum, and his eyes narrowed as he scanned the shadows ahead. "Four dozen men, including the volunteers, to hold off God knows what Jerry has lined up for us. Not exactly the ideal setup."

"Not ideal," Archer agreed, his voice low. "But it's what we've got. At least the volunteers seem steady. Corporal Barrett looks like he knows his stuff."

Pembroke's lips curled into a wry smile. "That's something, at least. Still, moving into a position we don't know, in the dark, with so few men...it's a gamble. But ours is not the reason why and all that."

Archer managed a wry smile, the strain of the situation settling on his shoulders. "Perditi sumus!" (We are lost). Pembroke raised an eyebrow, immediately catching the Latin.

"Oh, fantastic! Just what I needed to hear." Despite his words, Pembroke's expression softened though his tone stayed firm. "You're probably not wrong, Tom. Now, get D Company moving. I'll see what's waiting for us down the road." He paused, his gaze steady on Archer. "And keep an eye on the lads. It's been a hell of a day."

Archer drew a breath, straightened slightly, and replied, "I will, Sir. See you at the position."

Pembroke turned sharply. "All right, Corporal Barrett. Let's get the chaps moving. Follow me!" As Pembroke and the volunteers disappeared into the shadows, Archer turned back towards the café, his thoughts already racing ahead. Forty-six men—exhausted, battered, some wounded—none of them truly ready for what lay ahead.

Archer pushed open the door of the house that served as D Company HQ and stepped into the dim, smoke-filled room. The remnants of HQ Section were scattered; some men leant against walls while others crouched on the floor. Their exhaustion was palpable—mud-streaked faces, bloodied uniforms, and eyes that spoke of sleepless nights and relentless battle.

"Sergeant Major," Archer called, cutting through the low murmur of the room. Company Sergeant Major Dixon rose from a corner, his face drawn but alert. He crossed the room with deliberate strides.

"Sir?"

"Get the company ready to move," Archer said, firm but calm. "We're regrouping at the chapel ruins. Full kit, weapons, and whatever supplies we've got left. I want everyone assembled and ready in twenty minutes."

Dixon's brow furrowed. "Mr. Pembroke, Sir?" His tone was quizzical.

"He's fine, Sergeant Major," Archer replied briskly. "Now, get the men ready."

Dixon nodded sharply. "Understood, Sir." He turned on his heel, his voice booming as he began barking orders. "Right, lads! On your feet! Grab your gear and get sorted—double quick! Lewis!" He pointed to the company runner. "Get out to the sections and tell them to gather at the chapel ruins. Move it!"

The men stirred, their movements sluggish at first, then quickening as the urgency of Dixon's tone sank in. Archer stepped aside to let Dixon take charge as the room transformed into a scene of controlled chaos.

A little later, as the remnants of HQ Section trudged wearily towards the chapel ruins, CSM Dixon fell into step beside Archer.

"Are we moving out, Sir?" Dixon's voice his low but laced with quiet expectation. Archer slowed his pace, allowing the question to settle heavily on him.

He glanced at Dixon, then stopped, deciding to speak plainly. "Not quite, Sergeant Major. We drew the short straw—literally." He exhaled, his tone softening. "I'll explain everything to the rest of the company when we're all together." For a moment, Dixon absorbed the answer in silence, his expression unreadable.

Finally, he nodded once, his voice steady. "Sir."

As Archer stood before the chapel ruins, the darkness pressed in around him, broken only by the faint glow of the pale light of the half-moon. Long shadows swallowed the faces of the men gathered before him; their forms were little more than indistinct shapes in the night. In a strange way, the obscurity felt like a mercy. He couldn't see the exhaustion carved into their expressions or the silent questions they dared not voice. He didn't need to—he felt it in the stillness, in the way their collective breath seemed to hang heavy in the air.

Archer cleared his throat, his voice steady but low. "Listen up, lads. I know you're tired, and I know you're wondering what's next. Here it is: we've drawn the short straw. D Company's been chosen to stay behind and hold the line while the rest of the battalion makes for Dunkirk." He paused, letting the words settle into the quiet night. Around him, men shifted uneasily, the scrape of a boot against gravel breaking the stillness. Someone exhaled sharply, and the sound cut through the murmur of distant artillery. Others stared straight ahead. Their expressions were hidden by the shadows, but their tension was palpable.

"I'm not going to sugarcoat it," Archer continued. "This is going to be tough. But I've seen what you're capable of these past weeks. I know what D Company can do. And I know we're going to make every minute count—for each other, and for the lads in the battalion who are counting on us to get this done."

He glanced around, his eyes sweeping across the group. Though the darkness hid their faces, he could feel their eyes on him. "As I said, it's not ideal, but it's our lot."

Archer paused, letting the silence stretch, heavy but resolute, before continuing. "We've scraped together a small force: a couple of anti-tank guns from the RA, mortars, and a group of twelve volunteers. We're taking over some prepared positions on the Rue de Bergues: a natural bottleneck that Jerry will have to come through at some point, and we'll be waiting for him." He glanced towards Mallory as the moonlight caught the edge of his profile. "It's a good position, as far as I can tell," Archer added, more to himself than anyone else though doubt flickered briefly in his voice.

Mallory turned faintly, his focus already shifting to the road ahead where the real test lay. Archer continued. "We've been given the last reserves of ammo. That means we'll have the chance to stock up and give 'em hell."

Archer glanced over the men in an attempt to gauge their reactions. The announcement had hit hard, but the silence that followed wasn't one of rebellion: it was resignation, mixed with the kind of determination he'd come to expect from D Company.

Jacks muttered under his breath, breaking the quiet. "Same old story—someone's gotta stay behind."

Mallory, ever the steady hand, clapped a reassuring hand on Jacks' shoulder. "And someone always does," he said, his voice calm, but his gaze steady on Archer as if to say they trusted him to see them through this. Private Saunders, standing towards the back, shifted uncomfortably. His face, usually full of cheek and youthful energy, was tight with worry.

"Lieutenant," he piped up, his voice cracking slightly. "You think...we've got a chance?"

Archer stepped down from the slight rise he'd been standing on, moving closer to his men. His eyes settled on Saunders, who shifted nervously, his helmet slightly askew. Archer offered a faint, steady smile. "Saunders, when you're standing with us, I'd back this lot against anything."

A faint chuckle rippled through the group, breaking the oppressive tension like a crack of sunlight through storm clouds.

Saunders straightened slightly, the corners of his mouth twitching upwards in a timid smile. Even Mallory smirked as his gaze settled on Saunders with a mix of warmth and quiet authority.

"You hear that, lad? The lieutenant's got faith in you—and so do I. Just keep your head and do what you're best at. You'll be fine."

Webb, seated nearby and still nursing the bandage on his arm, grumbled, "Well, I suppose if we're stuck here, we might as well give Jerry a proper send-off."

Scouse Evans was knelt at the front. "Sir," he began, his Liverpudlian accent cutting through the gloom. "How'd we end up pullin' the short straw, then? Someone out there not like us?" A ripple of murmurs passed through the men. Archer, sensing a little discontent raised faint smile.

"Well, Evans, I know they don't like you. As for the rest of us, I'm not so sure." The quiet murmurs grew into more of a spirited laughter, lifting the tension in the air.

Raising a hand, Archer's tone softened as he continued. "But in all seriousness, Captain Pembroke drew the lot. Fair and square."

Scouse Evans smirked, tilting his helmet back slightly. "Figures, Sir. Captain Pembroke's luck is about as good as Saunders' luck with that French lass in Arras." The platoon erupted into muffled chuckles and knowing glances. Archer frowned slightly, clearly out of the loop.

Saunders flushed red, muttering, "That's not how it happened. I was—" Archer raised a hand, cutting young Saunders off, the chuckles still lingering among the men.

"All right, enough. If you lot spent as much energy fighting Jerry as you do cracking jokes, we'd have won the war by now." A faint ripple of laughter passed again, softer this time, but the weight in the air had shifted. The men were standing straighter, their eyes sharper as if clinging to the fragile sense of normalcy that humour had brought.

"Mallory," Archer continued, his tone turning brisk. "Get them ready to move. We've got a date with the Rue de Bergues, and I'd hate to keep Jerry waiting." The sergeant snapped a sharp nod, a smirk playing on his lips.

"Aye, Sir. But you'd best tell Saunders to leave his luck with the French girls behind—don't want him distracting the whole company."

More laughter followed as the men began gathering their gear, the light-hearted moment carrying them forwards into the night.

Archer lingered for a moment, watching them fall into step. A faint smile touched his face before it slipped away to be replaced by the steel of command.

"Let's go," he said quietly, turning towards the road ahead.

Chapter 5

The cool night air carried a sharp tang of smoke and scorched earth as D Company trudged through the darkened streets of Cassel. The faint glow of the waning moon cast long silhouettes over the shattered ruins; gutted buildings rose like sentinels on either side of the road. The town, once lively and bustling, now stood as a grim monument to the ravages of war. Archer glanced over his shoulder at the column of weary men moving in uneasy silence. Their faces were pale in the moonlight. Behind them, the remainder of D Company moved with the practiced efficiency of soldiers who had seen too much and survived against uncomprehensible odds. Striding a few paces ahead, Archer raised a hand, signalling the column to halt.

"This is it," Archer said quietly, his voice carrying over the stillness. The Rue de Bergues stretched ahead; its cobbled surface was uneven and strewn with debris. The road sloped gently downwards, framed by rows of damaged buildings whose jagged edges cast fractured shadows onto the rubble-strewn ground. Archer stepped forwards. His steps ground into the loose gravel as he surveyed the scene.

The road narrowed as it descended, hemmed in by centuries-old, stone structures on either side. Large piles of rubble from collapsed walls spilt into the street, creating natural barricades that funnelled the passage into a single lane barely wide enough for a vehicle. To the left, an abandoned cart lay tipped on its side; its splintered wood formed another improvised obstacle. To the right, the remains of a shop front leant precariously with its shattered windows and warped beams framing the gaping void where a door had once been.

Taking in the scene, Archer immediately understood why command had specified this area to hold. The terrain was unforgiving: a natural choke point that could stall even the most determined enemy advance. He left the men kneeling against the wall of a building who were resting in a doorway, and he crossed

76

the brick-strewn road to meet Pembroke.

"Tom, looks like Jerry will have to come straight down this road," Pembroke murmured, his eyes narrowing as he followed the road's descent.

"It would appear so, Sir," Archer responded matter-of-factly. Pembroke let out a soft hum, casting another glance down the street before turning back to Archer, his expression contemplative.

"Brigades got this one right, Tom. Jerry's going to have to come up this road, one way or the other."

Archer responded with a slight smirk. "It's the 'other' that worries me." Pembroke chuckled softly, pulling out his notebook and flipping it open to a rough sketch of the street ahead.

"Look here," he said, tapping the page with his pencil. "See how the road veers slightly to the right? That bend's where we set up the Vickers. It'll give us a perfect field of fire all the way down the street." Archer nodded, studying the sketched map intently, but he remained silent. Pembroke continued, his tone confident but measured. "If we concentrate our fire down the street, we'll make it bloody difficult for them to advance."

"What about armour?" Archer asked, his voice steady but tinged with concern.

Pembroke's expression brightened, almost invigorated by the challenge. "It's narrow, Tom. That's what works in our favour. We set up one of the anti-tank guns here—" he tapped the bend on his sketch, "—pointing straight down the street. If we're lucky, we can hit them before they even get a shot off. The second gun stays here, covering this end of the street as a fallback position. Once they push through, we'll pull back to this spot and hit them again."

Archer was fully alert, and his expression shadowed with concentration. "And if they try to outflank us? Come around the back of these buildings?"

Pembroke tilted his head thoughtfully as if anticipating the question. "That's where the lads come in. We'll split them into small groups—three or four men each—and position them in the buildings on either side of the street. They'll not only reinforce the main line from there, but they can also keep an eye on the rear. To be honest Tom, I'm hoping Jerry will push the flanks, and the only way he can do that will be with infantry, house to house. Our boys will be ready to meet them. This will slow any advance down which, ultimately my friend, is what we have been sent here to do."

Archer glanced back towards the darkened street where his men waited. "Ok, we make this as bloody and difficult as we can!"

Pembroke's smile faded slightly, his tone turning sombre. "Exactly, Tom. We make them bleed for every inch—that's all we can do." Pembroke's tone shifted, growing more practical. "Let's get the men into position. I've already got Barrett and the gun crews working on the first position."

Archer inclined his head slightly, his mind already running through the logistics before he turned sharply and started back towards the rest of the company. The cool night air seemed suddenly heavier as the weight of the task pressed down on him with every step. When he reached the gathered men, he found Mallory and CSM Dixon waiting, their faces grim but ready.

"Sergeant Major, Mallory," Archer began addressing both men, keeping his voice low but clear enough to carry to the men within earshot. "Here's the plan. We're splitting our defence into two parts. Pembroke's setting up the anti-tank guns—one at the bend to catch Jerry before they can reach us, and another here for a fallback position. Your job is to get the men into the buildings on either side of the street." Dixon's expression tightened in thought.

"Three to four men per building, Sir? Enough to hold their ground but able to fall back when needed?"

"Exactly," Archer confirmed. "We're creating overlapping fields of fire. The likelihood is that once we hit them in the street, they'll come at us from the rear. The groups can watch each other's backs. I want every man to know where the fallback position is." Archer went on. "Mallory, the volunteers we have picked up, get them integrated into the rifle groups. Keep them close to experienced men. I'm sure all of them are good, but they may need a steady man around." Archer allowed himself a moment to meet Dixon's and Mallory's eyes.

"Gentlemen, this is going to be a scrap...a real scrap. Every minute we keep them bottled up, the better the chances the battalion, hell, the British army, has of getting out."

Mallory stared back and asked, "What about us Sir, what are our chances of getting home?"

Archer stared straight back. "Let's cross that bridge when we get to it. I understand the ammunition reserves are over there in that shop. Get the men resupplied and then get to it."

With that, both men turned and began calling out orders. The calm night was quickly broken by the shuffle of equipment and low murmurs as the soldiers began to move into their positions. Archer lingered for a moment, glancing towards the horizon where the faintest hint of dawn would soon creep into view. There was no turning back now.

Archer made his way back through the darkened street, his feet crunching over the loose rubble scattered below his feet. Each breath felt like inhaling the battle itself—dust, smoke, and fear rolled into one oppressive weigh. As he approached the secondary position, he caught sight of Pembroke crouched near a partially collapsed building. The structure had once been a small townhouse, but now its roof was gone, and the remaining walls leant precariously inwards, jagged edges silhouetted against the dim light of the moon.

Pembroke was hunched beside the anti-tank gun, speaking with Corporal Barrett. The gun itself was positioned at the far end of the street, partially shielded by the ramshackle remains of a stone wall. Its barrel was pointed resolutely towards the southern approach; the narrow field of fire had already been carefully chosen to target any armour attempting to pass the primary position at the bend. A pile of loose bricks and broken beams had been hastily arranged into a crude barricade, offering the crew some cover.

The gun crew worked methodically, arranging their remaining ammunition into neat rows within arm's reach. The dull gleam of the shells caught the pale dawn light, and the hushed clinking of metal against stone carried faintly through the air. Pembroke's eyes flicked towards Archer as he approached with a focused but calm disposition.

"Tom," Pembroke said, straightening slightly. "We're about as ready as we can be here. Barrett's lads have done a fine job getting the guns into position."

Archer's gaze was taken from the gun's defence to a minor commotion he could hear coming from inside the shop where he'd sent the men to get resupplied. He approached the scene where the men were gathered, his movements disturbed the debris-strewn path. Inside, the weak glow of lanterns and flashlights illuminated the excitement rippling through the group as the crates of ammunition were pried open. A low murmur of approval spread among the men; their weariness was momentarily forgotten in the face of the unexpected bounty.

Jacks was the first to unearth a treasure, pulling out a Boys anti-tank rifle with a broad grin that broke through his otherwise grimy and tired face. "Look at this beauty!" he declared, hoisting the weapon like a trophy. The men around him chuckled, their spirits visibly lifting.

Archer stopped a few steps away. He rested his hands on his hips as he observed the scene with a small smile. In the corner of the room, a group of riflemen passed around bandoliers of rifle rounds; their hands worked quickly to load their pouches and swing bandoliers over their necks. Bren gunners picking up magazines with low but eager voices as they discussed plans for rationing their new-found supply. The glint of Mills bombs caught the dim light, and the sight of grenades being handled with careful reverence brought a sharp edge of hope to the atmosphere.

"Better than Christmas, this," Private Evans quipped, holding up a pristine grenade as if appraising a rare jewel. His Liverpudlian accent carried a note of humour that made a few heads turn with smirks and nods. Saunders approached Archer and passed him a bandolier and a Mills bomb.

"Thanks." Archer responded as if he was being passed a cup of tea.

Archer's gaze shifted to Jacks who was slinging the Boys rifle over his shoulder with an exaggerated air of pride.

"Planning to knock out a tank or two, Jacks?" Archer called; his tone was tinged with amusement.

Jacks glanced over. His grin was undimmed. "Just let me get one in my sights, Sir. I'll show Jerry a thing or two." The men laughed to lighten the oppressive mood that had clung to them since they arrived. Archer's smile lingered for a moment before he straightened, letting his gaze sweep over the group. There was an energy here—a spark of resilience—that bolstered his own determination.

His eyes settled on the crates being rapidly emptied as the men restocked their kits. The dull gleam of ammunition and grenades reminded him of the stakes, but also of the strength these men carried with them. They were battered, exhausted, and outnumbered, but they weren't beaten. Archer stepped back, letting the men continue their work. He turned towards Pembroke's position, his thoughts steady and resolved. Whatever came next, they would face it with what they had—and they would make it count.

The pale streaks of dawn were creeping into the sky, casting a muted light over the battered town of Cassel. Shrouded in the stillness of early morning, it seemed to hold its breath. A delicate chill lingered in the air, clinging to the stones and debris—a silent reminder of the night's uneasy calm.

Captain Pembroke led the way; his footsteps scuffed softly against loose rubble as he walked the line with deliberate movements and took in the defensive positions. Archer followed close behind, his rifle slung across his shoulder, while Company Sergeant Major Dixon brought up the rear, his gaze sweeping over the scattered positions with the practiced vigilance of a seasoned soldier.

The narrow street, hemmed in by its jagged ruins, had become a makeshift fortress. Sandbags had been hastily stacked in doorways to form crude firing positions. Men crouched behind broken walls and piles of rubble, their faces grimy and pale but resolute as they tightened straps, checked weapons, and adjusted helmets. The low murmur of last-minute preparations filled the air—a sharp contrast to the chaos they all knew was coming.

Pembroke paused near a section where the cobbled road curved slightly to the right. His eyes scanned the first anti-tank gun which was positioned to cover the length of the street. The crew, crouched low behind the weapon, whispered among themselves; each of their movements was efficient and deliberate. One man traced a hand along the barrel as though he was willing it to hold steady when the time came.

Pembroke turned to Archer and Dixon, motioning towards

the bend in the road. "This spot here," he began, his voice quieter, carrying a gentle edge of grim humour. "It's earnt itself a bit of a name: Dead Horse Corner." He stood with his hands resting loosely on his hips, sweeping his gaze over the bend in the road.

"When the East Riding Yeomanry passed through here, they found the road clogged with bodies. Not just men, mind you—horses too. One poor lad said it looked like a river of blood was flowing down the street. Turns out, it wasn't blood at all. It was red wine spilling from one of the horse-drawn limbers that had been hit. Took them hours to clear the mess, but the name stuck." Dixon let out a brief chuckle, shaking his head.

Pembroke's tone shifted, his eyes narrowing as they returned to the bend. "Point is, this spot's seen its fair share of death already. Now it's up to us to make sure it sees some more—Jerry's, this time."

Archer glanced down the road lingering on the long stretch of cobbles that led to their position. "Well, Sir, if Jerry's coming, this corner's as good a place as any to greet him."

Archer's gaze shifted down the street where the second anti-tank gun was concealed beneath the shadow of a collapsed roof. From this angle, the gun could target anything that broke through the first position. As they walked, Archer glanced up at a shattered window above where Saunders was crouched, peering out with a rifle in hand. He gave Archer a slight nod of acknowledgement as he scanned the street, and Archer could see the tension in his upper body. Archer allowed a faint smile to tug at the corner of his mouth.

"Saunders, how are you doing?" He called up softly. Saunders looked back, his grip tightening on the rifle as a nervous grin flickered across his face. "Just keeping an eye out, Sir."

Pembroke followed Archer's gaze and gave a low chuckle.

"He'll be fine once it starts. Nerves don't mean a lack of guts."

Archer was quick to respond. "That lad is terrified, yet he's one of the best under fire." They continued their walk: with every step, the tension wound tighter in their chests, like a noose being slowly drawn.

Pembroke turned to Dixon. His voice was quiet but no less serious. "Where have you placed the Brens?"

Dixon gestured towards the street. "We have four in total, Sir Two are placed above the Vickers covering the main road. Solid line of sight. One is back with the other gun, and the last one is with Sergeant Mallory in that house over there." Dixon pointed to a three-storey townhouse that looked remarkably untouched.

Pembroke acknowledged his approval by a small thumbs up. His sharp eyes scanned the positions. "Good. The men seem steady enough."

"They're nervous," Dixon admitted, his voice betraying the fear that gripped them. "But they'll stand!" Archer let the words hang in the air for a moment while his gaze shifted to the men scattered along the line. They continued to move with a calm purpose, adjusting their positions, checking their weapons, and sharing hushed words that carried a fragile resolve. Nervous, yes—but not broken. They'd been through too much for that.

He thought back to the many long days of retreat: the bridge they'd blown to stall Jerry's advance; the ambushes survived by sheer grit; and the desperate rescue mission that had pushed them all to their limits. These men had held the line when others would have faltered. They'd fought with courage borne not from glory, but from an unyielding determination to see each other through.

Archer felt a flicker of pride swell beneath the burden he'd carried for days. He knew what Dixon meant—these men would stand. They'd proven it time and again against impossible odds.

And as long as they stood, so would he.

But there was a part of him that couldn't ignore the question that was grinding in his mind: how long could they keep doing this? He heaved the thought aside, teeth clenched. It didn't matter. They would hold for as long as they could, and if the time came to fall back, they would do so with the same resolve they'd carried through every other challenge. Archer straightened slightly, the burden of leadership settling over his shoulders like an old, familiar armour. "They've stood this long," he murmured, more to himself than anyone else. "And they'll do it again."

Pembroke turned his head at the sound of Archer's voice. "They will, Tom," he said. His expression was unreadable as he spoke quietly, reading Archer's thoughts. "And we'll make damn sure it counts."

Pembroke glanced at Dixon. His tone was steady but carried a note of finality. "Sergeant Major, you'll take charge of the second gun. I want your eyes on the fallback line and those lads holding the rear. Keep them sharp. When Jerry pushes us back, we'll need every man ready."

Dixon gave a firm, resolute nod. "Understood, Sir. I'll make sure they're ready."

Turning to Archer, Pembroke's gaze softened just slightly. "Tom, you're with the first gun. Take position upstairs alongside the Bren gunners. That bend in the street is going to be the hottest point, and I'll need someone with a clear view to direct the fire."

Archer's response was immediate. He kept his voice calm as he buried the fear of the impending danger.

"Got it, Sir."

Pembroke's sharp eyes flicked between the two men, a gentle smile ghosting his lips. "Good. We know our places, then. Let's make Jerry regret every inch he takes."

As Pembroke moved to brief the gun crews, Archer lingered for a moment, his gaze sweeping over the line. The pale light of dawn had grown into a steady light, casting long shadows down the battered Rue de Bergues. He could hear the murmurs of the men, the continued adjustments of rifles and kit, and the rattle of ammunition boxes being set into place.

Dixon, ever the steady presence, clapped a hand on Archer's shoulder. "Good Luck Lieutenant." Archer met Dixon's gaze. The Sergeant Major appeared full of confidence, steadying something deep within him.

"Good luck to you too, Sergeant Major," Archer echoed, the words carrying both determination and finality.

Without another word, they moved to their positions; the quiet strain of the morning was thick with purpose. The waiting had begun, and with it, the certainty that when the time came, every man knew his place in the battle ahead.

Archer peered through the window of the crumbling attic he'd chosen as his vantage point. The building, perched above the gun position, seemed to defy gravity with its sagging walls and splintered beams. Its attic windows jutted out from the roof, and both were reinforced with sandbags where the frames had long since been blown away. The two Brens were already in position— one stationed at the next window, and the other manned by Webb, who lay prone, his barrel sighted through a breach in the roof that gave a clear view down the street. Archer rested his arms on the sandbagged ledge and raised his binoculars to hie eyes. He surveyed the road below him and the desolate expanse beyond.

Archer focused on the empty stretch of road. He'd walked the road, but now it looked different stripped of whatever life had once lingered. Hollow. It was as if the town itself was bracing for something it couldn't hold back. No movement, no sound—

just that brittle stillness that so often came before a barrage. His gaze passed over the ruined façades; their outlines were familiar but drained of meaning. He shifted his grip on the rifle. Whatever was coming, it would come through here. Smoke lingered on the breeze, curling faintly above the ruins to remind them all of the battles that had already scarred the town.

Directly below, the street was a maze of improvised defences. Sandbags and rubble were stacked in uneven piles, forming crude barricades meant to slow any advancing enemy. At Dead Horse Corner, the first anti-tank gun sat in grim readiness; its barrel was aimed unwaveringly down the narrow stretch ahead. The crew crouched behind it silently, and the strain was palpable as they awaited the inevitable moment when the weapon would roar into life.

Further down the street, Archer spotted the scraps of an overturned cart; its wooden frame was shattered and tilted at an awkward angle. Beyond that, the road disappeared into the gloom of more ruined buildings. On the upper floors of these structures, tentative movements suggested the presence of men stationed at windows, their rifles ready to sweep the narrow approach.

Archer's gaze shifted further upwards to the rooftops. One or two broken chimneys jutted at awkward angles with stark their silhouettes against the growing light of the sky. A low breeze stirred the air, dragging with it the bitter scent of charred wood and the distant, haunting stillness of the countryside.

The silence was deceptive. Archer knew that well. The road ahead appeared deserted, but every shattered window and crumbled wall seemed to promise its own deadly fight. As the dawn light grew stronger, so too did the expectance of the impending battle. Lowering the binoculars, he exhaled slowly and allowed himself a brief moment to take in the fragile beauty of the scene before him. He knew it was a fleeting calm before the inevitable storm. The sound of footsteps on the attic stairs pulled Archer from his thoughts. Pembroke stepped into view—calm, deliberate, radiating the kind of steadiness men clung to in chaos

"All nice and cosy up here, Tom?" he quipped, a wry smile tugging at his lips.

Archer turned to face him. "Well, it's not the Ritz, but we're comfortable enough." He glanced at Webb and Harding, both men remained fixed on the street below, their focus unbroken.

Pembroke dragged an old trunk across the floor and sat down, removing his helmet to reveal his blonde hair, damp with sweat and streaked with grime. He ran a hand through it, scratching at his scalp as he let out a weary sigh.

"Gosh, I could do with a drink. I've just been round all the chaps—everyone's as ready as they'll ever be." As his hand dropped from his hair, he noticed Archer holding out a familiar silver flask; its surface was dented and scratched but serviceable. Pembroke's brows rose in surprise.

"Bloody hell. You've still got that." Taking the flask, he brought it to his lips, savouring the warmth of the whisky as it spread through his chest. For a moment, the tension in his shoulders eased. "Didn't think the fight would last this long," he murmured, handing it back with a wide grin.

Archer took the flask, tipping it back for a quick nip before sliding it into his shirt pocket. "I can't see anything stirring out there," he muttered, moving back to the window. He raised his binoculars for another scan of the street. Pembroke joined him at the vantage point, leaning in slightly as Archer passed him the binoculars.

Taking them, Pembroke focused on the street below and the clouded distance beyond. He studied the view for a long moment before lowering them, turning the binoculars over in his hands. His gaze caught on the engraving near the hinge, and his face screwed as he read it aloud. "'Oberleutnant Erich Schneider.'" He glanced up at Archer, curiosity flickering in his eyes. "Who was he?"

Archer leant against the windowsill. His tone was quiet and reflective. "The officer who didn't make it out of that armoured car at the bridge. My first." He hesitated, his thumb brushing the edge of the binoculars. "These were his." He took a long, deep breath, and tightened his grip around the worn leather. "I said a prayer for him, you know. Didn't think it'd mean much, but it felt like the right thing." His voice softened to a whisper as he repeated the words: "'Domine, dona ei requiem, et ignosce mihi quod feci.'"

Pembroke's gaze didn't waver as he quietly replied, "Lord, grant him rest and forgive me for what I have done." The silence between them stretched for a moment before he murmured, "Amen." The single word carried a gravity that needed no further explanation, an understood acknowledgement of the burdens they both carried.

Pembroke's gaze drifted back to the horizon, his expression momentarily far away. Then, as if recalling the reason he'd come upstairs, his demeanour sharpened.

He cleared his throat and turned to Archer; his voice was brisk but quiet. "Right, Tom. Enough reminiscing. Sergeant Wallis got the mortars set up in a garden just west of the second gun position. It's a tight fit, but it'll do. They're well-concealed by the surrounding houses, and the range should cover both the road and the flank." He gestured towards the street below. "You've got the best vantage point, so you'll give the signal—a red flare—and he'll drop everything he's got onto the road." Pembroke paused, his hand brushing the holster at his side before drawing the very pistol. He held it out to Archer, meeting his eyes. "You'll need this," he said simply, the weight of the small device mirrored in his steady gaze.

Archer leant closer to Pembroke. His voice was low as he brought his mouth near to Pembroke's ear. "James," he said softly. Pembroke's eyes widened—it was the first time Archer had used his Christian name. "I'll fight hard here and at the next position. But I want to make one thing clear: I have no intention of surrendering or dying here in Cassel. When hope is lost, I'll need your permission to break off and break out."

Pembroke, momentarily taken aback by the directness of the statement, held Archer's gaze for a beat. A faint smile played at the corners of his lips as he straightened slightly and spoke with a calm but resolute voice. "Of course, old boy. Pretty sure we are all thinking the same." Pembroke placed a hand on Archer's shoulder, his grip firm but not heavy. The morning's fragile stillness was suddenly shattered by the distant, rolling thunder of German artillery. At first, the explosions seemed far off, just a low growl across the horizon. Then, steadily, methodically, the barrage began to creep closer, each detonation louder and more forceful than the last. Plumes of dust and debris rose into the air like dirty spectres to mark the inexorable advance of the shelling.

The ground beneath Archer's feet trembled as the bombardment reached the outskirts of Cassel. The methodical rhythm of destruction echoed through the streets, reverberating off the shattered buildings. Each vibration stirred clouds of dust that mingled with the choking tang of smoke and scorched stone. Archer ducked instinctively as a shell screamed overhead, its high-pitched wail giving way to a deafening explosion that obliterated a nearby building. Bricks and timber poured down in a chaotic cascade, sending a plume of smoke and ash curling through the air. The thick haze seeped through the town, weaving its way down the narrow Rue de Bergues like a hostage seeking refuge.

From his vantage point, Archer scanned the distance. Flashes of mortar fire flickered through the haze, their rapid succession marked a systematic effort to obliterate any resistance. He felt his fingers dig harder into the sandbags placed along the windowsill.

"Here we go, Tom!" Pembroke's voice cut through the fractured noise, barely audible but steady. He stood a few paces back, his eyes fixed on the horizon. Archer glanced over his shoulder to see him rigid, his face set with a grim determination.

The barrage crawled closer still, spreading not only along their front but across the town; it was a deliberate, calculated effort to pin down any British forces that remained. Archer's gut twisted with the devastating realisation—they still believed the British were here in force.

The bombardment dragged on, each thunderous impact stretching time into an agonising eternity. Archer cast a glance at the men below, crouched behind their defences. Their faces, pale and streaked with grime, were tight with fear, but their hands remained steady on their weapons.

The relentless destruction reached its crescendo with a final, ear-splitting assault that left Archer's ears ringing. And then, as abruptly as it had begun, the shelling ceased.

The sudden silence was almost worse than the noise: dense and oppressive as if the town itself held its breath.

Archer exhaled sharply. His heart pounded against his ribs. The rattle of shifting debris echoed in the stillness. He turned to Pembroke, who was already tightening the strap on his helmet with deliberate and calm hands.

"Good luck, lads," Pembroke muttered, his voice low but resolute. "I'm heading down to the gun, Tom. Remember red flare!"

Archer nodded slowly, tightening his jaw as he looked back out over the battered town.

An eerie stillness settled over the ruins like a shroud: the distant rumble of engines were low but growing in menace. It carried a chilling promise of what was to come.

Chapter 6

The low rumble of engines grew steadily louder, a deep, guttural sound that seemed to shake the very ground beneath them. The rhythmic clatter of tracked vehicles mingled with the grind of gears: a mechanical symphony of death that drew ever closer. Archer stood at the window of his crumbling vantage point, his fingers instinctively grasping his rifle as he scanned the haze-filled street below. The growing glimmers of sunlight pierced the smoky air, casting long, distorted shapes across the battered town. Raising his binoculars, Archer steadied them against the crumbling edge of the window frame, his hands firm despite the faint tremor of anticipation in his chest. Through the lenses, the subtle outlines of advancing tanks eerily emerged from the mist that parted just enough to reveal their angular forms—cold, mechanical shapes cutting through the gloom like blades through fabric. He adjusted the focus: the blurred shapes sharpening into the cold, mechanical menace of Panzer hulls. Their metallic sheen caught the pale sunrays, each glint of steel was a silent promise of destruction.

Archer's gaze lingered on the lead tank, a Panzer III. Its turret swivelled with predatory precision as its barrel swept across the ruins ahead, probing for resistance like an animal scenting its prey. More tanks rolled into view behind it, emerging one by one like predators from the haze and framed by the low flames and broken walls still bleeding smoke. Between the armoured behemoths, Archer could make out the shapes of infantry—lines of soldiers stepping cautiously, their helmets and weapons glinting faintly in the morning light.

As the tanks rumbled forwards, their angular forms began to melt into the chaos of the town. The lead Panzer vanished first, swallowed by the shattered buildings. One by one, the following tanks disappeared into the maze of crumbling walls and narrow streets, their dark shadows flickering and shifting through the smoke. The infantry, too, became little more than fleeting movements among the ruins; their presence was betrayed only by the glint of light off steel and the occasional shape darting between piles of rubble.

Archer lowered the binoculars for a moment. His head turned to listen to the growing, monotonous sound of grinding tracks and heavy engines that echoed through the confined streets. The enemy was no longer a distant, looming threat: they were here, threading their way into Cassel's heart, their progress being masked by the labyrinth of destruction.

He scanned further down the road, noting the methodical pace of the advancing column. Each vehicle and soldier moved with disciplined purpose. Their formation was tight despite the ruined, choked street.

Beyond the tanks, a heavier shape slowly emerged—broader and bulkier, with a squat shape that spoke of heavier armour. Archer's breath hitched. A self-propelled gun perhaps, or even an armoured recovery vehicle. Whatever it was, it signalled the Germans' intent to break through with overwhelming force.

"Steady," Archer murmured, his voice low but firm. Webb nodded without looking up, his fingers already resting on the weapon's grip, and his eyes fixed on the street below.

Archer yelled out, "Tanks! At least three, and Infantry!" The German tanks slowed as they approached the choke point ahead of Dead Horse Corner. Archer could hear the sharp hiss of air escaping their vents and the metallic clang of tracks shifting through Cassel's carcass. The lead tank, a Panzer III, swung its turret cautiously, the barrel scanning the ruins as if the machine itself were alive, preparing to execute.

Suddenly, a sharp, urgent shout echoed from below. "Prepare to fire!" Searching for the cause, Archer shifted his gaze to the men positioned in the buildings lining the street. From the shattered windows and improvised barricades, the soldiers of 6th Platoon and D company waited in gripped silence, their faces pale but determined. The Vickers gun crew crouched behind their sandbagged position, the water-cooled barrel trained on the road ahead. Nearby, a rifleman adjusted his helmet with trembling hands that betrayed the nerves that gripped them all.

The sound of the tanks grew deafening as they reached the edge of the defensive line. Archer's heart pounded in his chest: each beat an echo of the engines below. He forced his breathing to slow, the moment stilled, swollen with unsaid fears.

Across from Archer's vantage point, Jacks was positioned on the second floor of a battered commercial office and was adjusting the Boys anti-tank rifle against his shoulder. The cold, heavy steel felt reassuring in his hands, but he braced himself for the inevitable punishing recoil. The weapon kicked like a horse, and he'd seen more than a few novices walk away bruised—or worse—from their first shot. He wasn't about to let that happen to him. The morning light filtered through the shattered windows, casting sharp patterns across the dusty floor. From his vantage point, he had a clear view of the narrow street below with its uneven cobblestones framed by the ragged remains of gutted buildings. Jacks knew he'd be one of the first to spot the Germans as they advanced, and the thought sent a ripple of adrenaline through him.

He shifted his weight slightly, settling into the sandbags that shielded the window. He felt the grinding, mechanical growl that reverberated through the still air. Jacks squinted down the street, his rifle's long barrel steady as he sighted along its length. His breath slowed as he instinctively synched with the steady beat of his heart, and he scanned the shadows for movement. The first flicker of motion caught his eye: a dark shape emerging in the distance. He tightened his grip, the stock pressed firmly into his shoulder as the outline of a Panzer III materialised from the gloom. It moved cautiously, its turret repeatedly swivelling. Searching. Behind it, more shapes began to form: the hulking predators of more armour, followed by their infantry threading through the broken masonry like needles. Jacks swallowed hard: his throat dry as he watched the enemy column grow. Slowly, purposefully, he adjusted his aim slightly, aligning the sight on the second tank, knowing and hoping the gunners would take care of the lead one. The Boys rifle felt heavy in his hands, and its weight was a stark reminder of the role he'd been assigned. His mind raced with calculations—range, trajectory, the moment to fire—but his body remained still, coiled with anticipation: instinctively prepared for when the moment came.

"Come on," he muttered under his breath, his voice barely audible over the grumble of the advancing vehicles. "Just a little closer."

The sound of grinding tracks and the rhythmic clatter of boots overwhelmed the air and echoed off the ruins. Jacks could feel the tension building, not just in his own chest but in the street below where his comrades lay in wait. He shifted his focus, checking the window frames on either side of the road, searching for the signals he knew would come. As the lead tank inched closer, Jacks exhaled slowly, steadying his aim. The time for waiting was nearly over. He was ready.

On the other side of the road, Mallory was crouched behind the splintered remains of a counter in the café. The air inside was thick with dust, having been stirred anew by the recent barrage. It carried the faint, lingering scent of charred wood. The bombardment had left the building trembling, cracks were like spiderwebs over its walls and ceiling, but it still stood—barely. Around Mallory, the men worked with grim efficiency, their faces set and streaked with dirt as they finished the last of their preparations.

He cast his eyes along the line of buildings on his side of the Rue de Bergues, noting the large, rough holes punched through the interior walls. They had prepared three of the connecting buildings to form a single defensive stronghold, allowing the men to move between them without risking exposure on the street outside. Mallory had been meticulous in ensuring the openings were staggered between floors, avoiding the creation of a single continuous link that could become a death trap. It had been a hard, dirty job, made slower by the constant need for quiet. But it was done, and Mallory felt a sense of satisfaction knowing the fallback routes were secure.

Each building had been turned into a makeshift fortress. Furniture was overturned and piled into barricades against the windows, providing cover for the riflemen who were crouched behind them. Sandbags, salvaged from redundant positions, had been hastily stacked at the larger openings, while smaller firing slits were cut into the walls to provide clear lines of sight down the street. The remnants of iron railings had been bent into crude obstacles to block one of the doorways—an added defence designed to slow any German infantry bold enough to attempt a frontal assault.

Mallory adjusted his rifle and rose slightly, just enough to peer over the counter. He scanned the men nearest to him, their faces pale in the weak light filtering through the boarded windows. Private Saunders, barely more than a boy but hardened by battle, had proven himself time and again. Yet, Mallory could see fear still clutched at his soul; it was visible in the way his hands trembled on his weapon. Next to him, Scouse Evans muttered something under his breath, his fingers moving with practiced precision as he checked his ammunition pouches. The men were tense, but ready.

Mallory moved to the back of the room where a section of men had fortified the rear exit. Lance Corporal Matthews crouched by the door, carefully threading a length of wire around two unpinned grenades. His expertise with explosives was evident in the methodical way he worked.

"Tripwire's set," Matthews said, his voice low but steady. "Anything comes through here uninvited is in for a nasty surprise."

Mallory allowed a faint grin before sweeping his gaze over the improvised defences. "Good work. Make sure the lads know to steer clear."

He paused for a moment, letting the muffled sounds of the advancing engines fill the silence. The Germans were closing in. Mallory could feel it—their advance hung over him like a storm front rolling in. He stepped back to the front of the café, his boots cracking the broken glass scattered over the floor. The defences were as strong as they could make them. It was just a matter of time. Mallory took one last look at his men. "Steady now, lads," he murmured. "Let's show 'em we ain't going quietly."

Meanwhile, Pembroke was crouched behind the sandbags at Dead Horse Corner, his hand resting lightly on the firm barricade shielding the anti-tank gun. Their sandbagged position was carefully camouflaged, and a rough net draped across its rear to blend it into its surroundings. The three men who crewed it knelt motionless around him; their eyes were locked on the road ahead, their expressions taut with readiness. Each man knew his role. The quiet tension between them was sharper than words. The gun's barrel jutted resolutely down the narrow stretch of Rue de Bergues, having carefully chosen its position for maximum effect. The 2-pounder was a sturdy, compact weapon with a long barrel that extended from a robust cradle mounted on a two-wheeled carriage. The matte-green paint was scuffed and worn, bearing the marks of hard use, with faint scratches catching the dim morning light. The breech mechanism gleamed faintly. It had been meticulously oiled and prepped—a testament to the crew's diligence. Its low position nestled behind the sandbags, nearly invisible from a distance. The barrel's elevation was at the perfect angle and trained on the bend in the road where the first tank would inevitably appear. The gun's wheels were folded upwards, and its trail legs were locked firmly into the wreckage to brace against the recoil. Nearby, the 2-pounder's armour-piercing rounds, each one of them a simple solid shot forged from hardened steel, sat neatly in their cases. Designed to punch through thick armour with brute force, they lacked explosive filler, relying instead on kinetic energy to rip through steel and wreak havoc inside.

Pembroke scanned the road ahead, knowing that in this fight, the 2-pounder was their best chance to halt the enemy's advance—even if only briefly. He adjusted his helmet, the leather strap biting into his chin as he glanced towards the bend in the road. The distant growl of engines had become a heavy, relentless sound that reverberated through the rubble-strewn streets. Pembroke could feel it in his chest: an ominous, intimidating vibration that seemed to synchronise with the pounding of his heart.

"Eyes on the first tank," he murmured to the men, his voice barely audible above the din. Corporal Prosser crouched at the rear of the gun's breech and stayed motionless, already armed with the next round to pass to the loader. The crew were ready, their nerves tightly coiled but their training steadied their hands.

Pembroke squinted down the street, narrowing his gaze as the first Panzer came into view. The tank's hulking frame emerged from the haze, its turret swinging with a steady, unhurried confidence as if it had all the time in the world to find its next victim.

Behind it, more tanks followed, their bulks crowding the narrow approach.

He raised his binoculars, the view sharpening into a grim picture: German infantry methodically thread through the ruins behind the armour with purpose. Pembroke lowered the glasses and exhaled slowly.

"Wait," he ordered, his tone calm but unyielding. "Wait!" He locked onto the lead tank who had closed in on the mental marker he'd fixed in his mind. The gunner—a middle-aged man with steady hands—tightened his grip on the firing lever, his focus unwavering as he held his position.

Still, they waited, the tension coiling tighter with every passing second. Pembroke knew the first shot had to count, and he wasn't about to waste it.

The lead Panzer edged closer, its treads grinding over the cobblestones and scattering debris with every turn before the turret paused. Its barrel swung towards one of the buildings. Pembroke grimaced with concentration.

"Almost there..." His marker was 200 yards up the street, a good third of the way along the narrow road. He wanted to catch as much of the deadly column as possible in the confined space, so the gun and D Company could unleash maximum havoc.

The tank rolled on. Pembroke's hand shot up, and then down, slamming sharply onto the sandbagged barricade. "Fire!" The anti-tank gun roared. Its recoil jolted the gun back into its braced position as the shell streaked towards its target. The first round struck the Panzer dead-on but ricocheted upwards, the sloped armour had deflected the solid shot.

Pembroke's eyes widened in disbelief. "Fuck!" The word barely left his lips before the crew, working with practiced precision, realigned the gun.

"Fire!" Posser barked. The explosion was instantaneous this time: a flash of fire and metal as the Panzer's top hatch blew clear, followed by a plume of flame shooting into the sky. The tank ground to a halt. Smoke pouring from its shattered hull. The gun crew, moving with the rhythm of countless drills, were already pivoting to their next target. Corporal Prosser, his voice sharp and steady, called out commands as the second Panzer

100

tried to manoeuvre around the wreckage of the first.

"Tank! 200 yards! Traverse left! Fire when ready!" The gun thundered again. The solid shot screaming down the street at 2,600 feet per second. This round, however, slammed into the side of a building, shattering bricks in an explosion of dust and debris.

"Steady there, Mack!" Prosser snapped. "Reload!" The loader worked swiftly, ramming the next round into the breech as the gunner adjusted his aim, readying for another shot.

Archer had flinched when the first deafening blast of the 2-pounder echoed through the narrow streets. From his vantage point in the attic, he had seen the shell streak towards the lead Panzer and had watched its impact kick up a plume of mist and debris. The second shot, which had followed in quick succession, had lit up the ruins as the lead Panzer erupted in flame. Almost simultaneously, the sharp staccato bark of the Vickers rang out below. Its water-cooled barrel chugged rhythmically as tracer rounds stitched glowing arcs towards the advancing infantry. The heavy machine-gun's roar mingled with the sharper crack of rifles and the sharp cough of the Bren guns either side of him. The defenders of D Company were unleashing their fury in a co-ordinated storm of fire.

Archer bent low at the attic window, pressing his rifle into his shoulder as Webb and Harding fired short, controlled bursts from the Bren guns beside him. The rapid thump-thump-thump of the light machine-gun reverberated through the confined space, its muzzle flash lighting up the dust-choked air. Webb's face was set in grim concentration, his fingers steady on the trigger as he swept the weapon's fire across the road below.

The scene through the shattered window was a hellish view. The second Panzer ground forwards, its turret swivelling as it fought to navigate the smouldering remains of the first tank. Behind it, German infantry scattered, throwing themselves behind jagged walls or flat against the cobblestones. Archer tracked their movements, catching sight of a soldier who darted into a doorway. He fired, the recoil punching into his shoulder as the man crumpled backwards.

"More on the left!" Webb shouted. His voice was hoarse but cut through the chaos. Archer swung his gaze to the flanking buildings where shadows slipped through the swirling haze. The Bren gun roared again, its rounds sparking off the fallen walls as Webb tried to pin down the advancing Germans.

The attic trembled with the force of the 2-pounder's third shot, and the vibration rattling the fragile beams overhead. Below them, the Vickers continued its relentless rhythm, its tracers slicing through the mayhem. Archer leant out briefly, catching a glimpse of Corporal Prosser's crew reloading with practiced speed. Their faces betrayed no hesitation. Another explosion ripped through the street: this one was from the muzzle of the second tank. The shell screamed through the air and slammed into the building to Archer's right, tearing through the brickwork with a thunderous impact. The force of the blast sent shards of masonry and glass flying, and the attic shuddered violently, sending loose tiles falling and shattering in the street. Archer ducked instinctively. The sound rung in his ears as chunks of debris clattered around him. He glanced at Webb, who hadn't flinched, his focus unbroken as he kept the Bren firing in short, controlled bursts.

"Harding, how you doin'?" Archer called out, his voice cutting through the uproar. Harding, standing firm at the window, didn't miss a beat. The Bren cracked away in his hands, the muzzle flash strobing the room in bursts of light.

Without turning, he shouted back, "Never better, Sir!"

Through the smog-laden street, the second tank loomed into view, its angular silhouette slicing through the murky air like a shadow of menace. The Panzer halted briefly, swivelling its turret with mechanical precision, desperate to locate the source of the fire that had claimed its comrade. The grind of its treads echoed ominously as it started forwards again. It lurched to navigate the wreckage of the lead tank which was filled with the raging orange of flames; sparks flew wildly, and shards of ammunition popped and ricochetted in a deathly symphony of destruction.

The tank's heavy frame made easy work of crossing the crunched, scattered debris, and the scorched cobblestones groaned under its weight. Pausing briefly, the barrel suddenly swung deliberately towards the British positions, an unspoken promise of ruin. The machine's movements were slow but purposeful. Each lurch forwards betrayed its intent to obliterate anything in its path.

Without warning, the second Panzer's main gun roared. Its thunderous report shook the air and radiated heat through the veiled street. The high-explosive round streaked towards the defenders, striking the second floor of a nearby building. The impact sent a plume of pulverised brick and fractured timber into the air, and its force reverberating through the crumbling structure.

The building shuddered under the assault, and its weakened walls buckling as chunks of masonry rained down onto the street below. Shouts of alarm rose from within the British position as defenders ducked for cover, shielding their heads from the falling debris. The tank fired again. This time it targeted a sandbagged barricade at street level. The explosion tore through the defences, scattering sand and steel fragments in a deadly arc.

The Panzer's turret swung towards the anti-tank gun. Its cannon belched fire again as a shell screamed through the air, narrowly missing its mark.

Before the tank could adjust its aim, the 2-pounder fired,

the recoil slamming the gun back into its braced position. The armour-piercing round arched through the haze, hitting the Panzer's frontal plating with a sharp metallic clang. The shot failed to penetrate, glancing off and ricochetting into the ruins.

"Reload!" Corporal Prosser barked sharply over the din. The crew moved with swift precision and chambered another round as the tank lumbered forwards, dark fumes curling from its exhaust.

The gun fired again. This time, the shell slammed into the tank's right side. The round struck true, ripping into the exposed track. The grinding of treads turned to a violent screech as the metal links snapped and flew apart like shrapnel.

The Panzer lurched to the right, its weight dragging it off course. The crew inside scrambled to regain control, and the turret swivelled wildly as the tank veered into a pile of wreckage. Its damaged track locked in place. The tank ground to a halt with its massive frame blocking the narrow road. The high-pitched whine of its engine reverberated through the street, futilely straining to free itself.

Archer watched from the attic, his jaw tightening as he realised the unintentional boon. With its right flank exposed, the crippled second tank had become an impromptu barricade for the vehicles trapped behind it.

"They're bottled up!" he shouted. "Webb, Harding, hit them while they're stuck!" From below, the anti-tank gun fired again, a fresh round streaking towards the immobilised Panzer. The shell slammed into its side, and the explosion rocked the machine as fire and dark plumes poured from its hull. The Germans behind it scrambled for cover; their advance stalled by the wreckage clogging the road.

From his position on the second floor, Jacks had watched the chaos unfold through the broken window. The air had hung heavy with haze and the sharp tang of burning oil. With relief, he'd watched wreckage of the first Panzer belching dark, suffocating plumes as it blocked the road. Jacks' heart had pounded in his chest as he'd realised the opportunity they'd been given by the blockage in the road. He had adjusted the Boys rifle against his shoulder, its heavy steel frame digging into the sandbagged ledge.

"Right, lads," he growled, glancing at the three men crouched beside him. "Eyes sharp. They'll be trying to push past that wreck any second now."

Private Hawkins, twenty-six but feeling like an eighty-year-old, turned his head quickly. He maintained his firm grip of his rifle. Beside him, Lance Corporal Tug Wilson checked his Lee-Enfield with brisk, steady movements. A third soldier, a wiry man named Blake, from 7th platoon, cradled a grenade in his hands and fixed his gaze on the street below.

Jacks squinted through the rifle's iron sights, steading the long barrel as he had tracked the second tank. It had stalled just behind the wreck of the lead Panzer, desperately swivelling its turret. The Boys rifle kicked like a mule, and he knew he'd only get a few good shots before he'd have to pause to recover. His finger hovered over the trigger as he gauged the distance.

The second tank's tracks spun uselessly against the cobblestones, the noise grating in Jacks' ears. Finally, it shifted slightly, exposing its side as it navigated around the obstruction of the first tank. Jacks squeezed the trigger. The rifle thundered in his hands, the recoil slamming into his shoulder. The heavy armour-piercing round raced towards the Panzer, smacking the side with a loud metallic crack. The tank shuddered but kept moving, its armour deflecting the shot.

"Bloody thing's tough," Tug muttered, raising his rifle to cover the advancing infantry.

"Bloody thing!" Jacks replied through gritted teeth, his hands already working as he yanked back the bolt, ejecting the spent casing with a metallic clink before slamming it forwards to chamber the next round.

The German infantry were spilling into the street, darting between the scattered ruins and firing sporadically towards the British positions. Hawkins fired his rifle, the sharp crack blending with the beat of battle. Meanwhile, Blake hurled his grenade, the small explosive landing near a cluster of advancing soldiers. The blast delivered a cloud of dust and shrapnel, forcing the survivors to scatter.

Jacks adjusted the heavy Boys rifle against his shoulder, the bruising recoil from the last shot still radiating through his arm. He squinted through the iron sights to track the second tank as it lumbered forwards, fumes curling from its exhaust.

Jacks continued to work the bolt to eject the spent casing before slamming it forwards to chamber another round. He took aim again, this time targeting the exposed back side of the second Panzer's turret and fired. The rifle bucked violently, but the armour-piercing round ricocheted harmlessly off the Panzer's thick plating. He gritted his teeth as he chambered another round, but just as he lined up his next shot, the sharp crack of the 2-pounder split the air. Jacks flinched at the sudden roar, his sights momentarily shifting. He steadied the rifle again, only to see the Panzer lurch violently. Its right side dipped as its track exploded into a tangled mess of metal links, the screech of tearing steel echoing through the street.

Jacks lowered the rifle slightly, his eyes narrowing as he witnessed the second tank ground to a halt, its engine straining and roaring against its immobilised frame.

The beast screamed, filling the street with thick fumes of exhaust as the crew inside struggled desperately to regain control. Jacks watched as the 2-pounder struck again and then again. Each hardened steel round slammed into the tank's side with a deafening clang. The machine rocked under the impact. Its frame jolted violently with every hit. Suddenly, the top hatch flew open, and the commander scrambled out, followed by several crew members.

Jacks barely had time to react before the familiar chatter of Bren guns and the staccato bursts of the Vickers rang out, echoing through the ruins. He saw the bullets rip into the exposed crew. Their bodies jerked in quick, brutal motions as they fell one by one, systematically cut down by the defenders' relentless fire.

With the road choked by the burning wreckage of the first tank and the second almost closing the street, the third Panzer ground to a halt. Its engine idled as the crew assessed their options. The turret swivelled slowly, scanning the street and buildings with cold, mechanical precision to find where the British defences hid. Unable to push forwards, the tank settled into position, its intent clear. The Panzer's rumbling engine blended with the crackle of flames and the constant staccato of small arms fire. After a brief pause, the cannon fired. The high-explosive round tore through the air and smashed into the upper floors of a nearby building. The explosion ripped apart brick and timber in a violent eruption of dust and debris. Chunks of masonry rained down onto the street while the walls buckled and groaned, threatening collapse.

The tank adjusted its aim slightly, the turret grinding as it lined up another target. Another deafening blast followed, and another building along the British line shuddered under the impact. Windows shattered, and the defenders inside scrambled to reposition. They were forced to abandon weakened fortifications as the Panzer systematically dismantled their defences. Each shell left a mark of destruction: a cratered wall, a collapsed roof, the splintered remains of barricades once carefully constructed. Smoke billowed from the fresh wounds in the buildings, mingling with the thick haze that already consumed the street.

The German infantry began their advance, emerging cautiously from the blurred scene. Moving in small groups, they darted between piles of debris, using the wreckage of vehicles and shattered walls for cover. Meanwhile, the third Panzer continued its bombardment, each deafening explosion masking the sound of their infantry's advance over the hard ground as the enemy pushed ever forwards.

Despite the insane tension, the British defenders maintained a relentless rate of fire. With their Bren's, Webb and Harding poured bursts of .303 rounds into the advancing Germans; only the sharper cracks of rifles punctuated the steady rhythm of the machine-guns. The Vickers hammered away, its belt-fed ammunition sending glowing tracers slicing through haze. Bullets ricochetted off the shattered remains. Every step the Germans took was met with a hail of bullets, forcing them to hug the ground or scramble for shelter in the ruins lining the road.

One German squad attempted to move along the right side of the street, darting into the shadow of a partially collapsed building. A grenade arced through the air from a British position, landing among them with a sharp crump. The explosion threw dust and shrapnel into the air, scattering the soldiers who had survived the blast. The few who remained crawled into the building's tattered entryway, retreating under the relentless fire.

On the left of them, another group tried to push forwards, moving from cover to cover. A Harding tracked their movements, his fire cutting a line through the air. One soldier dropped. Then another. Their bodies turned under the vicious impact of the rounds. The survivors dove into a ruined store front, their shouts barely audible over the cacophony.

The third Panzer waited ominously in the street, its turret

methodically swivelling as it rained high-explosive shells onto the British defences. The surrounding ruins were cloaked in churning smoke, but the tank remained stationary, its path blocked by the wreckage of its predecessors. The closed hatches and idle engine made it an imposing target.

Dixon crouched low in what had once been a grocer's shop, the long front room now filled with debris and the faint smell of rotting produce. Broken shelves leant against the walls, their contents long since scattered in the chaos of the battle. He quickly surveyed his surroundings, his eyes darting to the partially intact staircase ahead of him. Slung over his shoulder was an old sandbag, rough-stitched and heavy with the weight of Mills bombs he'd packed earlier – it was his one change to do real damage.

Without hesitation, he sprinted forwards, hurdling over the debris in his path. He took the steps two at a time. The wooden stairs moaned under his pounding boots but held firm. Reaching the first floor in moments, he crouched low and crept towards the shattered remains of the front windows.

Outside, the tank's idling engine growled steadily below him. The sound was unmistakable—deep, mechanical, and unforgiving, reverberating through the floorboards and into his chest as he crept forwards. He didn't need to see it to know the turret would be moving, slow and deliberate, searching. Smoke coiled lazily around the tank's frame as it crawled into view; the wrecks of its fallen predecessors smouldered behind it in a backdrop of ruin.

Dixon moved cautiously, keeping to the shadows as he navigated the long upper floor. He stepped over a broken desk and past an overturned chair, his heart pounding as he approached the window closest to the tank. The rough frame offered a clear view of the Panzer's turret just below. He inhaled deeply, steadying himself, then crept closer to the edge. His boots shuffled slightly on the dusty floorboards as he gauged the distance. The tank wasn't directly below him, but a few feet out—close enough for an easy jump, though the thought of leaping onto the steel beast in the midst of the raging battle set his pulse racing. His lungs fought against the panic—shallow, rapid gasps struggling to become something calmer, something that wouldn't betray the fear crawling up his spine. One deep intake of a clogged breath, thick with dust and smoke, and he felt a little more in control. He watched as dust curled and danced around the tank's exhaust, the vibrations of its idling engine humming up through the floorboards like a warning.

Dust and exhaust coiled around the Panzer, its turret grinding with deliberate menace as the barrel swung towards another target. He felt the idling engine vibrating through the air; it was a constant growl that seemed to dare him to act. He tightly gripped the sandbag, feeling the weight of the grenades within, and he exhaled slowly. No room for hesitation.

With a surge of adrenaline, Dixon launched himself through the broken window. Air rushed past him in a blur. The ground dropped away as he aimed for the tank's turret. He landed hard on the steel frame, the impact jarring his knees and sending a metallic clang echoing around him. Mercifully, he hadn't been seen or heard.

He felt the Panzer shuddering beneath him, its engine reverberating through his legs. Dixon scrambled for balance even as the heat from the turret seared through the soles of his boots.

Moving quickly, he yanked the sandbag open and pulled the pin from one of the grenades. With practiced precision, he shoved the bag into the narrow joint between the gun mantel and the body of the tank, wedging it tightly against the exposed mechanism. Without waiting, Dixon leapt clear of the tank, landing hard against the cobblestones just as the first grenade detonated.

The explosion rocked the Panzer. A sharp crack echoed through the street as flames burst from the turret. The remaining grenades followed in rapid succession, and the explosion ripped through the turret with a deafening roar. Dixon was slammed violently to the ground as the shockwave hit him. The remaining grenades detonated in rapid succession, each blast tearing into the tank's barrel and gun mantlet. Leaving the barrel cracked and twisted, the concussive force rendered the tank's main weapon completely out of action.

Relieved to be breathing, Dixon pushed himself up on trembling arms, his ears ringing and his face streaked with soot. He turned to see the result of his work—a twisted barrel and smoke billowing from the turret. A grim, satisfied smile tugged at his lips. The tank's main weapon was silenced, and he'd bought the defenders precious time.

Ducking low, he weaved between cover as he made for the relative safety of a doorway. A sharp crack rang out. Dixon faltered mid-step. His body jerked violently as a rifle round struck him square in the back. He collapsed forwards, his outstretched hand brushing against the building's wall before he hit the ground. Dust rose around him, soaking up the dark stain spreading over the cobblestones.

From his position across the street, Mallory froze as he watched his old friend fall. The chaos of the battle seemed to fade for a moment as his gaze fixed on Dixon's lifeless form lying at the edge of safety in the doorway. He had seen Dixon face impossible odds before, but this time there would be no triumphant return: no barked orders or wry jokes to lift the men's spirits.

Mallory's face contorted. His grip on his rifle trembled as anger and grief surged within him.

"Bloody hell, Dixon..." he muttered under his breath. The crack of another rifle shot jolted him back into the moment, and he turned his attention to the street where the Germans were regrouping. The burning wreck of the third tank blocked their path, but the infantry were pressing forwards, using the confusion to push into the lower floors of the British-held buildings.

The fight inside the buildings was a vicious melee. Grime hung thick in the air, mingling with the acrid tang of ash and the bitter taste of sweat that lingered at the back of the defenders' throats. The Germans clambered through shattered windows and doorways and forced their way into the lower floors, crashing into obstacles deliberately placed to hinder their advance. Their boots could be heard thudding on the wooden boards and orders in harsh German were screamed out, echoing within the cramped spaces. The sounds were punctuated by the sharp crack of rifles and the deeper, bone-rattling roar of grenades from outside.

Mallory's head snapped towards the sound of splintering wood from a door farther down the corridor—the one Matthews had carefully rigged hours earlier. The Germans had found it.

An instant later, the door was blown apart, the carefully placed grenades detonating with a thunderous roar that shook the entire floor. Splinters of wood and jagged shards of metal ripped through the narrow hallway. The blast swallowed the shouts of the Germans caught in its path. Acrid haze and debris billowed outwards, choking the air as Mallory's ears rang from the shockwave.

"Hold your ground lads!" Mallory shouted; his voice was hoarse but resolute as he waved the defenders forwards. A rifleman to his left took cover behind a toppled dresser before sighting his weapon on the carnage at the top of the stairs.

Another soldier hurled a grenade through an opening in the wall; the explosion drew screams from the Germans trapped in the wreckage of the ground floor. For a moment, the attack faltered, the disarray granting the defenders a crucial opportunity to regroup. Bodies of German soldiers littered the corridor and ground floor. The booby trap had done its grisly work.

Across the street, Jacks crouched low behind a battered, fractured wall, his eyes darting over the shattered street and the men huddled beside him. The German infantry had been relentless; their last push had nearly broken his position. He wiped his forehead with a dirt-streaked sleeve, smearing sweat across his grime-caked battledress.

"Keep an eye on that corner," he barked to Hawkins who turned and shifted to cover a break in the collapsed remnants of a wall. Lance Corporal Tug Wilson was reloading his rifle, his hands moving quickly despite the tremor of exhaustion that had begun to set in.

The street fell eerily quiet for a moment, and the smoke hung like a shroud over the ruins. Jacks knew better than to trust this temporary reprieve. A sudden shout in German broke the silence, followed by a burst of rifle fire. Shadows darted through the haze as the next wave of attackers charged forwards.

"Here they come!" Jacks shouted. "Fire!" The Bren roared to life, its sharp staccato tearing through the air as Blake smothered the street with suppressive fire. Hawkins and Wilson fired their rifles in steady rhythm, picking off advancing soldiers as the Germans pressed towards the building's lower levels. Jacks pulled out his last grenade, arcing it through the smoky air. From their second-floor vantage point, Jacks watched as the grenade struck the jagged stones below before detonating with a thunderous blast. It was followed by screams as shrapnel found its mark. For a moment, the defenders held their ground, their fire cutting through the German ranks. Jacks shifted his aim and fired the last round for his Boys rifle, and the weapon's thunderous crack sent a round tearing through a soldier who had been taking cover behind a fallen beam.

But then, the low, terrifying crack of an anti-tank gun

echoed through the street. Jacks' stomach sank as the first round slammed into the wall to his right, shattering the brickwork and showering him in dust and debris. Another shot quickly followed, striking the corner of the building and sending chunks of masonry crashing to the ground.

"They've got a gun down there!" Jacks yelled over the din, and his thoughts started racing. "Stay down!"

As if to confirm his fears, a German MG34 opened up. Its rounds stitched across the shattered brickwork with deadly precision. Jacks ducked as bullets chewed through the remains of the wall, forcing his men to hug the ground. A sharp cry rang out, but it was cut short as Blake crumpled where he stood, a burst of rounds tearing through his chest. Jacks felt a moment of emptiness as he stared at Blake's lifeless body slumped against the crumbling floor, the Bren slipping from his limp hands. There was no time to mourn a good man—not here, not now.

The crash of splintered beams and shattered timbers snapped him back to the moment as another armour-piercing round slammed into the building, rattling its weakened frame.

"Jacks! We can't stay here!" Wilson shouted. His voice was almost drowned out by the relentless machine-gun fire. Jacks' face twisted in frustration, his mind racing as another round from the gun—this time a high-explosive shell—tore into the ground floor.

The impact was devastating, collapsing the ceiling and the floor above them. Falling debris crushed one of the men defending the ground floor: a young soldier barely into his twenties who had joined them in the night. His name was already a fading memory even if Jacks were pressed to recall it. The young lad had fought with the wide-eyed determination of someone eager to prove himself, but he'd been no match for the unforgiving chaos of battle. His muffled scream was cut short as the rubble settled, leaving the others no time to grieve.

"Fall back!" Jacks bellowed, his voice cutting through the turmoil as he waved his men towards the rear of the building.

"Move!" The floor beneath them trembled ominously. Large sections were already obliterated by the high-explosive round that had ripped through the building. Splintered beams and shattered masonry teetered on the brink of collapse, leaving little more than a precarious ledge for them to stand on. Jacks steadied himself against the crumbling wall, his eyes darting to Wilson and Hawkins as they leapt down to the rubble-strewn ground floor and scrambled towards the rear.

The collapsing building strained with each step, threatening to swallow them whole. Gritting his teeth, Jacks scrambled after the others, every nerve screaming to hold the line. He'd hated saying 'fall back' even as the words had left his mouth. Every instinct screamed at him to hold the line, to dig in and fight until the enemy was forced to break. But the gun a-PAK 38 and relentless machine-gun fire had turned their position into a death trap. The walls were crumbling around them, and every second spent here was a gamble with his men's lives.

Across the street, Archer crouched low in the attic, his rifle cradled against his chest as he surveyed the devastation below. The street was a broken graveyard. The scars of the battle were etched into every surface. The lead Panzer sat smouldering, its turret blown open and lifeless figures draped over its hull. Flames flickered faintly around the wreckage, casting eerie shadows across the churned-up cobblestones. Behind it, the second tank had been halted; its shattered track was tangled in the rubble of collapsed buildings. Smoke still coiled lazily from its exhaust, mixing with the ash that hung thick in the air.

The ruins of Cassel's buildings loomed like jagged teeth, their façades torn apart into gaping mouths. Windows were empty sockets with splintered and blackened frames. Remnants of the fight—spent casings, broken weapons, and the bodies of the fallen. Archer's gaze lingered on a young German soldier crumpled near the wreckage of the second Panzer, his rifle still clutched in pale hands. Closer to the British line, a sandbagged position had been torn open, a crimson stain marking where one of their own had fallen.

The distant rumble that Archer had dismissed as thunder now grew steadily louder. It was an ominous undertone that sent a chill through him. He glanced towards the horizon. The low growl of artillery was unmistakable. The defenders below shifted uneasily. Their pale faces were streaked with grime. They waited.

"Here it comes," Archer muttered, his voice lost in the rising wind. A sharp whistle cut through the air, high and menacing, before the first explosion ripped through the street with a deafening roar. The attic shuddered as debris cascaded around him. He exhaled, steadying himself.

The storm was just beginning.

Chapter 7

The first shells screamed in as the bright mid-morning sun illuminated the ruins of Cassel. Archer had barely registered the withdrawal of the German infantry when the building beneath him shuddered violently, the air splitting with the thunderous crack of artillery fire. A fraction of a second later, the first explosion tore through the Rue de Bergues, throwing more bricks, debris, and timbers into the choking air.

The artillery fire was relentless as the distinct shrieks of shells descended and blended with the deep, bone-rattling booms as they detonated. Waves of concussive force rippled outwards, shaking the foundations of already precarious buildings. Walls crumbled in great cascades of brick and mortar. The structures wailed like dying beasts before collapsing entirely.

Archer crouched low behind a crumbling section of the roof, and he pressed his back against the rough surface as he gripped his rifle tightly. Dust and debris coated his uniform, and the air around him was still thick with metallic bite of war. Sounds of distant and near explosions reverberated through the buildings, each jolting blast a reminder of how perilous their position had become.

He stole a quick glance through a new opening in the roof, his movements sharp and deliberate. The chaos outside was unrelenting: flashes of light and bursts of sound painted a grim tableau of destruction. Archer forced his breathing to steady, the weight of his rifle reassuring in his hands.

Thick and suffocating grit clouded the air and clung to every surface. It wormed its way into mouths and noses, mixing with the acrid tang of smoke and the metallic taste of blood. Around Archer, men coughed violently, some gagging as they tried to draw breath amid the choking haze. The relentless flashes of light from the shell bursts turned the street into a grotesque theatre, each illumination revealing new horrors before plunging them back into darkness.

Archer's ears rang with a constant whine beneath the broken rhythm of muffled roars and distant cracks. Nothing sounded real anymore. He ducked instinctively as another shell exploded only yards from his position, and the shockwave slamming into him with the force of a sledgehammer. The blast sent him sprawling against the rubble-strewn floor, his vision swimming as dust filled the air.

"Hold on!" he shouted hoarsely though the words felt meaningless, lost in the chaos that consumed them.

The attic shuddered violently. Its sagging rafters grumbled in protest as shattered tiles and wood fragments rained down like shards of shrapnel.

The blast sent him sprawling against the rubble-strewn floor, his vision swimming as dust filled the air. "Hold on!" he shouted hoarsely, though the words felt meaningless, lost in the chaos that consumed them.

A sudden, sharp crack from below preceded the whistling scream of another shell. This one struck closer. The explosion ripped through the building like a thunderclap. Archer felt the floor lurch beneath him, the fragile structure trembling as the shockwave threw debris in every direction.

"Harding!" he called out instinctively, his voice rising above the din. He turned. His heart sank as he caught sight of the gaping hole where Harding had been moments before. The edge of the attic floor had entirely collapsed; smoke and flame licked hungrily at the splintered wood. For a heartbeat, Archer just stared—frozen. It didn't seem real. One second Harding had been there, the next... nothing. Just fire, smoke, and a silence more deafening than the blasts around them. Choking smoke and the smell of scorched wood filled the air, mingling with the sharp, coppery scent of blood.

Webb, crouched with the Bren, stared in frozen horror at the devastation. His face was pale, lips pressed into a thin line as he gripped the weapon tightly. "Harding was right there..." Webb's voice cracked, barely audible over the pandemonium.

Archer followed Webb's gaze. His stomach tightened at the sight. Amid the rubble, a torn fragment of Harding's uniform fluttered in the smoky air, caught on a jagged splinter of wood. Nearby, the twisted remains of Harding's helmet lay half-buried beneath shattered beams and smouldering debris. Dark blood streaked the splintered wood and pooled where the floor had collapsed: a mute testament to the violence of the blast.

For a moment, Archer couldn't look away. The grim vision before him was a stark reminder of how quickly battle could claim them all. He forced himself to swallow the rising bile, and he reached out, gripping Webb's shoulder firmly.

"Webb, Webb!" he barked, shaking him slightly. Webb's wide, terrified eyes locked onto Archer's, pleading silently for some release from this maddening hell.

"Webb, come on now!" Archer repeated, his voice sharp, hard, and unyielding. "We've got this—hold it together!"

Startled, Webb blinked and snapped to attention. He started nodding quickly, his voice shaking but determined. "Sir—sorry. I'm alright, I'm alright!" The words sounded like he was trying to reassure both himself and Archer, his grip tightening on the Bren.

Below, Pembroke's gun position had become a vortex of activity. Sandbags that once formed solid defences were shredded, and their contents spilt like guts onto the street. Men scrambled to drag the wounded to safety with frantic but determined movements. Pembroke lay flat against the ground, his head slightly above the sandbags, shouting orders that cut like a blade.

"Stay down! We'll deal with the wounded later!" he bellowed, his voice sharp and unwavering. He caught sight of two soldiers rising to assist a fallen gunner, exposing them to fire.

"I said stay down!" he roared, the authority in his tone freezing them mid-motion.

A shell landed nearby with a deafening blast, and the shockwave ripped through the air. The explosion hurled the two soldiers off their feet, sending debris and dust cascading over the position.

Pembroke flinched. The ground vibrated beneath him as the explosion momentarily swallowed everything. He pushed himself up just enough to scan the carnage. His gaze locked onto one of the fallen men who was still moving. Crawling forwards, Pembroke grabbed the soldier by his webbing and dragged him towards the comparative safety of a collapsed doorway. Blood trickled from a gash on Pembroke's forehead, but he ignored it as he shoved the man into cover and barked to the others.

"Hold your positions! Stay low." Even prone, Pembroke's presence anchored the men as his calm but commanding voice cut through their fear and confusion. He exhaled sharply, wiping the dirt from his face with a blood-streaked hand, and scanned the line for the next crisis.

Meanwhile, Mallory was positioned in the gutted remains of a café farther down the street, pressed his back against the cracked plaster of a wall that barely stood upright. His rifle rested across his lap, and his breathing came fast and shallow. Every muscle in his body tensed with each fresh explosion. The café, once a bustling haven, was now a deathtrap: its walls sagged precariously, and its counters reduced to splinters.

He glanced at Private Saunders, who was crouched nearby, trembling uncontrollably. The young soldier clutched his rifle in a vice-like grip. He was rigid with tension.

"Keep your head down, lad," Mallory said, his voice gruff but steady. Saunders' wide eyes flicked to him, and he nodded though his grip on the weapon didn't relax.

The ground heaved again as another shell exploded directly

outside, and the blast shattered the last intact window, showering them with shards of the remaining pieces of glass and splinters of wood. Saunders let out a strangled cry, curling into himself.

Mallory reached over, gripping his shoulder tightly. "You're still here," he growled, forcing the boy's eyes to meet his. "Focus. It's the only way you'll make it through."

Saunders blinked rapidly, then nodded again, his breaths slowing just enough for Mallory to pull back.

Through the disorientation of noise and debris, Archer focused. He could just make out the shape of the second anti-tank gun nearly two hundred yards from Dead Horse Corner. Corporal Grant, who Archer had only briefly met, and his crew huddled behind it, their faces smudged with soot and fear. The gun's barrel was steady and resolute, but the weight of the fight bore down on its operators. Archer realised, they hadn't fired a round in hours, and the thought of taking aim seemed laughable amid the apocalyptic barrage.

Archer wiped a grimy sleeve across his face, but the effort only smeared the dirt deeper into his skin. He tried to peer down towards Pembroke's position on the ground floor where his voice rose over the chaos, barely audible. Another thunderous explosion shook their building, sending more dust and rubble cascading through the air. Archer coughed against the choking grit, and his vision was momentarily obscured. When the haze cleared, the street below had transformed yet again.

The cobblestones were torn apart and replaced by gaping craters. An abandoned horse-drawn cart, left to rot days ago, was now obliterated, and its wooden frame scattered in jagged splinters. The psychological toll began to show on all the men. Even hardened men like Mallory and Webb—steady as bedrock—shifted with a haunted air. Private Evans, normally a source of sardonic humour, sat hunched against a wall, his mouth moving silently as he rocked slightly back and forth. The unrelenting thunder of the barrage had battered their minds as much as their bodies, grinding away at their resolve.

In the attic, Webb muttered something under his breath, his hands fumbling as he reloaded the Bren. Archer reached over, steadying him. "We're still here," he said, his voice firm despite the knot tightening in his chest.

And then, as suddenly as it had begun, the barrage ceased. The silence was deafening, pressing on their ears like a physical weight. A ghostly shroud of dust hung over the ruins of Rue de Bergues.

Archer let out a shuddering breath, his knees trembling as he straightened out of his crouch. From below, Pembroke's voice cut through the mayhem, sharper now, calling his name.

"Archer! We're pulling back to the second gun!" Pembroke's voice carried both urgency and resolve. "The crew here's gone—two dead, the rest wounded. We're spiking the gun. Get what's left of the men down the street!"

"Understood!" Archer shouted back, though he wasn't sure Pembroke had heard him. Grabbing his rifle, his mind raced. The men further down the street—they had no idea the fallback had been ordered. He'd have to go himself.

He turned to Webb. "Get to Captain Pembroke and go with him." Archer descended the splintered staircase, leaping down with barely a footfall on the treads. Another shell exploded outside, tearing through what was left of the cobblestones with a deafening roar. Archer froze mid-step, his thoughts racing. Surely, it couldn't be starting again? The memory of the previous barrage clawed at him, but the single explosion told him otherwise—it was just a rogue shell.

Steeling himself, Archer pushed forwards and emerged into the ground-floor tumult. Pembroke and another man were crouched by the two-pounder, working hurriedly. He saw Pembroke jam a Mills bomb into the gun's breech with deliberate but tense movements. The sharp click of the grenade's pin being pulled sent a chill through Archer as he realised the gun would soon be useless to the enemy.

"Get down!" Pembroke yelled. Archer threw himself to the floor just as a dull thud echoed—the grenade detonating within the breech.

Without hesitation, Archer scrambled to his feet and bolted towards the street to warn the others. But the moment he stepped outside, he stopped dead. The world had turned savage. Craters ripped through the cobblestones, their edges blackened and smoking as if the earth itself had been clawed open. Shattered beams jutted from the rubble like broken bones. Smoke curled from doorways. A child's toy lay in the gutter, half-buried in dust.

One of the Panzers lay crippled, its tracks blown apart and its turret frozen at an awkward angle. Another bore scorch marks along its side; its blackened metal was evidence of a near-miss that had left it limping but still dangerous. Bodies lay scattered amid the debris, some motionless, others groaning faintly beneath the rubble. The foul mixture of burning oil and cordite clawed up Archer's nostrils—hot, metallic, and bitter—as it mingled with the choking dust drifting lazily from the ruined façades of nearby buildings.

As Archer tentatively stepped forwards, his boots crunched over shattered glass and fragments of brick as he pressed forwards. He weaved between craters and the wreckage of carts and sandbags which had been obliterated in the barrage. A shout cut through the din.

"Lieutenant, over here!" Archer slid to a stop on the crushed masonry beneath his boots, relief flooding him as he spotted Jacks emerging from behind a collapsed wall.

"Jacks!" he called, unable to keep the relief from his voice. "Get back to the second gun. Where's Mallory?"

Jacks pointed towards a battered café farther down the street. "Last I saw, he was in there!"

Archer nodded sharply. "Grab whoever you can and head back to the second gun. Move!" Without waiting for a reply, Archer turned and sprinted in the direction Jacks had indicated, his boots kicking up dust as he navigated the treacherous terrain.

Archer darted towards the café, skidding over the broken debris as the guttural shouts of German infantry reached his ears. A quick glance down the street confirmed his fears—dozens of enemy soldiers were advancing, their movements almost unhindered now that Jacks and the others had pulled back.

The sharp crack of a rifle echoed. It was followed by a burst of automatic fire. Archer swore under his breath and veered towards the closest patch of cover—a splintered cart half-buried in loose bricks that had once been the façade of neighbouring building. Bullets chewed through the air around him. Sprays of stone chips and dust shot up, and he threw himself behind the cart just as a volley of rifle fire erupted from above.

Archer looked up to see two familiar faces leaning out of a jagged hole in the second-floor wall. Evans and Saunders were firing down on the advancing Germans, their shots precise and measured. The sharp crack of Saunders' Lee-Enfield echoed as he dropped a soldier mid-stride. Evans quickly followed, picking off another who had taken cover behind a battered lamppost.

"Lieutenant!" Lance Corporal Matthews shouted between bursts of fire. "Over here, Sir!" Archer looked over to see Matthews kneeling in a doorway ten yards ahead, his Bren gun at the ready. "I'll cover you!" Matthews yelled.

Without hesitation, Matthews stepped into the maelstrom, the Bren at his hip unleashing its fierce rhythm of violence. The spray of bullets tore through the street, sending the advancing Germans scrambling for cover. The tearing of gunfire and Matthews' defence brought Archer the chance he needed.

Archer didn't think twice. Rising to a crouch, he sprinted across the open ground towards the café, adrenaline pounding in his veins as the Germans shifted their focus towards Matthews. Bullets cracked past Archer, some ricochetting off the cobblestones, but the relentless crack of Saunders, Evans, and whoever else had joined the fight, kept the enemy pinned in their positions.

Slamming through the café's doorway, Archer panted heavily as he pressed his back against the frame. The air inside was thick. A dim light filtered through broken windows. Jagged shadows circled the room.

"Mallory!" Archer called: his voice hoarse. "You in here?" "Mallory!" Archer called again, stepping farther into the café. The thick air made it hard to see, but then a shape emerged through a hole in the ceiling.

"Up here, Sir!" Mallory's voice was sharp, but his face told the story of a hard fight that still betrayed his exhaustion. He leant farther over the ragged opening, clutching his rifle tightly.

"Mallory, we're pulling back to the second gun," Archer said quickly. "The Germans are pushing hard down the street, and Pembroke's already moving. We're not holding this position."

Mallory turned his head for the briefest of moments. "Understood, Sir! Evans and Saunders keep the street covered. Be prepared to move!"

As Archer turned, a sharp yell cut through the chaos: "Grenade!" Before he could react, a tremendous shove slammed into his back, sending his entire body arching forwards. He hit the debris-strewn floor with a bone-jarring crash. The air was driven from his lungs in an instant. For a fleeting moment, he thought it was over—this was it. The pressure on his back pinned him in place, leaving him breathless and immobilised. The force of the impact reverberated through him, rattling his frame like a child's toy and leaving his senses dulled and his thoughts scrambled.

Momentarily paralysed by the weight on him, it took him half second to get his mind straight before he realised it was Matthews lying a top of him. He had thrown himself at Archer, pushing him to the floor to shield him from the effects of the

126

explosion. Their ears still rang from the deafening blast, and a clous of dust and smoke crept into their eyes, stinging and choking them with every shallow breath.

Suddenly, without warning, the distinct murmurs and groans of someone clambering through the remnants of a ground-floor window broke the tense silence. The shuffle of feet on debris followed. Archer and Matthews were instantly on their feet. The danger ahead was crystal clear; two grey-uniformed, steel-helmeted figures stood with their rifles held low. Without hesitation or command, both Archer and Matthews lunged at the intruders, instinct taking over. Archer veered left while Matthews ran right.

Summoning all his strength, Archer drove a fist straight into the nearest man's face. The German released his rifle as he staggered backwards, stunned by the speed and ferocity of the attack. Archer kicked the man's rifle away, closing the gap with a vice-like grip around his throat. The German fell to the floor under the sheer force, his eyes wide with shock and terror.

Pinned beneath Archer, the man's expression twisted as he clawed desperately at Archer's iron grip. His boots kicked wildly against the ground, his hands frantically grasping at Archer's arms, but the pressure on his throat was unrelenting. Archer's face hovered above, contorted into a grimace that the German would see as nothing short of demonic. Archer watched the man's vision blur, and his breath slip away. He felt the movement beneath him grow weaker, less frantic.

And then—stillness.

Archer knelt there, chest heaving, staring down at the lifeless body beneath him. He had killed the man with his bare hands. But there was no time for reflection. Out of the corner of his eye, he saw the other German gaining the upper hand over Matthews. Acting on instinct, Archer snatched up the German's discarded rifle from the floor and swung it with all his strength. The butt of the rifle connected with the side of the German's head, sending him sprawling against the wall. Without hesitation,

Archer swung again, the crack of the second blow echoing in the confined space.

The German slumped, motionless. Archer turned and grabbed Matthews, hauling him to his feet.

"Let's move," he said, his voice hard and urgent. Both men scrambled for their weapons and dashed towards the road, Archer shouting at Mallory and the others to move.

The street offered no safety. The moment Archer and Matthews exited the building, the Germans opened fire, forcing them to dive into the alcove of a nearby doorway. Bullets ricochetted off the stone arch above them, their meagre cover barely holding against the relentless onslaught.

Pinned down by the intensity of the incoming fire, neither Archer nor Matthews could even consider returning fire. Archer's eyes darted around desperately, searching for something—anything—that might get them out of their deadly predicament. But there was nothing.

Then came the familiar, rasping bursts of gunfire—a sound both Archer and Matthews knew all too well. It was the Bren. Each burst carried with it a glimmer of hope. Archer leant out of the doorway, straining to see the source. There, kneeling behind the turret of a stationary Panzer, was Jacks, calmly releasing precise, measured bursts of fire as if drumming out a retreat.

Archer and Matthews didn't need a second chance. This was it. Without hesitation, they broke into a sprint, racing towards Jacks and the relative safety the tank's cover provided.

"Thought you might need a hand!" Jacks called out with a grin, releasing another burst from the Bren.

"Got a mag?" Matthews asked urgently.

Jacks reached into his battle dress and pulled out a single magazine. "Only the one, mate—make it count!"

Archer, almost amazed at their nonchalant exchange in the midst of the anarchy, shook his head and took aim. He fired at the all-too-familiar shape of a German kneeling against a wall.

"A few more bursts, then we move, chaps," he said, his voice firm but steady.

As Pembroke crouched behind the second gun position, the stench hit him—burnt metal, singed flesh, and the raw stink of blood. It clung to his nostrils, thick and bitter, like he'd bitten into a spent shell casing. His eyes watered, but he didn't blink. Not here. Not now.

His gaze swept over the men huddled around him. Their faces were pale and streaked with soot, eyes bloodshot from exhaustion and grit. Even the most hardened among them carried the haunted look of men teetering on the edge.

Quietly, Pembroke took stock of their dwindling resources. Scattered among the debris were two half-empty boxes of two-pounder shells and a battered Bren gun, its barrel already showing signs of overheating. The weapon rested atop a hastily improvised barricade of sandbags, reinforced with timbers and old doors scavenged from the ruins. It wasn't much, but it would have to do.

His gaze lingered on his men as they worked their way up the street. Sergeant Mallory was barking orders, pointing, and positioning what was left of his exhausted section. Nearby, Corporal Grant knelt by the 2-pounder, calmly wiping grime from its breech. His hands moved with practiced precision. His lips pressed into a firm line.

"How many shells left, Grant?" Pembroke asked quietly, his voice low enough to mask the concern he didn't want the younger men to hear.

"Twelve," Grant replied without looking up. His tone was steady, but the gravity of the word was unmistakable. Twelve shells. Twelve chances to hold the advancing tide.

Pembroke lifted his head with an unreadable expression. He took a deep breath and leant back against the sandbags. His rifle rested across his knees. Slowly, he let his eyes drift over the men scattered around their position and rested on Private Horne, one of the volunteers who had joined them late the night before who was sat slumped against a splintered crate. His head was bowed, his shoulders trembling as he muttered under his breath—perhaps a prayer, perhaps nothing at all. Pembroke looked away and left the lad with his private moment.

Through the choking haze of dust and smoke, Pembroke spotted movement in the distance—a small group sprinting towards their position. His grip on his rifle tightened until recognition set in. Archer, flanked by Jacks and Matthews, emerged from the chaos, their movements urgent yet deliberate. Archer's head darted back and forth, scanning the street as he pushed his men forwards, urging them to close the gap. Jacks and Matthews, both carrying Brens, occasionally glanced over their shoulders, watchful for any sign of pursuit.

As they neared, Archer stopped briefly to confer with Mallory, gesturing sharply as he relayed instructions. Pembroke rose slightly, raising a hand and signalling them with a sharp wave. "Over here!" he called, his voice cutting through the air.

As the three men stumbled into the relative safety of the sandbagged position, Pembroke stepped forwards, his expression both stern and relieved.

"Took your time, Archer," he said, his tone clipped but not without a hint of dry humour. "What's the situation?"

"Not good," Archer said, his breath coming in sharp gasps as he wiped sweat and grime from his brow. "Tanks blocked the road, so their infantry's pushing up fast—both down the street and around the back of the buildings. We barely made it out."

Pembroke's jaw tightened, his gaze shifting towards the Dead Horse Corner where the enemy advance was steadily closing in. "How many did you lose?" he asked, his tone low but weighted.

Archer hesitated. His expression was grim. "Harding didn't make it. Jacks lost two more when their position collapsed, and we've had scattered losses pulling back. I've got maybe twelve or fourteen. What do you have?"

Pembroke responded grimly. "Ten, including the three gunners here."

Pembroke exhaled sharply, running a hand through his dirt-streaked hair. "Christ, we're running on fumes. Forty-six to start with, and we're almost halved at their first push." He glanced towards the anti-tank gun. Its crew was huddled behind the sandbags: their faces tight with tension. "We've got twelve shells left," he said grimly, nodding towards the gun. "They'll hold, but once those are gone, it's just rifles and grit."

Archer leant against the sandbagged wall, his chest still heaving. "Rifles and grit have gotten us this far," he replied quietly, though the edge of exhaustion was evident in his voice. He let his eyes drift over the remaining men who were scattered among the ruins.

"They're tired, James—bloody exhausted—but they'll stand. We'll all stand."

Pembroke's lips pressed into a thin line as he followed Archer's gaze. "They're good men," he murmured, almost to himself. "But good men can only hold out so long. What about ammo?"

"Not bad," Archer admitted. "A bandolier per man.

Enough to refill a couple of Bren mags for each gun."

Pembroke nodded absently, and his eyes scanned the shattered street ahead. He exhaled sharply and dropped down beside Archer, wiping his brow with the back of his hand.

"Tom, we've got to face facts," he said quietly, his voice just loud enough to carry. "Cassel is surrounded. If we're getting out of here, it'll have to be under cover of darkness."

Archer nodded slowly and fixed his gaze on the shattered street ahead.

"Then we hold until nightfall," he said, the words heavy but resolute. "We use every round, every shell, every grenade we've got. We make them pay for every inch they take."

Pembroke exhaled sharply, and his lips curling into a faint, bitter smile. "And when we're out of those?"

"Then we fix bayonets and fight," Archer replied, his tone unyielding. He looked at Pembroke, their eyes locking for a moment. "This is it, James. We hold them as long as we can. Then, we go."

Pembroke nodded, but as he opened his mouth to reply, Archer's gaze flicked to the very pistol on Pembroke's belt. His thoughts raced. The flare. His stomach twisted as he turned to Pembroke, his voice rising above the dull roar of the battle. "James, the mortars. Wallis and his crew—they're still out there. We never called them in!"

Pembroke froze for a moment, the realisation dawning on him. He groaned, rubbing a hand down his face. "Bloody hell. How the hell did we miss that?"

"Too busy fighting for our lives, I suppose," Archer muttered, half to himself in frustration. He straightened, his jaw tightening. "When the flare goes up, we don't just withdraw—we bring the mortars down on the street to cover us. It's our only chance."

Pembroke's expression hardened. "Right. We're bloody

fools for forgetting, but we'll make it work." He pushed himself up, his voice steadying. "Get the men ready. Every round, every Mills bomb—we leave nothing behind."

Archer turned, his voice cutting through the smoke and haze. "Mallory, Jacks, over here!"

Both Jacks and Mallory jogged over, their faces set and grim. Archer and Pembroke wasted no time, launching into the revised plan.

"Make sure the last of the ammunition is passed out," Archer began firmly. "We're going to hold until nightfall. That's our best chance to get out of here and make our way to Dunkirk."

Jacks and Mallory exchanged a glance. What happened to last man, last round? Both had already resigned themselves to fighting to the bitter end here. But now, a reprieve? Orders to withdraw? The faint glimmer of hope sparked something neither man had felt in days.

Pembroke picked up the briefing, his tone steady and authoritative. "We're holding this part of the street for as long as possible. When the flare is fired, the mortars will unleash everything they've got on the street ahead. Under cover of that barrage, you are to withdraw."

His gaze fixed firmly on the two NCOs, ensuring they were absorbing every word. "We'll conduct a fighting withdrawal up to Mont Cassel," he continued.

Archer's expression was stern as his eyes met theirs, reinforcing the seriousness of the plan. Pembroke closed the briefing, his voice softer but no less commanding. "Once night falls, we're heading northwest towards Watten. From there, we'll push north to Dunkirk—a total of about thirty miles."

Jacks and Mallory stood in silence for a moment after Pembroke and Archer moved off to relay the plan to others. Both men had the same thought spinning in their heads: hold until nightfall. Withdraw. Dunkirk. It sounded almost too good to be true.

Jacks shifted his weight and rested his hands on his hips as he glanced at Mallory. "Well, that's a turn, isn't it?" he muttered, his voice low enough to stay between the two of them. "Thought we were ready to go down swinging."

Mallory exhaled, rubbing the back of his neck. "Aye, but it's not exactly a picnic we're walking into, is it? Hold the street. Fight up to Mont Cassel. Then march thirty miles with Jerry breathing down our necks." His eyes narrowed as he watched the men farther down the line readying themselves. "It's a bloody miracle if we get half of them out alive."

Jacks grunted, leaning closer. "You think they'll hold, Sarge? After everything?"

Mallory didn't answer immediately. His eyes swept over the scattered defenders: their faces smeared with grime, eyes hollow from days of fighting. There was fear, exhaustion, and doubt in every expression. But beneath that, there was something else: resolve.

"They'll hold," he said finally, his voice steady. "Because they don't have a choice. None of us do."

Jacks nodded though his lips tightened. "Reckon it's a damn good thing, though, hearing 'withdraw.' Gives a man something to fight for. Bit of hope, you know?"

Mallory's expression softened slightly, but the edge of command quickly returned. "Hope's all well and good, Jacks, but hope doesn't get a bayonet in the guts. Go on, get the lads to fix bayonets. If Jerry pushes close again, we're going to meet them the hard way."

Jacks smirked faintly and adjusted his helmet. "Aye, Sarge. Nothing like cold steel to keep 'em honest."

Chapter 8

The street was a hellscape of ruin and fire. Smoke curled into the sky in thick, choking plumes, blotting out the fading afternoon light over Cassel. A twisted line of smouldering wreckage cut across the Rue de Bergues—the aftermath of the anti-tank gun's last stand and Dixon's bravery.

Three tanks lay broken along the road like fallen beasts. The first sat half-jammed against the edge of a bomb crater; its track had been blown clean through, the hull scorched and warping. The second had rolled to a stop against a stone wall, and black smoke still poured from its hatches. The stink of burnt oil mingled with something fouler—burning flesh. One of the crew had managed to clamber out before the fire took him, and his body was now slumped beside the turret, crumpled and blackened, limbs frozen in a final crawl.

The third tank lay farther up the street, slumped against the rubble with its gun twisted unnaturally upwards, and its turret ring scorched and buckled. Smoke still curled from the half-open commander's hatch, and a streak of something dark ran down the side where fire had licked through. A boot jutted out from the cupola, blackened and still. Nearby, a helmet lay cracked and empty on the cobbles, and its scorched lining fluttered faintly in the breeze. Dixon's final act had left its mark—lethal, desperate, and irreversible.

Scattered around the tanks were the dead of the supporting infantry. Grey-uniformed bodies sprawled in unnatural angles, rifles fallen from stiff fingers. Some lay in heaps where the Vickers had torn through them. Ragged holes had punched clean through chest and thigh while others bore the brutal neatness of rifle fire: a single shot, clean and final. One soldier had fallen against a low wall and a smear of blood traced the stone where he'd slid down. Another had died mid-charge, his hands still clutching a stick grotesque, suspended mix of rage and disbelief.

The Rue de Bergues had been held, but the cost hung heavy in the air—ash, blood, and silence.

To the east, two buildings burnt fiercely, and their flames licking hungrily at the night sky. The heat from the fires could be felt from a distance as it seared the air and cast long, dancing shadows across the shattered façades of nearby houses. Each crack and pop of collapsing timber mingled with the muffled cries of the wounded. It was a brutal reminder of the human cost that had been paid to hold the line.

Archer crouched behind a low barricade of rubble and sandbags. his rifle was placed across the sandbags. His eyes were fixed on the street ahead, momentarily mesmerised by the shadows that flickered in the light of the flames. Somewhere beyond the fire and smoke, the Germans were regrouping, preparing for another push; he could guarantee it. The distant bark of commands in guttural German drifted through towards him, growing louder with every passing moment.

"1400hrs, I make it. We need to buy ourselves at least four hours," Pembroke muttered beside archer with a low and grim tone. His uniform was streaked with dirt and blood, and his face was finally showing a hint of exhaustion. "They'll want to clear this street before they try anything else though."

Archer exhaled sharply, his hand grabbing at the stock of his rifle. His gaze swept over the burning ruins ahead to the makeshift barricades, and the scattered defenders crouched behind cover. Each face he saw was etched with grime and exhaustion, but their eyes still held that spark of defiance.

"We'll hold," Archer said firmly, more to himself than to Pembroke. "We have to."

A sudden crack of gunfire shattered the tense quiet, followed by the sharp, unmistakable zip of a machine-gun unleashing a burst from an elevated window. Bullets chewed through the wreckage in front of them, sending shards of wood and jagged metal spinning into the air. Archer ducked instinctively, pressing his back against the sandbagged barricade as the metallic ping of ricochets echoed all around.

"Get down!" someone shouted from farther up the street, their voice barely audible over the eruption of devastation.

The gunfire intensified. The steady rhythm of the MG34 swept across the street like a deadly scythe. Archer's chest tightened as he strained to make sense of the shadowy figures shifting in the haze. Then he heard it. The guttural bark of German commands grew louder, their words sharp and urgent.

"Stand too!" Pembroke shouted grimly, not that he had to. Everyone was aware: it was starting. Raising his head just enough to glance over the sandbags, Pembroke's face was pale, ingrained with soot, but his voice carried the same unyielding authority it always did.

Archer nodded tersely, gripping his rifle tighter. He dared a quick glance over the barricade; his heart sank at what he saw. Dark shapes were moving through the smoke and rubble ahead, every one of them crouching low as they advanced between the wreckage. Flashes of light glinted off helmets and rifles. The enemy's movement was methodical and precise.

"They're using the upper floors," Archer muttered, his eyes snapping to the shattered façades of the buildings on either side of the street. A German soldier darted into a second-storey window, the barrel of his weapon appearing a moment later to rake the defenders with suppressing fire.

"Grant!" Pembroke barked, his voice cutting through the din. "Get on that bloody machine-gun before they pin us all down!"

Corporal Eddie Grant didn't flinch. His calm demeanour seemed at odds with the chaos erupting around him. He turned towards the guttural crack of the German MG34 on the second floor, its muzzle flashes cutting through the smoke. His jaw tightened as he crouched beside the 2-pounder, and he moved his grime-streaked hands with practiced efficiency.

"Loader!" he barked, and Private Mason snapped to attention, already holding an armour-piercing shell. The dull-green casing glinted faintly in the light.

"Target, second floor, left window!" Grant ordered. His voice carried the calm authority of a man who knew his job even as bullets whipped past him. Mason slammed the round into the breech. The metallic clunk echoed sharply.

Grant's ungloved hand closed around the traverse wheel, adjusting the aim with deliberate precision. He leant into the gun, his one good eye squinting down the sight as he lined up the shot. The distant chatter of the machine-gun rang in his ears, but he didn't waver.

"Clear back!" Grant barked, and the crew behind him ducked instinctively.

With a sharp pull of the firing lever, the 2-pounder roared to life. The gun kicked back against its stabilizers; the force reverberated through the street. The armour-piercing round streaked towards the target, slamming into the second storey just below the window with a deafening crash. The building shuddered, and a cloud of brick dust and debris billowed outwards as the machine-gun abruptly fell silent.

"Direct hit!" Mason shouted with exhilaration. But Grant didn't pause to celebrate.

"Load!" he snapped, his hands already working to adjust the aim. Mason shoved another round into the breech; the action was quick and practiced as he ignored the havoc around them.

"Target, ground level, fifty yards. Infantry, near the overturned cart!" Grant shouted, his voice sharp and focused. He grabbed the traverse wheel, once again adjusting the aim of the gun with deliberate care. Through the haze, a cluster of German soldiers crouched behind a wrecked cart, their rifles snapping out fire at the defenders.

"Clear back!" Grant roared, his hand hovering over the firing lever.

The gun suddenly fired with a deafening crack. The barrel belched smoke and flame. The round streaked towards the wreckage, slamming into the cart with incredible force. The impact shattered what had been left of the wooden frame, sending splinters and shards of metal flying in all directions. Behind the cart, two German soldiers were hurled backwards, one clutching at his chest as a ragged piece of wood protruded through his tunic.

"Hit!" Mason shouted. This time, he allowed himself a grim smile to flash across his face.

Grant didn't pause. "Loader, call out the remaining rounds!" he barked, already recalibrating the gun for a new target. "Load!" came the cry again. Mason shoved another round into the breech, sweat dripping down his cheeks.

"Target, left side, seventy yards—group moving for cover!" Grant called, spinning the gun slightly to track a group of soldiers darting towards the relative safety of a doorway. One soldier crouched in the open, shouting commands to his comrades.

"Clear back!" The 2-pounder roared again. The recoil slammed into its stabilisers as the shell streaked towards its mark. The round struck the edge of the building, blowing apart the doorway and sending rubble cascading onto the Germans. A thicker cloud of dust and smoke erupted, swallowing the figures as they vanished into the dust.

Grant's lips pressed into a thin line as he adjusted the gun again. "Loader!" he barked, his tone strained but steady.

Mason yelled out "Nine!" as he slammed another round into the breech, his hands trembling slightly as the relentless pace of firing began to take its toll.

"Keep at it Grant! You're doing great!" Pembroke shouted from behind, his rifle barking as he took shots at advancing figures through the smoke.

Grant grunted in response, his focus never wavering. "Next target, fifty yards. Load!" Grant barked with unrelenting movements. Around them, the street was alive with the brutality of battle—machine-guns chattering, shouts ringing out, and the moans of collapsing buildings. But Grant's focus never wavered: every action was deliberate and efficient as though he were back in a training drill rather than the heart of the fight.

A burst of gunfire tore into the wall of sandbags, spewing dirt and debris with each impact. Archer ducked as bullets zipped overhead, the air hissing with their passage. The ground beneath him trembled with the pounding rhythm of every shot— whether German or British.

"They're not holding back," Pembroke said tightly, glancing at Archer with a grim but resolute expression.

Archer didn't respond and narrowed his focus as he took careful aim. Through the murky air, he caught sight of a grey helmet peeking over a pile of rubble seventy yards away. Steadying his breathing, he gently squeezed the trigger. A flash. a sharp crack. Then the helmet disappeared as its owner slumped behind the rubble. Without hesitation, Archer instinctively shifted his aim, searching for the next target. There was no shortage. Enemy shapes swarmed in and out of cover; the street crawled with them.

Beside him, the Bren gun clattered relentlessly. Its sharp, steady rhythm cut through the chaos. Webb crouched low, his hands firm on the weapon, each burst forcing a group of German soldiers to retreat into a derelict shop that lined the street. Webb's aim was merciless, his shots pinning them down with deadly precision.

Across the street, Jacks saw the opportunity. From his

perch on the first floor of a building, he stepped onto a small, cantilevered balcony jutting from a double window. The wood creaked under his boots as he pulled a Mills bomb from his webbing. He took a steadying breath, then gently lobbed the grenade out of the window and across the street. It arced cleanly through the shop's shattered opening.

The flash was followed by a sharp, concussive pop that echoed down the street. Dust and fragments erupted from the shop front as the grenade detonated among the cowering Germans. For a brief moment, there was silence. Then the faint sound of agony as screams leaked from inside the ruined shop.

Jacks, spotting the shifting shapes of the dazed Germans through the dust and smoke, followed up with several quick shots from his Lee-Enfield. Each pull of the trigger sent a round downrange. The bolt slid up and back in smooth, practiced motions before rechambering in seconds. He managed to hit at least two of the stumbling figures before he realised how exposed he'd made himself by leaning at the window.

A sudden burst from an MP40 rattled the brickwork to his left, sending shards of masonry flying. Jacks threw himself backwards, retreating into the building as his heart hammered in his chest. He cursed under his breath at his carelessness and silently blessed his luck. That was far too close for comfort, he thought grimly.

From behind him, Pritchard let out a loud, almost gleeful laugh.

"Careful there, Jacks!" he called, the wide grin on his face unmistakable. Kneeling against the internal wall with his rifle at the ready, Pritchard was doing what he did best—picking off targets with unnerving accuracy.

Pritchard's marksmanship was almost mechanical. He cradled the rifle as if it were an extension of himself, and the bolt glided effortlessly as he rechambered between shots. Each time he selected a target, he held perfectly still. His breath was measured and controlled as he whispered through the iron sights like a ritual. With smooth and deliberate movements, he was devoid of hesitation. When he fired, it was as though the rifle exhaled with him—a seamless extension of his will.

Jacks had shifted to a first-floor window, crouching low with his Lee-Enfield on the sill as he scanned the street below. To his right, Hawkins knelt behind the Bren. The weapon's steady chatter cut through the din of battle. Each burst forced the advancing Germans to dive for cover, stalling their momentum as Hawkins methodically swept the street.

"Keep it steady, Hawkins," Jacks muttered, pulling back the bolt of his rifle and rechambering a round. We have them pinned on the far side."

Hawkins grinned through the sweat streaking his grease-covered face. His eyes never left the sights.

"I'm on it, Jacks," he said, squeezing the trigger and sending another burst downrange.

To his left, O'Hara peeked through the shattered remains of a doorway, his rifle gripped tightly. His usually jovial expression was absent and replaced with a grim focus as he scanned for targets. A faint whistle caught his ear, and he flinched instinctively as a grenade landed a few yards down the street, sending up a shower of debris.

"Bloody close!" O'Hara hissed, ducking back into the shadows. He turned to Jacks, his voice threaded with tension. "What's the plan, Corp? We can't stay here forever, and Hawkins'll burn that bloody barrel out if we're not careful."

Jacks paused, his sharp eyes darting towards the rubble-strewn street. The Germans were regrouping again, small clusters darting between cover. He noticed one figure creeping along the edge of a derelict building. A grenade was clutched in his hand.

"We stay here until the flare goes up," Jacks said firmly,

raising his rifle back to his shoulder. "And if they want us out of here before that, they're gonna have to work for it." He steadied his aim, exhaling as he lined up his shot. A split second later, the German with the grenade crumpled to the ground, his weapon tumbling harmlessly from his grasp.

"Nice one!" O'Hara said, a flicker of his usual spirit returning. He quickly shifted his focus, firing a shot of his own and forcing a soldier to dive back into cover.

Hawkins, unfazed by the exchange, shifted the Bren slightly and unleashed another burst, the rounds chewing through an overturned cart.

"Come on, Jerry," he muttered under his breath, his tone almost mocking. "I'll keep you dancing all day."

Across the street from Jacks and the others, Mallory pressed his back against the crumbling wall, sweat streaking his face as he listened to the chaos unfolding below. He could hear the Germans moving methodically below, clearing the lower floors room by room. The sharp crack of rifles and the dull thump of grenades echoed up the staircase, followed by the heavy thud of boots rushing the cleared rooms.

"Wilson, Saunders—how's that wall coming?" Mallory barked, glancing over his shoulder.

Saunders, his sleeves rolled up and dirt smearing his forearms, swung his entrenching tool into the plaster like a pickaxe. Each strike sent chunks of brick and mortar crumbling to the floor, the dust stinging their eyes and throats. Lance Corporal Wilson worked beside him with frantic but effective movements.

"Nearly there, Sarge!" Saunders grunted, his voice strained. "Just a bit more."

"Make it quick," Mallory said grimly, turning his attention back to the door. "Evans, cover the stairs. Don't let them get up here."

Evans knelt at the top of the staircase; his rifle was steady as he aimed down the narrow, dimly lit steps. The doorway leading to the stairs had been blown apart earlier, and its frame hung shattered and splintered. Beside him, Corbett—a burly volunteer who looked more like a dock worker than a soldier—clutched his rifle tightly, a grenade balanced in his free hand, ready to lob if the Germans pushed too close.

Across the room, Pike—one of the dozen volunteers who had joined them at Cassel—crouched near a shattered window, his pale face streaked with dirt as he peered nervously through the smoke-filled courtyard below. His hands trembled slightly as he gripped his rifle; the tension in his knuckles betrayed his fear.

Mallory stepped closer to Evans, gripping his shoulder firmly. "If they get too close, let me know. No hesitation."

"They're already close, Sarge," Evans muttered, his eyes fixed on the shadowy figures moving at the base of the stairs. "Too bloody close."

The unmistakable clink of a stick grenade landing on the wooden floor snapped Mallory into action. Without a second thought, he lunged forwards, snatching it up and hurling it back down the staircase. The explosion that followed shook the room, rattling the broken windowpanes and sending a cloud of dust cascading from the ceiling.

"They're not stopping," Corbett said, his voice tight as his gaze flicked nervously to the door frame. "They're gonna come through that stairwell any second."

"Then we buy Saunders and Wilson the time they need to break through that wall. It's our only way out of this mess," Mallory snapped, turning towards Pike. He motioned for the younger volunteer to shift position. "Pike, cover the window. If Jerry gets around the side and into the courtyard, we're done for."

Pike nodded quickly, swallowing hard before shifting his

position to get a better view. He froze for half a second as he spotted a German soldier climbing over the rear wall into the courtyard. His hesitation passed in an instant as he fired, the rifle's crack ringing out. The German fell backwards with a thud, disappearing into the smoke.

From behind them, Wilson gave a triumphant shout. "Got it, Sarge! There's enough room to squeeze through now!"

Mallory turned sharply. "Right, move! Wilson, Saunders—you're first. Corbett, hold this spot and cover them."

Corbett moved and took up position near the hole by a doorway, gripping his rifle tightly, and his eyes flicked towards the stairs as the pounding of German boots grew louder.

The two men scrambled through the jagged hole in the wall. Their arms and legs scraped against the broken brick and plaster as they disappeared into the neighbouring property to relative safety. Corbett stood by the opening, his rifle at the ready, waiting for Mallory's signal to follow.

But the Germans didn't wait. A burst of gunfire tore through the opening where there once was a door, and a second later, German soldiers charged through. Evans fired first, his shot catching one in the chest, but at least three others surged forwards, throwing themselves up the staircase in a flurry of shouts and rifle fire.

"Evans!" Mallory roared, grabbing Evans by his webbing and dragging him back. They both fell into position near the narrow landing, Mallory's bayonet already fixed. "Corbett, go—now!"

Corbett hesitated for a fraction of a second, then dove through the hole in the wall, leaving Mallory and Evans to face the rushing enemy.

Evans fired one last shot before his rifle clicked empty. "Arhhhhhhhhhhhhhh!" he screamed, his voice raw with adrenalin as he pointed his bayonetted rifle forwards.

The first German soldier burst onto the landing, his rifle partially raised, but Mallory was faster. He lunged forwards, driving the bayonet deep into the man's gut. The German let out a sharp cry, collapsing against Mallory who wrenched the weapon free, spinning to face the next.

Evans was already engaged, grunting with effort as he drove his bayonet into another soldier. Blood sprayed across the narrow landing, the confined space forcing the fight into a brutal, frenzied attack. Mallory felt a sharp burn across his arm as a German bullet tore through his sleeve, but he ignored it, thrusting his blade upwards into the next man's chest with a savage yell.

"Evans, move back!" Mallory yelled, his voice hoarse. "Through that hole!"

But Evans didn't answer. He was grappling with another soldier, the two of them locked in a desperate struggle that sent them crashing into the wall. Mallory swung around, and in a single motion, drove his bayonet through the German's side, sending him sprawling to the ground.

"Evans, now!" Mallory shouted again, grabbing his shoulder and pulling him towards the hole. Evans turned, and for the briefest of moments, their eyes met. In that instant, they were no longer men—they were animals with their blood up. Killing was second nature: primal and instinctual.

With one final glance at the blood-soaked landing, Mallory reached into his webbing and pulled out a grenade. He yanked the pin free with a sharp tug and tossed it towards the staircase. The small, green canister clinked as it bounced down the steps. "That'll keep 'em busy," he muttered, grabbing Evans by the shoulder.

The two men scrambled through the jagged opening in the wall just as the grenade detonated with a deafening crack. The blast shook the walls, sending a plume of dust and splinters cascading through the room. For a moment, the pounding of German boots below them faltered, shouts and cries rising in their place.

Mallory and Evans collapsed into the neighbouring property, coughing from the dust and their own exhaustion, as Corbett and the others pulled them to safety.

Mallory slumped against the wall, chest heaving, the blood on his arm soaking through his sleeve. He wiped it with the back of his hand, smearing it further without thinking. His mind reeled—raw from what they'd just survived—but there was no time to dwell on it. No time to regroup, no plan to speak of. Just breathe and be ready to go again. The sound of German footsteps returned, echoing through the room they'd barely escaped, closer now, deliberate

Then, the barrel of an MP40 appeared, poking through the hole in the wall. It spat fire in short, controlled bursts, sweeping from left to right and back again. The nine-millimetre rounds tore into the plastered walls opposite where Mallory and Evans had paused. The sharp cracks echoing in the confined space.

Mallory's stomach dropped. He watched as Pike staggered backwards, then crumpled to his knees before falling face-first to the floor. A dark pool of crimson quickly spread beneath the lifeless body, staining the dusty floorboards.

Before Mallory could react further, a German soldier foolishly leant through the hole in the wall. His head twisted as if to inspect the aftermath of his grisly work. Without hesitation and with renewed, revengeful instincts, Mallory lunged, driving his bayonet into the back of the man's neck. The blade sank deep, and the German let out a strangled cry before collapsing and slumping against the floorboards.

Mallory staggered back, chest heaving. There was no room for anger. Not now. Just get up, get moving. His eyes flicked to where Pike had fallen—still, pale, and far too young. Mallory felt a tight pull in his chest, but there was no time to stop. Not for grief. This was survival now. He needed to act. He turned and slipped into the corridor, scanning for movement. Evans was ahead, falling back through the smoke. Mallory moved quickly and headed for the far end of the building, drawn by the sharp crack of rifle fire and the steady snap of a Bren gun. From here, he could just make out Webb working his Bren, and the 2-pounder still firing beyond the wreckage. That was Archer's line. They'd work their way back to it—intent on causing as much devastation to the pursuing Germans as possible.

The battle for Rue de Bergues had become a nightmare of fire, smoke, and blood. The street, once a narrow thoroughfare of quaint brick homes and shop fronts, had been reduced to a vision of hell. Flames roared from shattered buildings, and their orange glow twisted and flickered amongst the choking plumes of smoke that curled into the day's sky. The air was drenched with the stench of burning timber, cordite and spilt blood. Every second was punctuated by the sharp cracks of rifle fire, the endless chatter of machine-guns, and the thunderous roar of explosions tearing through the ruins.

Archer crouched behind the makeshift barricade of sandbags and rubble near the bend in the Rue de Bergues, his rifle tucked tight into his shoulder as he fired into the haze ahead. He had no idea where Mallory or Jacks were, or if they were even still holding. There had been no runner, nor had any signal made it back. Between shots, Archer had stolen a few glances down the Rue de Bergues, trying to take stock of the situation. Once or twice, he'd glimpsed the odd figure moving past a shattered window—too fleeting to identify. Then came the crack of a rifle, and the muted thump of a grenade. He couldn't tell if it was friend or foe, but it was enough to confirm one thing: the fight was still going. He watched the Germans pushing forwards, their disciplined figures weaving through the smoke and debris, flitting between cover like shadows. The muzzle flashes of their weapons illuminated their helmets and faces for fleeting moments before they disappeared again into the ruinous landscape.

A round zipped past Archer's ear, sending a spray of pulverised stone into his already wounded cheek. He gritted his teeth and pressed lower, taking a breath before snapping his rifle up to fire again. He wasn't sure where, but he hoped it'd make a difference.

The street ahead was a chaotic mess—dead Germans lay sprawled at grotesque angles where they had fallen. Some of their bodies were half-buried beneath the rubble. More were advancing though, stepping over their fallen comrades with their own machine-guns suppressing Archer's position with brutal efficiency. It seemed futile to shoot, but he knew he had to try.

Further down the street, both Mallory and Jacks were locked in brutal, close quarters fighting, Jacks group on the east side and Mallory with his men on the west. The Germans had pushed into the shattered buildings, forcing the British to defend every room, every stairwell, every pile of rubble. The sounds of their battle echoed through the ruined walls—rifle butts cracking against skulls, bayonets flashing in the dim firelight, the brutal wet impact of bayonets finding flesh. Grenades exploded in deafening bursts, sending splinters and bodies flying.

Mallory and Evans had moved into a ruined townhouse, their boots crunching over shattered glass and splintered wood as they navigated the debris. The Germans were in pursuit, sweeping through the lower floors, their shouted commands echoing through the ruins. Mallory and his group had made their way back through the buildings. Corbett had positioned himself in the crook of an old brick doorway, firing directly down the street. The 2-pounder, set on the bend twenty yards behind him, kept up its steady rate of fire, while the Bren to its left hammered out its relentless staccato bursts. Mallory had taken up a position in the building behind Corbett, rifle raised. The others spread out around them, finding cover where they could—behind overturned tables, battered cupboards, and whatever else the buildings offered. They steadied themselves, weapons ready, bracing for the fight to inevitably reach them.

Above the noise and dust, the steady thump of the 2-pounder and the rattling bursts of the Bren gun still echoed up the street. It was a brutal rhythm that carried more than firepower. It was reassurance. Proof they weren't alone. Each report was a reminder that others were still holding the line, still fighting. And for now, that was enough.

To their rear, Corporal Grant and his 2-pounder gun crew worked furiously, hammering German positions with devastating fire. One of his rounds slammed into the upper floor of a nearby building, sending brickwork and bodies tumbling onto the street below. The gun's recoil rattled through the barricades, but Grant barely flinched, already shouting for another round to be loaded.

Despite their losses, the Germans showed no hesitation. More figures darted between cover in the street; some were pressed into ruined shops and houses, attempting to outflank the British positions. Machine-gun fire rattled from upper-floor windows, pinning defenders down.

Pembroke suddenly appeared beside Archer and crouched to scan the scene with growing concern. There were too many gaps in their line, too little time left to hold. They'd gone from being prepared and organised to being totally reactive to each German manoeuvre. The situation was quickly slipping beyond their control, and soon, they would have no choice but to fall back or be overrun.

Back at Mallory's position, Saunders and Tug Wilson were set up at the rear of the townhouse crouched low behind the collapsed remains of a kitchen wall. The battle raged all around but then came something far nearer: the unmistakable clatter of an MG34 being mounted, just twenty yards away. Tug's breath caught. If it opened up, they'd be torn apart.

Wilson pressed his back against the brickwork, his breath steadying. "That sounds like trouble," he muttered to Saunders who peered through the smoke and dust, his eyes narrowing. A small German fire team had positioned themselves behind a half-collapsed wall. Their MG34 was mounted on the debris, and the gunner had already settled behind the sights. Wilson realised immediately they had set up to put fire on the 2-pounder and Archer's group on the bend. The gun had been sighted to take advantage of a gap in the row of buildings which gave a direct line of sight. If they got that thing firing, it would tear through that position.

Wilson's fingers tightened around his Lee-Enfield. "We can't let that bastard open up."

"Agreed." Saunders exhaled sharply. "I'll move right, get close. Son as I fire, you hit them hard."

Wilson gave a firm nod, gripping his rifle in preparation.

Saunders moved fast, darting through a hole in the crumbling brickwork of the house, and he moved low through the ruined building. The Germans were focused ahead of them, taking a bead on the 2-pounder, unaware as Saunders came from their right. He raised his rifle, sighted the gunner's profile—then fired.

The bullet punched through the German's throat. He dropped instantly. His loader turned in shock, but Wilson's rifle cracked a fraction of a second later, taking the man through the chest. Another German quickly scrambled for the MG34, but Saunders surged forwards, his bayonet flashing as he drove it deep into the enemy's gut. The man gurgled, collapsing against the wreckage.

A moment of silence hung in the air. Then, Wilson strode forwards, already reaching for the MG34. He slung his rifle down, gripping the German weapon with a grin that was all teeth and danger.

"Well, well," he muttered, feeding in the belt of ammunition. "Follow me Saunders!"

As Wilson turned, Saunders yanked the belt of spare ammunition from the man he had skewered with his bayonet moments before. Slinging it around his neck, he turned and followed Wilson.

With Saunders in pursuit, Wilson sprinted towards the neighbouring building—the one they had defended earlier—unleashing a burst of fire at the doorway as he crashed through. He turned right into another room and let off another burst, moving with ceaseless efficiency. He repeated the process, clearing each space as he advanced.

Reaching the staircase, he glanced back to see a sweat-soaked Saunders following, ammunition draped around his neck. A quick assessment told him there were maybe 50 to 80 rounds left—enough for ten to twelve good bursts.

Wilson pointed his gun up the stairs that Pike had been defending less than an hour before and fired, sending rounds tearing into the darkness above. He surged forwards, taking the steps two at a time, firing from the hip as he went. His gunfire ripped through the rooms. Germans dropped in his wake. Saunders followed close behind, adding to the onslaught with his rifle and bayonet. The two men systematically cleared the first floor in a brutal, unforgiving assault.

Wilson moved to an opening—the remnants of an old window overlooking the street. From this position, he had the advantage of being behind the advancing Germans.

Without needing to be told, Saunders was already at work, linking the belt of ammunition from his neck to the last few rounds still loaded in the MG34.

"You're good," he muttered to Wilson before chambering another five rounds into his rifle.

Wilson was already firing from the window. On the street below, three or four Germans dropped in the initial bursts. Another two fell before the rest even realised they were being cut down from behind. Panic erupted as the survivors scrambled for cover.

Wilson quickly shifted his sights to a machine-gun nest on the first floor of a building farther down the street. He didn't realise it was the same gun that was pinning down Archer and the men at the barricades. He unleashed burst after burst, hammering the position. Whether he had killed the crew or simply forced them into cover, he couldn't tell—but the machine-gun went silent.

Archer saw the advantage shift. The Germans were reeling, caught between fire from Wilson's position and the stubborn resistance in the barricades. It wasn't a breakthrough, but it was enough—a momentary hesitation in the enemy's assault.

He turned to Webb crouched to his side, his face streaked with sweat and grime.

"Reload...... Follow me! Charge!"

Without hesitation, the two men surged forwards, followed by two of the volunteers. Rifle and bayonets at the ready, Webb releasing small bursts from the hip. Gunfire snapped past them as the enemy, still dazed from the sudden turn of events, scrambled to react. Archer fired as he ran, putting a German down mid-turn. His men crashed into the stunned infantry. Pembroke, realising the moment was changing momentum, called on Corporal Grant and Private Mason to grab their personal weapons and follow. The seven men with bayonets and rifles at the ready headed straight into the disorientated Germans butts and bayonets slamming into bodies as they pushed through the street.

For a few mad moments, they gained ground, forcing the Germans back towards cover.

Then the shift came again.

A sharp, whistling sound cut through the din. Mortars.

The first explosion struck behind them, throwing up a spray of dirt and debris. Then another. Closer this time. The Germans had adapted, abandoning their immediate assault in favour of hammering the British positions with indirect fire.

"Take cover!" Archer bellowed, diving into the remains of a building. He was followed by Webb and Pembroke and two others as they scrambled for any shelter they could find as the bombardment intensified.

The street became an inferno. Shells struck rooftops, sending tiles and splinters raining down. Cobblestones cracked and shattered under the impact, sending deadly shards in every direction. Smoke and dust choked Cassel, killing visibility as the relentless, incessant barrage hammered their position.

One round hit the barricade Archer had been behind minutes before. It blew apart sandbags and the wooden supports. Another shell screamed in, slamming into the emplacement of the 2-pounder gun. The explosion sent pieces of the anti-tank weapon flying. The wreckage burnt. The gun was silenced. A critical piece of their defence was obliterated.

Archer risked another glance towards the barricades. He saw devastation, then he saw the sprawled-out bodies of Grant and Mason, caught in the street by the mortar fire.

Another explosion struck closer, pelting him with rubble and dirt. Then came the sounds he dreaded: shouts and boots pounding forwards.

Under the cover of the mortar barrage, the Germans were committing fresh troops to the assault. Archer witnessed a German lieutenant bellowing from behind a smoking wreckage, gesturing for his men to flank left. The assault teams moved with grim precision and determination, rifles snapping to their shoulders as they advanced.

Archer pushed himself up, wincing. He could see the enemy pouring forwards, rushing towards the shattered British, their rifles and submachine-guns ready.

"We need to get back to our gun position... pull back to the gun!" Archer shouted to his men.

He moved first, leading them to fall back towards the remains of the 2-pounder's position without the need to communicate his intention. He turned, took a knee and fired as the men bound beyond him. Then, in turn, his men turned and fired as the group retreated in bounds, trying to cover their movements. Alas, at least one man went down in this movement. As Archer withdrew, he turned and raised his arm, signalling to anyone left.

"Move back!" he called, motioning for them to fall back.

From both sides of the street men were firing from the windows and openings as they gave up their hard contested positions, the men worked in bounds providing cover so, ensuring the enemy couldn't press forwards too quickly. Their rifles cracked in steady, controlled shots, keeping the Germans at bay as the withdrawal continued.

Pembroke knelt behind the wreckage of the 2-pounder, surrounded by the wreckage and debris caused by the mortar hit. His breath was ragged. His mind raced as he tried to make sense of the chaos around him. What was left? What could still be salvaged?

His eyes locked onto Archer who was leading a handful of men in a desperate dash towards him. Behind them, flashes of grey uniforms moved through the smoke—Germans, advancing, slipping into cover as they pressed forwards.

Pembroke gripped the sandbagged parapet, frozen. What

could they do? No order came to mind, no clever tactic. For the first time, his calm was failing him—cracking under the weight of it all. He was watching his men run for their lives, and he had no answer.

Archer eventually reached the wreckage, chest heaving. Around him, the men instinctively melted into cover, weapons ready. He swallowed hard, catching his breath then, Pembroke appeared beside him, eyes scanning the advancing enemy.

"Tom, this is getting a little too dicey!"

Archer turned, his eyes comically wide, mouth slightly open, head tilting as he deadpan humour, "Really, Captain?"

Pembroke let out a breath, then chuckled at Archer's expression. The absurd understatement of the moment hit them both, and before they knew it, Archer's face split into a grin, a quiet giggle escaping him. Pembroke shook his head, his chuckle turning into full laughter. The tension broke—if only for a moment.

Still grinning, Pembroke pulled his flare pistol, raised it towards the sky, and fired. The flare burst into a vivid arc of red, streaking high above the smoke-choked street, its trail hanging defiantly against the grey afternoon sky—a signal, a call, and a warning all at once.

Chapter 9

Just off the Rue de Bruges, the mortar pit was set up in the garden of a small townhouse, a once-charming home that had been left battered and hollowed by war. Its whitewashed walls were streaked with soot, and the roof was partially collapsed to expose the charred remnants of wooden beams within. The front door hung awkwardly on one hinge, swaying slightly in the faint breeze, while shattered windowpanes framed the dark, empty interior like vacant eyes staring out at the battlefield.

The garden, though overgrown and neglected even before the fighting had reached Cassel, had once been carefully tended. A low stone wall, now half-collapsed, ran around the perimeter. Its fallen sections formed natural cover for the mortar pit. What had once been a flower bed was now churned-up dirt and debris, and the dead remains of lilac and rose bushes had been crushed beneath heavy boots and scattered casings. A wrought-iron bench, rusted but still standing, leant at an angle near the back of the garden; its wooden slats splintered. The last few surviving leaves of a fruit tree were coated in dust and grime as was the broken wheelbarrow which lay on its side at the foot of the tree.

The pit itself was nestled between a crumbling garden shed and a pile of fallen masonry from the house. It was well-concealed by the surrounding structures. The mortar crews had dug shallow trenches and reinforced them with sandbags scrounged from abandoned positions, ensuring they had at least some protection if the enemy countered with artillery or mortar fire of their own.

Beyond the broken wall, Cassel smouldered in the distance. A heavy shroud of smoke rolled over the town, blotting out sections of the sky. The mortar team could imagine the taste of acrid cordite, scorched wood, and burning flesh from their position. For them, there was just the faintest trace of damp earth and crushed vegetation—a sickly reminder that this had once been a home, not a battlefield.

Sergeant Frank Wallis adjusted his grip on the tube of one of the two-inch mortars, and the familiar chill of steel bit into his fingers. Beside each weapon, he had carefully laid out the ammunition—five rounds per gun to start with. In the last few hours, he'd got his men scouring old positions, and stripping anything they could find to bolster their meagre arsenal. They had scraped together another four rounds per gun, along with three smoke bombs.

Wallis knew his orders: when the flare went up, he'd fire everything he had—then head for Mont Cassel. Simple enough in theory. In reality, it felt like a death sentence.

He exhaled slowly, rolling the tension from his shoulders as he knelt beside the two-inch mortar, and fingers ran absently over the smooth casing of a high-explosive round. The familiar chill of steel under his touch was oddly reassuring. Nine rounds per gun. Three smoke bombs. Not nearly enough. He'd fired more in training exercises than he had now to stall an entire German assault.

Wallis had been a soldier long enough to know how this would go—a desperate last stand with no guarantees. The Germans would hit hard, fast, and relentlessly. He doubted his mortars could do more than slow them down for a few minutes, but that was the job. Buy time. Nothing more.

He glanced at the men around him, their faces dimly illuminated by the dull grey sky. They weren't regular mortar crews—just a mix of riflemen and stragglers pulled from whatever was left of the battalion who had been handed mortars and ordered to hold.

Private Dunlop, barely twenty, shifted nervously beside his gun, his hands worrying the strap of his webbing. His lips moved in a silent mumble. Not far from him, Corporal Briggs—an older, hard-faced veteran with a streak of white in his hair—sat with his back against the half-collapsed wall, methodically rolling a cigarette with stained fingers. His expression was unreadable. Cool under fire, but not blind to what was coming. Private Holt crouched nearby, methodically checking the fins of a mortar round, his movements deliberate and precise. Young, but he had a quiet focus that spoke of determination rather than fear. Farther down the pit, Private Lewis was bent over his mortar, muttering calculations to himself, checking and rechecking the distances they had scribbled down earlier. The rain had smudged some of the ink, but it hardly mattered. He knew that when the signal came, they'd fire every last round, accuracy be damned.

Wallis' fingers tightened on the mortar round in his hands. He wasn't afraid of dying—not really. But there was something disturbing about waiting for it. The limbo between action and destruction. He wondered how long it would take for the Germans to zero in on them. A minute? Two? Less?

Sergeant Frank Wallis crouched low in the shallow hastily dug mortar pit, pulling his lips into a tight line with a slow, knowing sigh. Years of hard training had etched the routine into his bones. His men moved around him with quiet efficiency—they trusted him to read the ground, to call the arc, to get it right. His eyes flicked to the distant town where Cassel smouldered behind veils of thick smoke. He imagined the men still holding the main street, waiting for the same flare that would send hell raining down from his mortars. Did they know he was here? Would they feel it when he fired? Or would it all be swallowed in the chaos, they were already in. Nothing but a footnote in the battle?

Cassel had been burning all morning. The fighting had ebbed and surged, relentless and unyielding. From his position west of the Rue de Bergues, Wallis had heard it all—the dull, rhythmic thud of artillery as German gunners pounded the British lines, the distinctive chug of a Vickers gun rattling away in

161

controlled bursts.

Somewhere to the east, they'd heard a tank gun fire—a short, deep bark that had sent a shell screaming through the ruins. The explosion had followed a second later, a dull, heavy crump that had sent a ripple through the ground even at this distance. Wallis had exhaled slowly and tightened his fingers around his mortar tube.

Then, the tempo had shifted again. Rifles had cracked in sharp succession, overlapping like snapping twigs, and the unmistakable rip of a Bren gun had cut through the distant haze. At that point, Wallis had known they were still holding, still in the fight. But then the Germans had pushed again.

When the sound he'd been dreading had come—the rapid, mechanical chatter of an MG34, firing in short, precise bursts—Wallis clenched his jaw. The waiting had been excruciating. Now the fight was close. He imagined the terror in the town—the lads trapped under fire, crouched behind broken walls, counting on him to hit back. Still no flare. Wallis scanned the sky, jaw tight. How much longer could they hold? How close did it have to get before the signal came?

At 16.15 hrs, Wallis glanced at his watch. The lads had been at it all day. Rifles, Brens, the two-pounders—all holding the town through wave after wave of attacks. He hadn't been called upon yet. Not a single round fired. Not a single mortar round dropped into action. And yet, while Cassel had burnt with smoke thick enough to choke the sky, he knew his time was coming.

It had been at least two hours since he'd last seen Pembroke, back when the captain had come through with orders to withdraw to Mont Cassel when the time came.

But still, nothing. It gnawed at him. The men around him shifted uneasily, waiting, watching. Dunlop brushed a layer of dust from his trousers, his uniform stained with sweat. Briggs took another slow drag of his cigarette. They all knew the guns had never stopped—not really. Somewhere in the ruins, their comrades were still fighting. Still dying.

Overhead, the whistle of incoming rounds had made the air feel tight. Then, a sudden muffled detonation, followed by a second, closer one. Mortars. Not his. German. They were starting to bracket the British positions.

He swallowed. His mouth was dry.

A few of the men near him shifted uneasily, eyes flicking towards the town. They could hear it too. Dunlop swallowed hard, his hands tightening around his rifle.

Briggs, still leaning against the broken wall, naturally realised something was about to happen, and he exhaled smoke as he muttered, "Sounds like Jerry's got his teeth into 'em now." He took up his position at one of the mortars.

For the slightest of moments, his eyes locked on the sky where the flare arced high: a streak of red against the grey afternoon.

"Prepare to fire!" he said with a loud, firm but calm voice.

Around him, the mortar crew snapped into action. Men hunched over the tubes, their hands moving with practiced efficiency. They'd been ready for this moment for too long. Private Holt already had the first round cradled in his hands. His face was a mask of dirt, broken by gleaming trails of sweat.

"Fire," Wallis said calmly as if merely asking someone to pass the salt at dinner.

Holt dropped the smoke round into the smooth bore of the tube.

Thump. A second thump followed from the neighbouring tube.

Briggs leant forwards and checked his sights.

Wallis silently held both tubes, listening for the impact of the first two rounds. Frustratingly, he couldn't hear the distinct puff of the smoke bombs detonating on impact.

"Ready H.E. Fire one!"

A single thump followed moments later. Wallis arched his neck, tracking the shot. Crash! He knew the explosion had struck the cobblestoned street. He couldn't be certain, but he was convinced enough—they were on target.

"Rapid fire!" His voice came louder now, a guttural bark as tension tightened his body.

The men snapped into motion. One man passed rounds to Holt with practiced speed; he took each shell, dropped it into the tube, then turned away as the thump sent the bomb off to do its deathly work. Briggs leant forwards, checked the sighting, then turned away, ready for the next.

One after another, the bombs went on their voyage. Both tubes fired in tandem—not planned, but instinctive. Thump. Thump. A deadly rhythm: steady as a drumbeat. The air filled with the rhythmic cough of mortars. It was a relentless, brutal chorus. Their last few crates sat half-empty. With each round fired, they edged closer to the inevitable—no more support, no more firepower. Just a rifle and a bayonet left.

In Cassel, Leutnant Klaus Reiner had been watching the British line buckle while his men pushed forwards, machine-guns hammering the final defensive pockets when hell itself split the sky open.

Until that point, for what felt like hours, he had stood just behind the forward line and watched the battle advantage constantly shifting as wave after wave of German infantry had surged up the shattered street. He had seen friends and comrades charge through the smoke only to be torn apart by unseen rifles or cut down by the unrelenting chatter of Bren guns. The attack up the main road had been relentless. Bodies lay sprawled across the cobblestones; some were motionless while others still twitching in their final moments. Blood pooled in the potholes, seeping into the cracked stone alongside the blackened stains of burning fuel.

164

To the flanks, his fellow officers had attempted to break through, sending men scrambling through alleyways, across ruined storefronts and into the broken remnants of houses. Each time, the British had met them with fierce resistance—grenades lobbed into tight spaces and rifle fire picked them off as they tried to advance. The wreckage of a tank had continued to smoulder all morning; its metal was twisted and charred, and the bodies of its occupants were slumped in grotesque angles.

Time had seemed to pass quickly as the air had thickened with the choking smell of scorched stone and earth and burning flesh. The smoke had mingled with the late afternoon haze, making it difficult to see beyond a few dozen metres. Throughout, Reiner had heard the groans of the wounded, and the frantic shouts of medics dragging men to cover while the occasional sharp crack of a British sniper still lurked somewhere in the ruins. His men were exhausted. The relentless attacks had taken their toll. Yet despite the carnage, he felt no hesitation.

It was his turn. His platoon—his men—would be the ones to break the defenders for good.

Reiner's mouth tightened as he turned to them, the confidence in his voice unwavering. "We finish this."

The street ahead was a wasteland of death and destruction, but he believed in the plan. He believed in their training. He would lead from the front through the shattered remains of the previous assaults, over the bodies of the fallen, and into the teeth of the British guns. This time, they would not be stopped.

Klaus Reiner surged ahead over shattered brick and shell-scarred cobblestones, his men advancing in disciplined waves. They moved through the wreckage without hesitation—stepping over bodies, smoke curling from the ruins as it masked the retreating enemy.

The suffocating smoke masked the British, but Reiner could see them—British soldiers scrambling back, darting between wrecked vehicles and rubble-strewn doorways to flee.

A grin flickered across his face. They were breaking. His machine-gunners dropped to their knees mid-stride, bracing their weapons against the ground. The chatter of MG34s filled the air, hammering rounds towards the retreating British.

Reiner caught sight of one enemy soldier—a lanky private running hard with his rifle swinging from one side to the other—before a burst of fire shredded him. The man stumbled forwards, arms flailing before he crashed onto the bloodied stone. Reiner nodded.

Shots spat from the first-floor windows of a ruined shop front as his men stormed past. A British straggler had taken position there, desperate to hold for a moment longer. Too slow. A sharp burst from a German rifle sent him toppling out of the window, hitting the ground with a lifeless thud.

The enemy was still fighting as they withdrew, but Reiner knew it wouldn't be enough. Reiner's men pressed forwards: disciplined, ruthless, unstoppable.

Ahead, one British soldier—an officer, from the look of him—dived behind an improvised barricade of furniture and sandbags, barking orders to the few men still at his side. Reiner tracked him for a split second, raising his MP 40, but before he could fire, a sharp crack echoed through the street.

A German beside him—Hoffman—jerked back with a strangled gasp and dropped onto the stones, his helmet rolling free.

The sniper.

Reiner's eyes snapped up, scanning the ruined façades ahead. Somewhere, hidden in the skeletal remains of the buildings, a British marksman was still picking his men off.

"Up! Keep moving!" he roared, stepping over Hoffman's

still-twitching body. The platoon surged forwards, returning fire as they stormed up the street. A German grenadier dashed ahead, pulling the chord on a stick grenade before hurling it through a shattered doorway.

Boom.

The explosion sent dust and debris cascading into the air. Satisfyingly, no more shots came from that position.

Reiner kept moving, pressing forwards into the storm of gunfire. The British were running.

He barely had time to register the distant thump of the British mortars before the first bomb struck the street ahead of him. The round burst with a dull whump, belching thick, acrid white smoke that billowed into the air, curling and expanding with unnatural speed. The pungent stench of burning phosphorus hit his nostrils, sharp and chemical, even as the second bomb struck higher, slamming into the upper façade of a nearby building.

The explosion was sudden. Violent. Shards of masonry and glass showered down, but the phosphorus was worse; it sent a cascade of burning fragments through the air like molten stars, sticking to walls, the street, and anything unfortunate enough to be caught beneath.

A scream tore through the haze. One of Reiner's men reeled backwards, shrieking, clawing at his sleeve where a glob of the burning gel had splashed across his tunic. Flesh sizzled beneath the fabric as he thrashed, the fire eating into him with a mindless, clinging hunger. The others barely glanced at him—there was no stopping for the damned.

Reiner swore, instinctively ducking down, knowing there was no way to smother phosphorus once it took hold.

Then came the third bomb.

There was a moment of eerie silence before the ground seemed to convulse. A thunderous crack erupted barely twenty metres away, hurling up chunks of cobblestone, dirt, and shattered brick upwards. The shockwave punched into Reiner's chest, rattling his teeth. Men flung themselves down, instinct taking over.

And then the real barrage began.

The next rounds fell in rapid succession—thump-whump-thump-whump—explosions overlapping in a deafening, gut-churning cacophony.

Smoke and dust turned the street into a choking, blinding nightmare. The air was thick with burning ash and the metallic tang of blood. Somewhere through the anarchy, Reiner could hear the panicked shouts of his men scrambling for cover.

Then, the mortars found their range.

A blast ripped through a section of wall barely ten metres from him, flinging a storm of bricks and debris like shrapnel. A soldier was caught mid-step, his body twisting unnaturally before he crumpled, and then lay unmoving. Another round detonated against the remnants of a collapsed shop front, blowing out the last of its charred wooden beams. It sent a cascade of bricks and debris crashing onto the street. A shattered wooden door, wrenched free by the blast, spun through the air before smashing into the ruins of a café across the way.

Another barrage: this one closer.

The air itself seemed to shake as another round exploded in the centre of the street, obliterating a trio of his men who had been diving for cover behind a pile of rubble. A pressure wave slammed into Reiner, forcing him low, his ears ringing. He barely had time to register the next blast before the shockwave knocked him sideways.

More men fell. Screams, which rose above the din, were then quickly lost beneath the relentless pounding of the bombardment. Blood slicked the cobbles. Figures staggered through the smoke. Some clutched wounds: others dragged the dying into what little cover remained.

Through the shifting haze, Reiner saw Feldwebel Möller waving him down. The sergeant's voice was drowned in the infernal barrage, and his mouth formed words Reiner couldn't hear. Then another round struck home.

A direct hit.

The blast engulfed Möller and two others in a maelstrom of fire and debris, and their forms vanished in an instant. Reiner felt himself thrown backwards. His back slammed against something hard. Pain exploded through his ribs, and for a terrifying moment, his vision darkened.

Then, silence.

A lull.

With his ears ringing, and his lungs burning, Reiner forced himself up onto his elbows. The street was a smoking ruin. Half of his men lay dead or dying while others were stunned, their faces streaked with dust, blood and shock.

He coughed. His throat was raw from smoke and dust. His hands trembled as he pressed down against the cobbles, forcing himself onto one knee. Every inch of him ached. His ribs screamed in protest. Around him, the street was a wasteland of craters, bodies and smouldering debris. The British mortars had done their work well.

A few metres away of Reiner, a young rifleman clutched his head: his eyes were wide and unseeing, and his lips moved in silent prayer or with madness. Another man groaned nearby, dragging himself across the rubble to leave a dark smear in his wake. Those still alive were dazed. Some were half-buried under the wreckage of the street.

But then—movement.

Through the lingering haze, Reiner saw figures advancing. Then a hand seized his tunic, yanking him upright. He barely registered the contorted face inches from his own, spitting orders at him.

Kapitan Münster screamed at him, "Aufstehen! Move, damn you!"

The words snapped through the fog clouding Reiner's mind. He sucked in a breath, planted his boots, and shoved himself forwards, barking orders to his men. "On your feet! Forwards! Now!"

Münster was leading another German platoon, who were fresh and moving with purpose and was pushing forwards through the battered ruins, undeterred by the British shelling. Their Feldwebel barked orders and gestured for men to spread out with their rifles up. They were ready to seize the momentum.

The Germans were committing to the attack.

Reiner shook off the haze. Adrenaline kicked in as the realisation hit him—if they were moving, he needed to move with them.

With a grunt of effort, he staggered to his feet and wiped blood from his brow with a shaking hand. The ground swayed beneath him, but he forced himself steady. His own men—what was left of them—needed direction.

"Los!" he rasped. His voice was hoarse, but it was enough.

A few heads snapped towards him. Those still capable of fighting pushed themselves up, instinct taking over. He grabbed one of them—a Gefreiter with a bandaged arm—and pulled him close.

"Regroup," Reiner ordered, his breath coming fast. "We're moving forwards."

The soldier hesitated, blinking through the dust. "The bombardment—"

"It's ending." Reiner cut him off, his eyes locked onto the advancing platoon. "We're not staying here to die." He turned, waving a signal. One by one, his battered men dragged themselves together, reloading, stripping weapons from the fallen, steeling themselves for the next fight.

The moment of hesitation was gone.

Reiner's entire body screamed in protest. Bruises were already blooming beneath his uniform, and his ribs were a solid ache. But none of it mattered.

He was still standing. The fight wasn't over. Not yet. Tightening his grip on his rifle, Reiner fell into step beside the advancing troops. They would finish this.

Gunfire snapped through the air, sharp cracks of Lee-Enfields. The occasional chug of a Bren gun answered the renewed German assault. The street was complete chaos. It was filled with the fading echo of mortar blasts and the steady drumbeat of advancing enemy's fire within the acrid bite of lingering smoke.

Pembroke knelt beside Archer. His rifle was held in one hand as he watched a few riflemen crouched behind scattered debris, firing into the shifting haze. The Germans were coming again. This time in force.

Pembroke exhaled sharply. "Tom. Time to go."

Archer ground his teeth. His ears still rang from the bombardment, but he forced himself to focus. Withdrawal. Now.

Before he could respond, Jacks and his group emerged from a side street, moving fast and low, their weapons at the ready. Mallory followed a moment later, leading what was left of his detachment. Saunders, Matthews, Wilson—all faces Archer was relieved to see.

A flicker of tension eased in his chest. For now, they had made it.

Jacks gave a tight nod, his face smeared with dirt and glistening with sweat. "What's the word?"

Jacks glanced towards the German lines; his expression was unreadable. Archer was staying. Of course he was. He exhaled through his nose. "Figures."

Mallory, hearing they were to stay, immediately took charge of the remaining men, gathering them quickly and moving them into cover before the Germans could reorganise after the mortar barrage. The phosphorus smoke was still thick in the street, obscuring their movements, but through the haze, the enemy's screams and shouts made a renewed push evident.

"Into cover, now!" Mallory's voice was sharp and commanding.

The men scrambled for any shelter they could find: behind the remains of shattered walls, furniture that'd been dragged into the street, and doorways barely standing. The stench of smoke burnt in their throats, but it was cover. However temporary. He didn't have to tell them to reload; every man knew what was coming.

Then silence.

Not peace—but the kind of silence that presses in, thick and unnatural, the battlefield holding its breath. Muffled footsteps echoed somewhere ahead. A faint clatter of metal. The whine of something distant and fast—too fast. Someone whispered a prayer. Another checked his rifle with trembling hands.

Through the shifting haze, figures loomed—Germans, moving cautiously with their weapons raised. They were hesitant, obviously shaken by the mortar strike, but they weren't stopping. The attack was still coming. Across from them, Mallory's men had bayonets fixed, bracing for the inevitable clash.

"Hold your fire," Mallory ordered, eyes narrowing as he tracked the advancing enemy. "Wait for my mark."

Jacks shifted beside him. His rifle was tight in his grip, and his face was smeared with a grim mixture of fear and sweat. "They're still coming," he muttered.

Mallory's gaze flicked across the scattered figures of 6th Platoon. Each man had braced into the ruins, waiting for the moment the Germans pushed through the haze.

Webb, ever reliable, had his Bren rested on the broken remains of a shop counter and scanned for emerging movement through the smoke. His hands moved with practiced ease, setting the next magazine close by. He didn't need orders. He knew when to fire.

Matthews, the Royal Engineer Lance Corporal, knelt low near a shattered doorway. A Mills bomb was in one hand, and his rifle rested against the other. There was a cold pragmatism to him; he knew this was just another demolition job. Only this, it wasn't steel and brick, but men.

Close by, Saunders, the youngster of the group, shifted nervously, but his grip on the rifle was firm. He'd grown in the past few days—still wide-eyed, but steady when it counted.

Lance Corporal Tug Wilson crouched behind an old dresser, checking his bayonet with the weary familiarity of a man who'd been in enough scraps to know what came next. A professional soldier through and through: he worked best when things got ugly.

To Mallory's right, Private Scouse Evans tucked himself against the rubble of a collapsed wall, muttering something under his breath—probably a Liverpool curse at the enemy they couldn't yet see. He was a scrapper, quick with a quip but quicker with a rifle.

A little farther along, Hawkins adjusted his webbing, rolling his shoulders as if limbering up for a fight. His arm still bore the leftovers of a bandage. It was a reminder of the wound he took at the farmhouse, but he wasn't about to let it slow him down.

And then there was Pritchard—the best shot in the platoon, the battalion: a calm, unflappable presence amid the chaos. He lay prone near the edge of their cover, his rifle steadied on a shattered windowsill, sighting through the murk. He wouldn't waste bullets. When he fired, it would count.

Mallory shifted. The movement tugged at the gash on his forearm. He glanced down, examining the dried blood smeared across his palm and the crusted wound along his sleeve. It had stopped bleeding hours ago, but the dull ache remained—more an irritation than a real hindrance. He flexed his fingers, grimacing slightly at the sting before shaking it off. No time for that now.

He exhaled, steadying himself, and turned his attention back to the street. They were as ready as they could be.

Archer adjusted the grip on his rifle, shifting against the jagged remains of a doorway. His breath was steady, but beneath the surface, he felt the exhaustion pressing in. It wasn't just the hours of fighting, the weight of his equipment, or even the growing list of names he wouldn't be calling at roll.

It was something deeper. A creeping, leaden fatigue in his bones, the kind that came from days of running on little more than instinct and duty. He wasn't sure how much more they could all give, but he knew they'd give it a bloody good go!

He stole a glance at his men—what was left of them. Webb, steady as ever with his Bren. Wilson who tightened his grip on his bayonet, knowing exactly what was coming. Pritchard, calm and patient, had his rifle already sighted on the advancing enemy. They had fought like hell to hold this street, and now, the inevitable was coming for them.

There was no doubt in his mind. He wasn't leaving Cassel.

It wasn't some grand sacrifice, nor some heroic last stand. It was just what needed to be done. He wasn't going to lead his men in a mad, glorious charge. He was going to hold. Buy time. Give the others a fighting chance to get clear. That was all that mattered.

His fingers curled tighter around the rifle stock, and his jaw tightening as he let out a slow breath. The phosphorus smoke was thinning now, carried away on the breeze, revealing the shifting shadows beyond. The Germans would be through any second.

He rolled his shoulders, steadying himself. One more fight. One more hold. Then it was down to fate.

The Germans were coming.

The phosphorus smoke lifted just enough for Mallory to make out movement in the street beyond. Shapes emerged through the haze. Germans, advancing cautiously, had their rifles at the ready, and their machine-gunners set up on a wrecked vehicle for better cover. The chatter of an MG34 ripped through the street again, stitching bullets into the masonry above their heads, forcing the remaining men of 6th Platoon to keep low.

Mallory wiped the back of his hand across his forehead, smearing dried blood from the earlier graze. The wound was barely more than an irritation, but it stung all the same. He flexed his fingers, shaking it off. Pain meant nothing now. Only survival mattered.

Webb crouched behind the remnants of the counter, his Bren gun nestled against his shoulder. "They're getting ready to push again," he muttered, checking the magazine before nodding towards Mallory. "Say the word."

Mallory glanced at Archer, who was pressed against a doorway, rifle up, and watching the German advance with cold, calculating eyes. There was no hesitation when he gave the order.

"Wait until they commit. Then hit them hard."

The Germans crept closer, rifles darting left and right, methodical now—learning from the dead, but not slowing. One gestured ahead, calling something to his squad. His voice was muffled by the lingering smoke. But Mallory knew that this was the moment.

"Fire!" Mallory barked.

The street erupted in gunfire. Webb's Bren roared first,

sending a hail of rounds straight into the leading Germans. One went down instantly. Another staggered, a sharp cry escaping before he collapsed. Pritchard fired from his cover, his Lee-Enfield cracking once—twice—and another enemy soldier crumpled in the street.

The Germans scrambled for cover, returning aimless fire. Bullets snapped against brick and shattered what little glass remained in the shop fronts to send shards flying through the air. A grenade arced from the enemy's position, bouncing once on the rubble-strewn street.

"Grenade!" Evans shouted.

Wilson was already moving, booting it away just before it detonated with a sharp crack, sending debris skittering harmlessly across the ground.

"Close one," Wilson muttered, barely winded.

More Germans were moving up. Archer fired, dropping one as he tried to rush between cover. Another German ducked behind an upturned table, firing wild shots in their direction, forcing them to keep their heads down.

"We can't hold here forever!" Jacks called over the gunfire.

Archer knew that. He knew they were to fall back to Mont Cassel. But if they moved too soon, the Germans would press them hard. They needed to break the enemy's momentum first.

"One last push," he said, shifting to reload. "Then we go."

Mallory nodded. "Webb, unload into them. Make it count."

Webb grinned and set himself. "Aye, Sir."

The Bren rattled to life again, pouring fire down the street, forcing the Germans to dive for further cover. As soon as the gunfire peaked, Archer shouted the command.

"Fall back!"

The men knew they were to withdraw in pairs. Matthews and Wilson moved first, darting from cover, and they sprinted towards the next position behind a collapsed wall. Saunders and Evans followed, keeping low as bullets snapped past them.

Webb let off one final burst before he and Mallory peeled away, moving fast. Only Archer and Jacks remained.

It was a single road uphill to Mont Cassel, and the men bounded towards it in twos, covering each other—four men on each side, taking turns to fire and fall back.

Archer fired twice more, covering the retreat before Jacks grabbed his shoulder and gave him a rough shove. "Come on, Sir! Time to go!"

Archer hesitated for half a heartbeat. His eyes scanned the street one last time. The Germans were still coming in bounds as were the British. Gritting his teeth, he turned and sprinted after Jacks, pushing hard to catch up with the others.

Archer turned and sprinted after his men. They weren't out of it yet.

Chapter 10

The air over Mont Cassel hung heavy with smoke and the sharp tang of burnt metal, the aftermath of battle clinging to every gust. Dust swirled through the narrow lanes like ash from a dying fire, coating the cobbles and settling in the ruins of once-stately buildings. The town of Cassel—perched atop this ancient Flanders hill, known locally as Mont Cassel—had become a shell of itself. Its steep streets, once bustling with market day chatter and the clatter of carts, now lay silent beneath the weight of war.

Days of fighting had taken their toll. Stone façades were punched through by shell blasts, rooftops lay caved in, and centuries-old walls had been reduced to rubble. The damage bore the unmistakable signature of Stuka dive-bombers and relentless German artillery, each strike peeling away another layer of the town's proud history. What had once been a natural fortress was now a crucible, and the men who remained within it knew they were fighting not just for survival—but to buy time.

Blackened skeletons of buildings lined the roads. Their façades were pockmarked by shrapnel and riddled with bullet holes. Fires still smouldered in the distance, their dying embers casting a dull orange glow against the deepening dusk. The cobbled streets, which had once bustled with life, were now a wasteland of rubble, spent shell casings, and the bodies of the many fallen—both British and German.

Captain James Pembroke crouched low behind the remains of an old stone wall on the uppermost part of the town, peering out over what was left of his command. The position had been reinforced as best as possible, but he knew it wouldn't hold much longer.

This was no fortified redoubt, no trench line to fallback behind. It was a defensible patch of ground in a town that had been bombed into submission. Fourteen men had made it with him to the uppermost part of town; every one of them was grim-faced and hollow-eyed. Each one carried the weight of exhaustion and the knowledge that this battle was nearing its end.

Pembroke didn't realise that another twelve men were still fighting their way up the ruined street, trying desperately to reach them before the final German push. He just hoped they were.

He knew the defences were pitiful.

Sandbags, once stacked in firing positions, had been shredded by shrapnel, their contents spilling uselessly onto the street. Windows and doorways that had served as firing points had become jagged, gaping holes, their upper floors either collapsed or on the verge of giving way. The makeshift rifle pits, which had been dug into courtyard gardens and collapsed store fronts, had caved in under relentless bombardment.

A wrecked lorry, its engine block still smouldering, had been shoved across an alley as a makeshift barricade—but it would do little to stop the continued German advance.

It was the first time Pembroke truly noticed the litany of British Army vehicles littering the streets—lorries, Bren gun carriers, even tanks, all abandoned and useless: silent relics of a battle already lost. He turned and glanced at his men. They were spread out in whatever cover remained—hunched in the doorways of shattered houses, crouched behind rubble piles or pressed into the shadows of alleyways. All of them waiting. Waiting for the end.

He had ordered the Vickers machine-gun back to this position several hours ago. Its crew had set up in the corner of a townhouse, whose façade had long since been removed by war, giving them a clear view of the street as it wound up the hill.

He had ordered the Vickers machine-gun back to this position several hours ago. Its crew had set up in the corner of a townhouse whose façade had long since torn away by war. It gave them a clear view of the street as it wound up to the mount. Ammunition was dangerously low, and the Bren gunners clutched their final magazines like lifelines. The riflemen had maybe a handful of clips each.

Pembroke exhaled slowly, scanning the battlefield with an experienced eye. The street leading up to their position ahead was a shattered ruin, thick with smoke and the cries of soldiers who were locked in the struggle of war.

Archer and his men were still scrambling up the incline, their footfalls hammering against the cobbles as they bounded from cover to cover. The Germans were closing in. Their shouts echoed through the wreckage. The sharp crack of rifle fire snapped at the retreating British.

Through the thinning haze, Pembroke spotted the enemy pouring forwards in disciplined waves, using the wrecked buildings and shattered walls to close the distance. The bark of orders in German carried across the battlefield. Their officers were urging them on, sensing victory.

A distant growl of engines sent a shiver through him—vehicles, likely half-tracks or light tanks, were creeping forwards through the ruins, their silhouettes flickering in the smoke-filled distance. Though they had no anti-tank defences left, Pembroke knew whatever was coming would do so with overwhelming force. It would be minutes, maybe less, before the enemy surged up the street in full strength.

He clenched his jaw and turned back towards the battered British line. "We hold this ridge as long as we can. Make every shot count."

His gaze flicked to the dimming sky. If they could survive until nightfall, they had a chance. Under the cover of darkness, they could slip away, disappear into the fields, and make for Watten—then north to Dunkirk. He realised it was a long shot, but it was all they had left.

A sudden burst of automatic fire tore through the quiet and snapped Pembroke's focus back to the street. One of the last men still fighting their way up was calling out, his voice hoarse and ragged.

Pembroke turned towards his battered line, his eyes darting between the last fourteen men.

The mortar team—Sergeant Wallis, Corporal Briggs, Privates Dunlop, Lewis, Holt, and Mason—had long since abandoned their tubes and now stood armed with rifles and bayonets, preparing for the inevitable. Then, he caught sight of the remnants of 6th Platoon arriving. As he arrived, Jacks crouched low, reloading his rifle with swift, practiced motions, while Mallory was already taking careful shots. His face was impassive with his eyes fixed ahead as if the retreat had been routine rather than a running gauntlet.

Tug Wilson and Scouse Evans knelt behind a pile of rubble, selecting targets with grim focus before firing. Saunders pressed himself against a shattered barricade, breathing heavily, his hands trembling around his weapon.

Webb and Matthews threw themselves into a rifle pit, while Pritchard sprinted for the first floor of a townhouse, seeking the advantage of higher ground. Nearby, Tanner, Carter, and O'Hara huddled behind the broken remains of a low stone wall, rifles tight in their grips, eyes locked on the advancing darkness.

Each man knew they had minutes—maybe seconds—before the Germans were upon them.

Archer threw himself behind a section of the collapsed wall, sucking in gulps of air, his rifle still gripped tightly in his hands.

"We're out of time, Captain!" he gasped, shaking off the exhaustion threatening to overtake him. "They're pushing hard, and we're barely keeping them back!"

Pembroke turned to face Archer, and his face was grim but composed. "I know. But we still have men left, and we're not done yet." His eyes flicked over Archer's shoulder to the darkening ruins beyond. "How many made it up?"

Archer took a moment to catch his breath, his chest rising

and falling heavily. "Thirteen, including me."

Pembroke gave a firm nod. His expression didn't betray either relief or frustration—just the cold calculation of survival.

"That brings us to twenty-seven. Not many, but it'll have to do."

He turned his gaze over the battered remains of the Mont Cassel position. "We've got three Brens, but ammo's really low. The Vickers is still in play, but not for long—one good belt left. Other than that, it's rifles, grenades, and whatever's left in the lads' pouches."

Archer removed his helmet and ran a hand through his sweat-matted hair; his body ached from the relentless fight. "How long are we supposed to hold?"

Pembroke's jaw clenched. "Until nightfall. If we can't hold them here, we'll withdraw to the Hôtel du Nord"—he pointed north to the solid stone structure—"and fight until darkness!"

But could they really hold out that long? Could they keep this up until nightfall? The thought gnawed at him. They had no choice. Darkness would be their saviour, but sunset was still at least an hour away—maybe two.

Archer glanced around at their position, at the men locked in the brutal rhythm of combat—reloading, taking aim, firing. Once again, he felt a surge of admiration for the soldiers around him. Men he commanded. Men still standing.

Archer froze as a deep, guttural rumble rolled in from the darkness—a low, metallic growl of steel grinding against shattered stone. The sound clawed at his nerves. Armour. And it was getting closer.

Archer stiffened. "That sounds like armour."

He snatched up his binoculars and lifted them to his eyes. The smoke was thick, hanging like a veil over the ruins. But then he saw it. Past the shattered façades, the street below them was clear. Too clear. The silence was unnatural. It was the kind that came before something terrible.

His stomach gripping tighter. "They've cleared the way. Fuck."

Pembroke took the binoculars, scanning the battlefield himself. A beat of silence. Then—

"Tom, I'm afraid you're right. Fuck."

The ground beneath them started to vibrate as the unmistakable clatter of tank tracks ground against the cobbles and echoed through the ruined town. Then it came into view—a hulking shadow emerging from the smoke, turret swivelling, scanning for targets. A Panzer IV.

Pembroke exhaled slowly, his voice low and firm. "Shit. This is going to liven things up!"

The German infantry had melted away, slipping into doorways and ducking behind shattered walls to give the tank an unimpeded path up the street. It moved with deliberate menace, each grinding inch was a promise of violence as its tracks crunched over bricks and shattered timbers, and all the while, its 75mm gun slowly rotated, seeking a victim.

For a brief moment, the street was eerily quiet, nothing but the distant crackle of burning buildings and the grinding of steel on stone.

Every man had paused, breaking the rhythm of what had moments earlier been an unyielding torrent of fire. Then—

"Fire!" Sergeant Wallis bellowed, his voice raw with defiance.

The British line once again erupted.

Rifles barked, Bren guns chattered, and a storm of bullets hammered against the Panzer's thick hull. The rounds pinged and sparked off the armoured beast, ricochetting uselessly into the early evening light. It was futile, but it was defiance.

The Vickers roared to life, its water-cooled barrel spitting a stream of .303 rounds straight into the tank's advancing frame.

For a heartbeat, it almost felt like they were fighting back.

Then came the first explosion.

The Panzer's main gun thundered. A high-explosive shell screamed towards the Vickers' position. The impact ripped through the gun and its crew, shattering sandbags and bodies. It sent men tumbling backwards in a globule of blood and broken steel.

A flash of fire, a shower of debris—the Vickers was silenced.

"Jesus Christ!" someone shouted. The panic was clear in his voice.

Wallis didn't hesitate. "Keep firing! Don't let the bastards think we're done!"

The men obeyed. Their rifles cracked, but the Panzer barely seemed to notice.

Then, the turret shifted slightly.

Wallis saw it too late.

The second shell hit like a hammer blow, exploding against the ruined street where he and his men had taken position.

The blast extinguished him in a storm of fire and shrapnel. One moment he was there, shouting orders, the next—nothing but smoke, blood, and the scattered remnants of the men around him.

The shockwave threw the rest of the men to the ground, dirt and splinters raining over them. Before anyone could process the loss, the Panzer's hull-mounted MG34 rumbled to life. A deadly arc of bullets swept across the street, kicking up dust and chipping away at brick and flesh alike.

"Get to cover!" Pembroke roared, dragging a dazed private back behind a crumbling wall.

Heart hammering, Archer dropped down behind the crumbling wall. They had no answer to this. Nothing but rifles against a steel giant. He cursed under his breath, shoving another clip into his rifle.

"So much for holding the line, we are going to get murdered!"

The Panzer kept coming.

Pembroke didn't respond immediately. His gaze flicked towards the growing shadows in the distance. Clear of the smoke, the Panzer IV loomed fully into view, its turret already scanning, deliberate and unhurried. Another shell slammed into a nearby ruin, sending debris cascading across the street. The Germans were pressing forwards with renewed ferocity: their riflemen and machine-gunners were advancing under the protection of the armoured beast. Pembroke could almost feel their excitement, their growing belief that victory was within reach.

The tank's rumble grew louder. The ground beneath them shook with each grinding rotation of its treads. The sound echoed through the ruins like a death knell.

The Germans were closing in fast.

Pembroke turned sharply to Archer, his voice loud and firm. "We're moving. Hôtel du Nord. You lead. I'll bring up the rear."

Archer gave a quick nod, already scanning the battlefield, calculating the safest route. The men needed direction and fast.

"Prepare to move!" he yelled the order.

The battle raged around him: a storm of fire and steel. The sharp, rattling bursts of German MG34s chewed through the rubble, kicking up more dust and shards of stone. The boom of the tank's main gun followed, and the force of the explosion slammed against Archer's chest, making his ears ring.

Somewhere ahead, a British Bren gun answered back. It chattered defiantly, but it was running low; its bursts were shorter, more sporadic. A rifle cracked nearby. Followed by another. The defenders fought on, but the advantage was slipping — momentum now with the enemy.

Archer ducked as a German round smacked into the bricks

near his head, spitting fragments into the air. He ignored it, his mind worked through the options—they couldn't just run blind. Not through this hell.

He spotted Mallory, who was crouched near a shattered wagon, rifle tight against his shoulder. Scouse Evans and Tug Wilson were beside him, alternating shots with grim faces. Pritchard had just darted from cover, heading for the second floor of a ruined house. It was one last stand before the withdrawal.

To Archer's left, Jacks was already beginning to move, shaking men out of their stunned state, shouting above the noise. He was doing his job.

Archer took a breath, steeling himself. He had to rally them. Now.

He opened his mouth to shout, but his voice was swallowed by the storm of gunfire and explosions. No one was hearing a damn thing. Frustration flared. He needed to get through to them. They had to move. Now.

Then it hit him. He reached into his battledress pocket, fingers brushing against the crumpled field dressing he'd stuffed there earlier. He pushed past it, rummaging until he felt the cold metal of the policeman's whistle that had been issued to him when he first drew his kit.

He tore it free and blew hard: one sharp, piercing blast.

The shrill note cut through the commotion. It was a sound drilled into them from training, a sound that demanded attention. He blew the whistle a second time.

Heads snapped towards him.

"On me! We're moving!" Archer bellowed, pointing towards the hotel. They had to move as one, or not at all.

Pembroke was already grabbing Jacks, relaying orders. "Make sure they're all moving! No one gets left behind!" Jacks didn't hesitate. He turned and grabbed Tanner, Carter, O'Hara, and Saunders, motioning them towards Archer and the escape route.

In the midst of the rallying call, Mallory had no intention of leaving quietly. He took to one knee in a doorway, screaming at the men to get to Archer. He chambered another round and fired again, hitting a grey uniformed German in the torso. The man slumped to the ground, and Mallory took aim once more. Beside him, Pritchard appeared crouched alongside him, breathing hard. His face was pale, streaked with days of dirt. His grip on his rifle was steady.

Mallory glanced at him.

Pritchard smirked, chambering a round. "I think Mr Archer wants us to join him, Sarge."

Mallory smiled at the old pro. Then the two men rose as one, firing into the dull light of the evening, defying the inevitable just a moment longer.

Archer surveyed the area. He saw the men were moving into cover around him, and he moved first, signalling the men to follow. They broke cover in twos and threes, keeping low, moving fast. Scouse Evans, Tug Wilson, Saunders, and O'Hara were close behind him, dodging through the rubble-strewn street.

The Germans were already pressing forwards, their shapes flickering like wraiths in the swirling smoke. Their figures darted between the wreckage, crouching low, rifles raised. The muzzle flashes of their weapons flared like jagged lightning in the gloom to briefly illuminate ghostly glimpses of field-grey uniforms and grim, determined faces. Their voices were sharp, urgent. Harsh commands barked over the din. It was a mix of clipped orders and the raw, guttural urgency of men pushing forward under fire, determined to break through.

Boots crunched over shattered brick and twisted metal as the dull thud of bodies shifted in the haze. Somewhere to Archer's right, a wounded man groaned. It was a ragged, choked sound that was quickly lost beneath the haste to retreat.

Behind Archer, Pembroke watched the movement carefully, keeping count. He saw Tanner and Carter fall into line, moving fast—too fast. Their steps were rushed...too frantic.

Then came the sound. A deep, rattling burst.

The tank's MG34 opened up again, spitting fire into the street. A streak of glowing tracers cut through the smoke, stitching across the cobbles. Tanner barely had time to react. His body jerked violently mid-stride. The rounds tore through him. He crumpled, crashing onto the broken stones.

Carter barely had time to process it before the tank's turret let loose another high-explosive round. The thunderclap of the blast obliterated the air, and a shockwave of fire and shattered masonry engulfing the space where they had just stood. Pembroke staggered; the breath had been knocked from him as rubble crashed down around them. Dust and smoke billowed in choking waves, swallowing everything.

For a heartbeat, no one could see.

Then, as the dust thinned, Pembroke saw a dark shape slumped against the shattered ruins. Carter. His rifle lay forgotten beside him. His body twisted at an unnatural angle. He hadn't made it.

Archer's stomach twisted, but there was no time. No saving them now.

He locked eyes with Pembroke, who had seen it too. No words were needed. There was no time to grieve. More gunfire erupted behind them, but at least they were still moving.

The Hôtel du Nord was up ahead. It was their last chance to regroup before making their escape. The retreat wasn't over yet.

The hotel was dark and silent. No flickering lanterns. No voices inside. There was just cold stone walls and dust-covered furniture left behind in the brutality of war.

The Hôtel du Nord had once been a grand establishment: a place of fine dining, polished wooden floors, and warm lamplight that spilt out onto the cobbled streets of Mont Cassel. Now, it was just another ruin in a dying town.

The exterior bore all the scars of battle. Shrapnel had torn through its façade to leave jagged holes in the once-pristine stonework. The upper windows were shattered: their glass had long since blown out by artillery concussions. One section of the roof had partially caved in, leaving splintered wooden beams jutting like broken ribs. Crooked on their hinges, the front doors looked as though they'd been forced open—either in a desperate flight or by an explosion's blast.

Inside, the grandeur of the past was buried beneath layers of the war's debris. There were signs that the thick dust which coated every surface had been stirred by the boots of the retreating soldiers. The lobby's once-polished floors were now scuffed and littered with broken glass. Fallen plaster and abandoned luggage lay haphazardly, and the grand mirror behind the reception desk was cracked down the centre, distorting reflections like a fractured memory of what the hotel had once been.

In the corner, a few rickety chairs and an overturned table told of a last, failed attempt to barricade the entrance. The bullet holes, which peppered the walls, were signs of a fight fought and lost.

The air was stale, carrying the lingering scent of gunpowder, smoke, and something metallic—blood maybe? Or the rust of time creeping into what war had left behind.

It was shelter. It was temporary. And it was all they had left.

Archer's breath came in ragged gasps as he ducked inside, and the last of the men filtered through behind him. No German fire followed them—not yet.

Last of all, Pembroke pushed through the debris-littered lobby and turned to Mallory.

190

"Mallory, get the men in defensive positions," he ordered.

Mallory looked at him, then at Archer. There was no more talk of retreat. No more fallback positions. This was it.

Our final stand.

The words settled like iron in his mind. For hours, he'd known this was how it would end, but hearing it unspoken between them made it real. No more pulling back. No more fighting for another position to delay the inevitable. They had reached the end of the line.

Mallory exhaled slowly, running his tongue over dry, cracked lips. He'd been in tight spots before—fights that had seemed hopeless, and times when survival had been a roll of the dice. But this was different. The odds weren't just stacked against them; the dice had already been thrown. And yet, he felt no fear, no panic. Just a cold acceptance. The kind that settled into a man's bones after too many years of war.

He glanced around at the men—faces he knew well; faces he'd fought beside. Jacks, crouched low, gripping his rifle like it was part of him. Pembroke, jaw set in that stubborn way of his, refusing to let the exhaustion show. Even Archer, barely more than a boy when all this had started, standing there with that same steel in his eyes.

Good men.

He swallowed hard, his chest clenched with a pressure he couldn't shake. If this was the end, they'd meet it on their feet, with rifles in their hands, and blood on their knuckles if it came to that. They wouldn't surrender, wouldn't break.

A ghost of a smile tugged at the corner of his lips. If the bastards wanted Cassel, they were going to have to fight for every last stone of it.

Mallory nodded. "I'll get them set." He turned to the

others. "Evans, Wilson—watch the main entrance. Saunders, O'Hara, cover the rear. Jacks, get up top. If there's a rifle position, I want eyes out there!" The men moved into action, no arguments, no hesitation. They understood as well as he did. This was all they had left.

Archer and Pembroke left Mallory to organise the men and rushed up a ruined staircase, boots kicking up dust as they climbed towards what was left of a balcony overlooking the town. The railing was shattered, and part of the floor had caved in, but it was high enough to give them a vantage point over the ruins of Cassel.

Outside, the town was eerily quiet.

The distant hammer of machine-gun fire had faded and had been replaced by the crackling of burning buildings and the occasional burst of scattered rifle fire from somewhere deep in the ruins. But there was no return fire. No hurried shouts. No sharp cracks of British rifles. No sounds of the battalion still holding the line. Only silence, save for the slow collapse of Cassel into German hands.

Archer lifted his binoculars to scan the streets. His gut twisted. He passed the binoculars to Pembroke who also monitored the streets.

The streets below were swarming with dark shapes: Germans moving in force with armoured cars, and infantry clearing buildings, dragging bodies, and taking up positions all over Cassel. The one good thing was the Germans were not in pursuit of them. As Pembroke continued his gaze, he exhaled sharply before dropping the binoculars down and passing them back to Archer.

He then wiped a hand down his face. "They're gone," he muttered.

Archer turned to him. "The battalion?" Pembroke gave a slow, grim nod.

"The battalion. The whole bloody army. Looks like it's just us now and the whole bloody Wehrmacht!"

The words settled between them like the last shovelful of dirt on top of a coffin. For a moment, neither man spoke. The fight was over, at least for Cassel. Their job—delaying the Germans, holding them here for as long as possible—had been completed. The battalion had gone. The brigade had gone. The British Army was in full retreat, falling back towards Dunkirk.

A strange, almost hollow satisfaction settled in Archer's chest. They'd done what they had been ordered to do. They'd held. Against all odds, against everything the Germans had thrown at them, they had stood their ground.

But the feeling was hollow, blunted by fatigue and the brutal cost of good men they'd never see again. They stood beside each other in the half-ruined room, smoke curling through the broken buildings. Somewhere out there, among the ruins, lay the dead — friends, comrades, men who had stood beside them. Archer couldn't dwell on it now, not yet. But the ache pressed hard in his chest — dull, constant, like a wound that wouldn't close. They had to face the reality of what came next. The battle had been won, but the war within these streets wasn't over. They were surrounded and battered, and their numbers had drastically dwindled. The orders had been clear: hold until nightfall, then make their escape. But how many of them would still be standing by then?

A flicker of doubt gnawed at him. Had it been worth it? The lives spent? The blood soaked into the rubble? He shoved the thought away, locking it down. Doubt had no place here. All that mattered was what lay ahead.

He turned his gaze back down the battered streets where the enemy was regrouping for the next assault. His grip tightened on his rifle. They weren't done yet.

"What now, Sir?" asked Archer.

Pembroke let out a slow breath, casting one last glance towards the shattered town ahead of them. Then he turned, without a word, and stepped into the dimly lit foyer of the hotel, his boots scuffing against the dust-covered tiles. The building had seen better days. The building had seen better days. Its grandeur had become a shadow of itself. The chandelier above them had lost most of its glass and symbolised the situation they were in. A faint smell of damp mingled with the staleness of abandonment.

Pembroke exhaled, rolled his shoulders, and then turned to face what remained of his command.

"Gather round," he called firmly but not unkindly. There was no need to bark orders—not anymore. Those who had made it this far didn't need reminding of discipline. They needed direction and the sense of steady authority.

One by one, they came. Some limped, some rolled their shoulders as if trying to shake the battle from their bones. Each face bore the same look of utter exhaustion. Days of grime streaked their skin, and their uniforms were stiff with dried sweat and blood. Yet despite it all, they stood, waiting, their eyes turning to him and Archer.

Archer shifted slightly beside him, aware of the pressure in their eyes. He wasn't just their officer anymore. He was their lieutenant. Every man here had fought and bled beside him. They had survived together.

Jacks and Mallory were among the first to step forwards, standing side by side out of habit rather than thought. Jacks shifted his rifle onto his shoulder, ever ready, while Mallory rubbed at the wound along his forearm, his eyes scanning the room, ever watchful.

Next came Wilson with his rifle slung low. His uniform was still marked from the last fight. Then, Saunders and Evans followed. Evans muttered something under his breath in that familiar Liverpudlian drawl, but his sharp wit was momentarily subdued by exhaustion. Saunders looked more ragged than usual. His usual quick movements were slower, and his face was drawn tight.

Matthews, the engineer, cracked his knuckles absentmindedly as he came to stand beside them. His hands still bore all the grime of battle. Pritchard, the sharpshooter, was quiet. His face was impassive although his eyes flicked across the room, noting every entrance, every potential threat.

Next O'Hara entered, adjusting his helmet. His mouth twitched into something that might have been a smirk if he weren't so damned tired. Webb, the Bren gunner, followed close behind. His uniform was torn at the shoulder where the day's fighting had nearly taken him out.

Finally, there were the men who had joined them later: the men who were survivors from Pembroke's side. Brookes, Finch, Button, Hastings and Wade. They stood together, not quite part of the old unit, but not outsiders either. The battle had forged them into one whether they had started with Archer or not.

The silence stretched for a heavy moment. No one spoke, but the toll of what they had just endured pressed down on them all.

Archer glanced around the room, nodding slightly to each man. Sixteen left. That was all. Sixteen out of the forty-six who had stood with them at the start of this battle.

And D Company?

At full strength, D Company had been 120 men strong. Three full rifle platoons, machine-gunners, signallers—all gone. The company had been fighting since the first days of the retreat. There had been bleeding men at every turn. They'd been cut down in ambushes, bombardments, and desperate rearguards.

Finally, after days of holding the line, after the sickening toil of Cassel—D Company was finished.

Sixteen men. That was all that was left.

It hit him low in the chest — not pain exactly, but something harder to name. The names of the dead pressed in at the edges of his mind, but he forced them aside. There would be time to remember them if they made it out of here.

The men stood in the dim interior of the ruined hotel and gathered around Pembroke and Archer, waiting for the final word. Outside, they could all hear the distant rumble of enemy movement that signalled time was running short.

Pembroke took a step forwards. His voice steady but firm.

Gentlemen, we have achieved our objective. The battalion and the brigade have withdrawn from Cassel. From what I can tell, we are the last British forces left in the town.'"

His words hung in the air. No one needed to be told what that meant. He scanned their faces. These men had fought through hell. These men had given everything.

"Every single one of you has done his duty and more. There's not a man here who has anything left to prove. Archer and I cannot, in good conscience, ask any more of you."

He paused, allowing that to sink in. Then he squared his shoulders. His tone was resolute.

"So now, the decision is yours. There are two options. We can make a break for it and head north to Dunkirk. It won't be easy, and there are no guarantees. But if we stay sharp, and have a bit of luck, we might just make it."

His gaze swept over the men once more before he continued.

"Or, you can call it a day. No shame in it. No honour lost. If you decide to lay down arms, I will not think any less of you. None of us will."

Silence.

A few men exchanged glances, but most just stared at him, listening.

Then Pembroke drew a steady breath and delivered the last

196

line: the one that mattered most.

The silence stretched for a long moment after Pembroke's words. Their decision hung in the stale air of the ruined hotel. Then Archer stepped forwards. His voice was quieter but no less firm, and it cut through the stillness.

"Alright. Let's be straight about this." His eyes moved over the faces of the men, making sure they were listening. "Dunkirk's about twenty miles away, but the route we're likely to take will stretch that to forty. Maybe more. We all know our situation. Food and water's low. Ammo's not great, and Jerry has us surrounded."

He let that sink in. His grim but steady expression met every man's eyes.

"So, this isn't going to be a march. It's going to be a crawl, moving at night, resting up during the day. No fires. No noise. No mistakes. Slip up, and we don't get a second chance."

A few men shifted uneasily. They all knew what he meant.

Archer exhaled, rubbing the grime from his jaw. Then, with a wry shake of his head, he added, "And let's be honest—fuck, we don't even know what's at Dunkirk. For all we know, it's a bloody disaster."

A murmur rippled through the men, some nodding, some exchanging wary glances. They all knew that uncertainty was part of this war, but hearing it put so plainly only reinforced the unease of the journey ahead.

Archer straightened. His voice was firm again.

"But I'll tell you this—standing here and waiting for Jerry to round us up isn't an option. For Captain Pembroke and me, we're making a go of it. Gents, if you join us, it's by your decision. It's not an order."

The room was silent, the decision pressing on every man like a held breath. Then, after a long beat, Mallory exhaled through his nose, adjusting his webbing as he stepped forwards.

"Well, that settles it then," he said, matter of fact as if it had never been in doubt. "We're in."

A ripple of nods followed. No one spoke, but there was no hesitation either. The choice had already been made in their minds.

They had fought and bled together—none of them were about to walk away now.

Archer glanced at Pembroke, then back to the men. "Alright. Get your gear together. Let's go."

Chapter 11

The fires of Cassel still burnt as night crept in, and their glow cast flickering orange light against the darkening sky. Smoke continued to coil between the shattered buildings, rising in thick plumes that carried the stench of destruction. The town was dying. Its streets were littered with death. The air was heavy with the distant rumble of artillery as the Germans took over.

Sixteen men moved through the ruins: shadows in the devastation. They stayed close to the broken walls, stepping carefully over rubble and shattered glass in an attempt to remain unseen and unheard. The sporadic crack of gunfire echoed in the distance, and it was a stark reminder that the enemy was tightening its grip on the town. Somewhere, an engine rumbled. It was unmistakably the deep mechanical growl of German armour repositioning and securing its dominance.

Archer led the way with his rifle gripped in his hands. His jaw was tight, and his senses were alert. Pembroke moved alongside him, guiding the men towards the town's western edge where open ground lay beyond. Every step was a risk. Every moment was a chance for the Germans to catch sight of them and end their desperate bid for survival.

The streets were a labyrinth of wreckage. Bombed-out homes and crumbling shop fronts formed jagged silhouettes against the firelit sky. They passed the ruins of a bakery; its sign was barely clinging to its rusted chain, and the smell of scorched flour and burnt wood lingered in the air. A toppled cart lay on its side. Its contents had long been plundered or turned to ash. Ahead, the road forked, giving them a choice between an open boulevard strewn with debris or a narrower alleyway swallowed in shadow.

Pritchard emerged from the darkness, crouching low as he moved back to Archer and Pembroke.

His face was slick with sweat, but his voice was steady. "Boulevard's too open," he murmured. "Wreckage, no cover. Germans are probably watching it. The alley's tight, but if we move quick, we're more likely to stay unseen."

Pembroke exhaled, nodding towards Archer who studied the alleyway's jagged walls.

"Plenty of cover," he murmured to Pembroke.

Pembroke gave a short nod. "We take the alley. Keep low, move fast."

A breeze stirred within the ruins. Silence.

Pritchard turned and quickly led the way, slipping into the darkness. Pembroke gestured for the others to follow. Archer moved first, followed by Jacks, and O'Hara, then the rest.

The cobblestones beneath their tired feet were rough and uneven, and coated in dust and dried blood. Their boots barely made a sound as they advanced, slipping between the ruins like wraiths.

A cat darted through the rubble and vanished into the dark, making Evans flinch. Behind him, Saunders—nervous as ever when not in action—gave a silent giggle at Evans' reaction.

Up ahead, Pritchard led them further into the alleyway, his movements swift and practiced. His rifle was held tight against his chest. The space was narrow and hemmed in by the ruins of buildings that had once been quaint homes and shops. Their façades had all been shattered by shellfire. The men followed in single file, pressed close to the jagged walls, and their boots stepped lightly over the debris.

Archer glanced around. The alley was barely a few feet wide in places, and the upper floors of the ruined buildings leant inwards as if they might collapse at any moment. A length of tattered laundry still hung between two of them, swaying slightly in the night breeze. It was eerily silent. Too silent.

A sudden, metallic clatter broke the quiet.

Everyone froze.

O'Hara, second in line behind Pritchard, had caught his

boot against a loose tin cup, sending it skittering against the cobblestones. He sucked in a sharp breath and became rigid. Behind him, Saunders visibly tensed, gripping his rifle tighter.

Pritchard shot a look back at Archer. His expression was unreadable as he raised his fist to signal hold position.

The silence stretched.

Somewhere in the distance, the low murmur of German voices drifted through the ruins. It was faint, impossible to tell how far. Webb slowly exhaled through his nose and gripped the Bren gun across his chest. After an agonising moment, Pritchard gave a slow nod and pressed forwards, the others following with heightened caution. Ahead, the alleyway constricted further and forced them to move carefully around a pile of collapsed masonry. As Archer rounded it, his foot sank into something soft. He stopped.

Looking down, he saw a German boot sticking out from the rubble. His stomach lurched. The leg inside it was motionless. The uniform was coated in dust. A corpse, half-buried.

Jacks came up beside him and gave a low grunt. "Must've been here a while," he muttered. "Collapsed building took him out."

Archer exhaled and kept moving.

Pritchard suddenly stopped, raising his hand again. He crouched, peering around the next turn. Archer reached his side, careful to keep low.

Pritchard crouched just short of the alley's mouth; his rifle was held ready as he scanned the open ground beyond. The road stretched from west to east. It was a scar of broken tarmac and scattered debris lined with the wreckage of war. Burnt-out civilian cars and an overturned truck that lay abandoned along its edges were twisted frames bathed in the faint orange glow of fires that still smouldered in Cassel's ruins.

Beyond the road, a low wire fence ran parallel, sagging

where artillery blasts had torn the posts from the ground. And beyond that—nothing but open fields. Vast and empty, they rolled away under the night sky, a sea of deep blue shadows. No buildings. No cover. Just an endless stretch of trampled farmland that had once been golden with wheat but was now scarred by marching boots and tank tracks.

Pritchard moved first, stepping onto the road. He kept low, his boots rolling carefully over the cracked surface, and his eyes darting between each wreckage. Archer followed, keeping close. His heart pounded in his chest. O'Hara and Jacks moved after them, slipping between the charred remains of a civilian car, blown apart by a blast. At the roadside, Pritchard knelt by the fence, scanning the fields ahead. Archer turned, lifting a hand—the signal for the others to follow.

Then, the sky ignited.

A German flare shot up, bright white, bursting open like a second sun above them. For a heartbeat, everything was frozen in harsh, unnatural light.

The British soldiers were caught mid-motion. Saunders, already halfway across the road, widened his eyes in horror. Evans flinched at the sudden glare. Tug Wilson, who was next in line, instinctively raised his rifle, turning towards the source of the flare.

And then—there they were.

A German patrol: nine men. Some stood with their rifles low in their hands; others had them slung lazily over their shoulders.

Pritchard and Wilson reacted in unison, rifles rising.

The Germans appeared relaxed, unhurried—almost as if they had fired the flare out of curiosity rather than with any tactical intent.

Pritchard and Wilson didn't stop to question it. They didn't care why the flare had been fired—only that it had, and that its harsh, daylight-bright glow had exposed the enemy to them.

Crack. Both men fired simultaneously.

A split-second later, shots rang out from the far side of the road; Archer, O'Hara and Jacks were adding their fire to the ambush.

The Germans, despite having initiated the action, were completely caught off guard. The first few shots dropped two men instantly: one slumped forwards, the other crumpled where he stood. Another stumbled back, gripping his side. Then came the ripping burst of a Bren gun.

The rounds thudded into the chest of a hapless soldier, lifting him off his feet before he crashed to the ground.

Pembroke signalled to the men still in the alley. "Follow me!"

Mallory was first behind him, followed closely by Brookes, Finch, Button, Hastings, and Wade. All seven men surged forwards, rifles up, rushing the German patrol. They fired from the hip, sending a volley of rounds into the enemy, cutting down at least two more Germans.

Pembroke dropped to one knee with Mallory alongside him. Both men chambered fresh rounds and fired. Their shots snapped through the night towards the remaining Germans.

That was enough. The survivors broke and ran, disappearing into the ruins.

"Let's get out of here—move!" Pembroke barked, already turning.

The men sprinted towards where Archer and the others had crossed the road and were vanishing into the fields and the safety of darkness.

The last remnants of D Company slipped away from Mont Cassel as the first hints of night stretched across the sky. A dull orange glow lingered over the town, smudges of smoke rising from burning buildings. Behind them, occasional bursts of small-arms fire and distant artillery thuds reminded them that the battle was still raging. Ahead lay the open countryside and miles of hostile ground between them and Dunkirk.

For now, they were clear, not safe, but away. The brief lull was a gift. Archer took the lead, crouched low as he moved along the edge of a sunken road. The terrain here was a blessing. The road had been cut into the landscape years ago, leaving high banks lined with thick hedgerows. The deep ditches running alongside the track provided extra concealment. With a hand signal, he gestured for the men to move in pairs, keep low and step lightly. The road curved ahead and disappeared into the dark. It was flanked by open fields on one side and a line of trees on the other.

Pembroke followed closely behind Archer, checking their rear as the rest of the men filtered along the ditch. Their gear barely made a sound. Exhaustion had gnawed through them, but the adrenaline kept them moving. No one spoke. The only sounds were the occasional crunch of boots on dirt and the rustling of leaves in the faint breeze.

They had barely covered half a mile when Archer suddenly raised his fist. Halt. The column froze. He turned his head slightly, listening. Faint voices. German. The crackle of a radio, and the murmur of a conversation just ahead. He eased forwards, pressing himself against the embankment and peering through the thick foliage.

A German patrol, half a dozen men at least, were clustered near a break in the hedgerow where a narrow track intersected their sunken road. The glow of a cigarette flared briefly in the gloom. One of the Germans muttered something, and another laughed under his breath. A sergeant stood apart from the group and scanned the darkness with his rifle held loosely at his side.

Pulling back, he steadied his breathing as he assessed the situation. He glanced at Pembroke, who was already looking back at the men behind them. No words were needed. This couldn't be avoided. It had to be dealt with. Silently.

Archer tapped Mallory and Jacks and then pointed to the left. Pembroke gestured to Pritchard and Evans, indicating the right. They knew what to do. Knives, rifle butts—quick and quiet.

Slowly, Archer crept forwards, feeling the damp earth shift beneath his boots. The Germans were relaxed. Their rifles were slung casually, and their focus was elsewhere. He moved like a shadow, closing the distance.

A moment of stillness. Then, a flurry of controlled violence.

Jacks struck first. His blade flashed as he drove it up beneath a man's ribs, silencing him before he could even gasp. Archer followed, seizing another by the collar and slamming his bayonet into the base of his skull. The man crumpled; a strangled gurgle escaped before darkness took him.

On the right, Pembroke struck hard, his rifle butt crunching against bone before his target slumped lifelessly. Evans thrust his knife deep into another's throat, holding him firm as the body twitched. The last German turned, eyes widening but too late. Pritchard drove his knife in, twisting hard before lowering the body to the ground.

Silence returned. Six dead. No shots fired.

Archer exhaled slowly, wiping his blade clean on a dead man's tunic. No time to linger.

Pritchard and Evans crouched down, moving fast, patting down pockets and webbing. Pritchard yanked open a pocket to find a chunk of stale ration biscuit and, miraculously, a small bar of chocolate. He shoved it into his tunic and moved on to another. Evans grinned as he plucked a half-full cigarette tin from one of the bodies.

"Bit of luck," he murmured, slipping it into his pocket.

Archer gave the signal to move, and they melted into the

night once more, leaving the corpses cooling in the damp grass.

They pressed on, angling their path away from the road. The terrain grew rougher as the trees thinned out ahead and gave way to open fields. Beyond the tree line, the land sloped downwards into a shallow valley where the faint outline of a barn and a few low structures could be seen in the distance. A farm.

Pritchard, who had gone ahead, returned to Archer and Pembroke. They dropped to one knee, the others following suit.

"Motorised German unit," Pritchard reported in a low voice. "Motorbikes, half-tracks, and armoured cars. At least two companies' worth. Not even trying to keep their position secret. Lights everywhere. This must be where that patrol came from."

Pembroke exhaled sharply. "They think they've already won." His voice carried an edge of irritation.

"I think they have," Archer said quietly.

Pembroke stared at him, and for a moment, neither man spoke. The shared understanding of the comment lingered between them. They both knew the truth.

"No point in boxing around and heading for Watten," Pembroke said finally. "They're probably there too." He adjusted his grip on his rifle. "We turn north now. Stay alert for more patrols."

By the time the first hint of dawn crept over the horizon, and a thin band of pale grey stretched across the sky, they knew they needed to disappear. Archer wiped the sweat from his brow, feeling the exhaustion settling deep in his limbs. They had been moving all night, picking their way through fields and sunken roads, staying low to avoid detection.

Pembroke, who was a few paces ahead, suddenly raised a hand. The group halted instantly, dropping into a crouch. He turned back to Archer who came running up, and he pointed towards a small wood nestled at the edge of a ploughed field about five hundred yards to their front.

"Dawn is approaching, fast. Not sure we can trust finding any further cover, so we will hold up in that wood for the day."

Archer glanced around. The landscape was opening up: fewer hedgerows, less cover, and too many exposed stretches of open ground. The small wood ahead was their best chance of staying out of sight before daylight fully broke.

As they neared the treeline, no more than a hundred yards from the small wood, Archer gave the slightest of whistles: sharp and brief, just enough to catch Pembroke's attention. The group instinctively dropped to a knee, rifles ready, breathing heavy from the relentless march through the night.

Archer jogged up to Pembroke, keeping his voice low. "Sir, hold here. Let me take Jacks and Pritchard forwards and check it out."

Pembroke gave a curt nod, his eyes scanning the thinning shadows. No one needed to be told what would happen if the woods weren't empty.

Archer motioned to Jacks and Pritchard, and the three of them peeled off from the group, moving towards the trees as one in a low, steady crouch. The sky was already lightening — black giving way to grim grey. Day was coming fast, and with it, came danger.

It was the worst time to move—too much light to be invisible but not enough to see clearly. They had no choice.

The wood loomed ahead. It was a jagged cluster of trees clawing at the sky—dense enough to provide decent cover but not so thick as to restrict movement. Gnarled tree trunks stood close together, their branches intertwined like grasping fingers, offering pockets of darkness beneath their canopy. The ground was soft and uneven, thick with damp leaves, fallen branches, and patches of tangled undergrowth. The scent of wet earth and rotting foliage rose from the soggy ground.

As they slipped between the first trees, Archer glanced at Pritchard. The man moved like he belonged here, his steps were near silent, and his body slipped through the brush without disturbing so much as a twig. A lifetime of poaching had made him ghost-like in places like this. While the others—including Archer—had to think about every step, Pritchard simply flowed, instinct guiding him where training guided the rest.

Jacks, who moved beside them, was competent—quiet, alert—but next to Pritchard, even he felt loud. Archer had seen men freeze in battle, but he had also seen men come alive in certain environments. This was Pritchard's element. His rifle was hung loose in his grip, but Archer had no doubt he would drop it in favour of a blade in an instant if it meant keeping silent.

The three of them pushed deeper, pausing every few steps to listen. The world was waking; birds shifted in the trees, and a breeze whispered through the branches. But no voices. No movement that didn't belong.

Archer gave Pritchard a glance and saw him give the smallest of nods. Clear—for now.

Jacks turned and headed back towards Pembroke's position, raised a hand, and signalled for the others to move up. They had found their shelter, for however long it would last.

Pembroke motioned for the men to spread out. The air smelt of wet bark and churned earth. It mingled with the faint, distant scent of smoke on the wind. He didn't like it. Smoke meant destruction. And destruction meant Germans.

They gathered in a shallow depression near the base of a large oak which was shielded on one side by a tangle of brambles. It wasn't perfect, but it would have to do.

As the rest of the group reached the trees, Archer and Pembroke got to work, setting up a concealed spot to lie low until nightfall. The men were exhausted; their movements had been slower, but the discipline held. There was no talking beyond what was necessary.

Archer turned to Pembroke. "We set four on watch. Rotate every two hours. That gives the rest time to sleep."

Pembroke gave a quick nod, rubbing a hand over his face. "Agreed. We need eyes on all sides. If a patrol sweeps through, I want to know before they're on top of us."

Archer scanned the group and pointed. "Jacks, Evans, Pritchard, Saunders—first watch. One north, one east, one south, one west. Keep low. Stay alert. Rotate every four hours. One NCO per guard. Inform me every change. Wake me if necessary." More than anything, he needed to know the guard was set.

The four men moved into position without a word. Pritchard melted into the trees as if he'd always been there while Saunders took up a spot where he had a clear view back towards where they had come from. Jacks and Evans settled in, rifles ready, eyes sweeping the dim surroundings.

The rest of the men unbuckled their webbing belts, placed their weapons within reach, and found whatever space they could to lie down. The ground was damp and uneven, but nobody complained. At this point, rest was more valuable than comfort.

Archer dropped into a crouch near the base of a thick tree, stretching out his legs. He exhaled slowly. He would rest—but only for a few hours.

Pembroke, still kneeling beside him, spoke quietly. "If we're lucky, we'll get through the day without trouble."

Archer didn't answer right away. He glanced towards Jacks who was barely visible against the shadows of the trees. Then he looked to Pritchard, blending in as though the forest had swallowed him. Then Archer turned back to Pembroke.

"Let's hope we're lucky," he muttered, closing his eyes.

Archer blinked awake. Fatigue still dragged at his limbs, but his body had taken the rest it could. Six hours. More sleep than he'd had in days. His limbs ached, and his uniform was stiff with dried sweat, but for the first time in what felt like an eternity, he didn't feel like he was on the verge of collapse.

He rolled onto his side, propping himself up on his elbow. The trees gave way to open ground ahead, and from where he lay, he could see across the fields stretching into the distance. Beyond them, a German column rumbled past, no more than three hundred yards away.

Archer realised the entire road was alive with steel and movement: half-tracks, trucks, motorcycles, and the steady procession of men. Their engine noise droned, constant and oppressive, drowning out the usual sounds of the countryside. Dust billowed in thick clouds as it was kicked up by the passing vehicles and hung in the midday air.

They'd been rolling past for at least five minutes. No urgency. No caution. They moved like an army that knew it had already won.

A presence at his side. Pembroke.

Archer glanced at him and saw the same grim recognition on his face. Pembroke lay flat beside him, rifle resting in the crook of his arm, and he watched the enemy roll past with a quiet, detached focus.

"They're moving a lot of men up," Pembroke murmured.

Archer didn't look at him, just kept his eyes on the column. "Yeah."

He had counted at least a dozen trucks already and more were still appearing over the crest of the road. The men inside them weren't expecting a fight. Helmets were off, some men were smoking, others laughing—no sense of urgency. Just confidence.

"They're pushing hard towards Dunkirk," Pembroke said, his voice barely above a whisper. "Probably reinforcing the perimeter."

Archer exhaled slowly. If the Germans were throwing this much towards Dunkirk, the window to escape was closing faster than they'd thought.

For a brief moment, he considered the rifle resting in the crook of his arm. He could take a shot. Drop the officer riding in the front of that half-track. Maybe two if he was quick.

But what then?

Another truck rolled past: another squad of Germans looking fresh, clean, well-fed. The complete opposite of the sixteen men lying in the woods, barely hanging on.

Archer shifted slightly, watching, waiting. The war was still moving around them.

The day crawled by in a haze of cool air and silence. The men had found what little cover they could under the trees and had got a few hours of sleep while keeping vigilant watch. The usual tension was heavy in the air. Every small noise that was amplified in the quiet of the woods, every movement of leaves or distant noise from the enemy, seemed like a threat.

Archer found a place for himself at the edge of their hideout and leant against the trunk of an old oak, pulling out the small notebook he kept in one of his battledress pockets. He flicked through the pages, his fingers lingering over the names and dates he'd written. He looked down the list and started crossing through those who hadn't made it: Tanner, Carter, Brewer...each time he read a name, he paused for a brief reflection on the man behind it.

He let out a long sigh, glancing at the men resting around him. It was hard to know what to make of it all. He didn't know whether these men would even survive the next few days. As the light filtered through the trees, Archer's eyes fell on Pritchard who was sitting nearby, sharing his last tin of bully beef with young Saunders. They were calm and silent except for the faint tinkling noise as Saunders scraped the mush of meat from the tin. Archer's thoughts turned back to the list.

He hadn't planned on keeping the list. It had started out as a way of remembering the men's names, but now it had become a conscious note to make sure no one was forgotten. Each name had a face, with stories, with laughs and jokes that had brightened the hellish days of retreat.

He paused on Richards' name: the first to fall. The sound of his voice was still fresh in Archer's memory. Richards had always been a steady one and well-respected amongst the men. Archer knew Jacks had taken his loss hard especially when he thought of Richards' two little girls.

Pembroke came over after a while, catching sight of the book in Archer's hands. Archer hadn't even realised he was still looking at the names.

"You're still keeping that?" Pembroke asked quietly.

Archer looked up before glancing back briefly at the names.

"Somebody has to," he said simply. "They deserve to be remembered."

Archer closed the book, pocketing it again. The men around him were quiet. Each one was lost in their own thoughts, whether it was the horror of the war, the fear of the next battle, or simply the relief of surviving one more day.

The afternoon passed slowly. The dull sky was overcast and grey, and Archer had to force himself to ignore the growing ache in his bones. They had to keep moving soon before the Germans closed in or they ran out of time. But for now, there was no choice but to wait.

As the shadows lengthened and the light began to fade, Archer felt the pull of duty and determination return over him once more. He glanced at Pembroke, who was keeping watch, and then at the men around them. They were still alive. For now, that was enough.

Eventually, the grey sky cast shadows through the trees. Archer lay beside Pembroke. They had moved to the edge of the woods, keeping their movements low and slow just enough to ensure they weren't too easily discovered. The light was fading, and it wouldn't be long before they could move again.

Pembroke pulled the map from his battledress, the paper crinkling in his hands. It was old, barely legible in places, but it was the only thing they had.

"How far do you think we made it last night?" Pembroke asked, squinting at the horizon.

Archer glanced at the map, tracing their path with his finger. "Hard to say. I'd estimate about seven to nine miles—give or take a few." He folded the map slightly, holding it up to the fading light. "We've been following this route parallel to the Rue de Bergues." He gestured towards the road where they had been observing German troops moving along all day.

Pembroke continued, "We'll stick to this route. Keep low. Keep quiet. If we keep our heads down, we might make it through the night without a hitch." He hesitated, looking at Archer. "Let's not stop. Not for anything. We keep a steady march, and we'll make it to Dunkirk in the morning."

"Alright," Archer said, glancing at the map one last time. "North it is. Keep moving until we can't move anymore."

Just as they finished their conversation, Mallory appeared by their side.

"Sir," his voice showed concern. "Jerrys, heading this way." He pointed towards the road. Some three hundred yards away, towards the south, a German unit had broken through the hedgerow running along the road and was heading towards the woods.

"Fuck, Fuck, Fuck!" Pembroke said, fuelled with irritation.

Chapter 12

The woods were thick with shadow, the canopy above turning the last remnants of daylight into shifting patches of darkness. Damp earth muffled the sound of their boots as Archer and his men moved cautiously between the trees, their forms barely visible in the gloom. The distant thunder of artillery rumbled beyond the horizon. But here, among the trunks and undergrowth, the world was eerily still.

Archer crouched behind a tree, its bark rough and gouged against his back as he scanned the scene ahead. The Germans had halted their advance—for now. He could see them beyond the tree line, silhouettes shifting in the twilight...waiting. Their hesitation sent a prickle of unease through him. They weren't rushing in blindly. They were planning something.

Pembroke knelt beside him, whispering, "I think they know we're here."

Archer gave a small nod, and his fingers tightened around his rifle. They had little time. If they stayed, they'd be surrounded before long.

"It's not good," Archer muttered. "We can't hold them off. There's a whole bloody German army on that road!" He locked eyes with Pembroke. "We need to make a run for it."

"Agreed. Let's get the chaps moving. If we pull back with the woods at our backs, it might give us some cover." Pembroke wasn't convinced, but he said it anyway.

The order rippled through the ranks. Mallory and Jacks signalled the men, urging them to slip deeper into the woods. The first groups moved quickly, staying low and navigating through the undergrowth with trained efficiency.

The trees were dense but only in patches. There were gaps where light filtered through, revealing the thinning cover. The woodland stretched barely a few hundred yards before breaking into open fields. If the Germans pushed forwards, they'd be pinned before they could reach proper concealment. It wasn't a forest; it was a fragile barrier and one that wouldn't shield them for long.

Then came the first distant thump.

A heartbeat later, the first mortar round exploded against the tree line: a brilliant flash, then a deafening crack. The blast tore through the undergrowth, sending shattered branches and clumps of earth whipping through the air mixed with deadly shrapnel.

Archer barely had time to flinch before the shell struck—right where he and Pembroke had crouched seconds earlier. The blasts gouged a crater of churned soil and splintered wood. The ground shuddered beneath them. The shockwave rolled through the trees, and leaves and debris cascaded down like a sudden storm.

The stillness of the previous moments was obliterated in an instant.

"Go! Move!" Archer bellowed.

The intended calm, efficient withdrawal from the woods turned into a desperate sprint. Men darted between trees, ducking low as more mortar rounds screamed overhead. Another shell hit, tearing through a cluster of saplings to throw Finch backwards with a cry. The woods lit up in flashes of fire and fury.

Then came the armour.

The first German half-track lurched into view beyond the trees, its machine-gun rattling to life. Tracers zipped through the undergrowth, cutting another man down as he ran. The mortar fire intensified, a relentless barrage that tore through the trees in violent bursts. Each explosion slammed into the earth with a deafening roar, shaking the ground and shredding trunks into jagged splinters. The forest shuddered with every impact, branches crashing down as the air thickened with dust, bark and the glow of burning embers.

Archer turned, searching for Pembroke, but another explosion tore through the space between them. They had to keep moving. A roaring blast sent another shockwave through the trees, and a wall of smoke and debris rushed over him, choking the air as he threw himself to the forest floor.

When he staggered up, coughing, he saw the woods had dissolved into complete disarray. Figures raced past him, breaking from the tree line, their forms barely visible through the swirling dust. Some men had already reached the open ground beyond, sprinting across the darkened fields in the distance while others stumbled or fell, lost in the confusion.

More shells slammed into the trees behind Archer. The crack of splintering wood merged with the sharp retorts of rifle fire. The cover of the woods was gone—the only option now was to run.

Jacks grabbed his arm. "Sir! We have to go!"

Archer hesitated, scanning the burning woods, but there was no time. He had Saunders, Webb, and Matthews still with him. They had to keep moving.

Another mortar struck to close for his liking, and it sent a tree crashing down behind them, followed by the whizzing of bullets and tracer rounds, some ricochetting off trees and branches.

"Run!" he bellowed, his voice raw, fierce, cutting through the chaos.

They sprinted into the open ground. Archer caught sight of a soldier turning, raising his rifle—hesitating.

"Keep moving! Don't stop!" Archer shouted to him.

In the distance, Archer could make out a hedgerow: two hundred yards ahead—their only cover.

"Head for the hedgerow!"

The ground was uneven, each step jarring his body as Archer sprinted forwards, lungs burning. His boots pounded against the damp earth, but the roar of gunfire behind them drowned out everything. As he ran, bullets whipped overhead, and tracer rounds sliced across the field like fiery threads. The stuttering rip of machine-guns and the distant thump of mortars filled the air with chaos. Each jarring step sent a shock through Archer's legs as he sprinted across the uneven ground, lungs searing. Gunfire roared behind them, deafening but his mind was louder: this was it. The end. No more time. Fear soaked him to the bone. Every breath came ragged. Bullets snapped past, tracer rounds lighting the dark like sparks from hell.

Bullets cracked past his ears, kicking up more dirt and splintering into the ground around him. A burst of fire raked the field from the left, and someone else went down with a choked cry. Again, there was no time to check who it was.

Archer's pulse thundered in his skull. His chest heaving. His heart hammering. His legs burning—but he knew he couldn't stop. He held the rifle tight, but it felt weightless — lost in the blur of fear and falling back.

A mortar round suddenly exploded somewhere behind him, and the shockwave punched through his chest like a hammer. The impact sent heat licking at his back, but he forced his legs to keep moving.

Ahead, the hedgerow was still too far. Two hundred yards felt like two miles. The open ground stretched out before him, endless, exposed. Every second out here was borrowed time.

The shriek of incoming rounds, the shouts of men, the crash of bullets snapping past—all of it blurred together, but instinct kept him moving. Move. Run. Survive.

When the hedgerow loomed ahead right in front of them, they realised how thick and tangled it was, but they knew it was their only chance. Archer threw himself forwards, slamming into the thorns and branches, and felt them tearing at his uniform, at his skin. The weight of men behind him pushed him through, boots sliding on damp earth as he tumbled into cover.

Bodies crashed through beside him—Jacks, Saunders, Webb, Matthews—gasping, covered in mud, and eyes wide with exhaustion and fear. Someone groaned, clutching at a grazed arm, but there was no time for more than a glance. They had made it. That was all that mattered.

Gunfire still lacerated the field behind them. Somewhere out there, men were still running—or had fallen. But Archer couldn't look back. He wouldn't. Not yet.

He pressed himself against the hedgerow, sucking in deep, shuddering breaths. His chest ached. His pulse thundered in his ears. Every inch of him screamed to rest, but they couldn't stay here.

He scanned the faces of the men crouched beside him—sweating, shaking, alive. That was all that mattered.

But where was Pembroke? Mallory? How many had actually made it? And how the hell were they going to get out of this?

His hands clenched around his rifle. No time to think. No time to grieve. Only one thing mattered: what next?

Archer hauled himself upright, taking ragged breaths at every movement. His hands shook as he gripped his rifle. The gunfire still raged behind them, but they were through. For now.

He turned, scanning the men who had pushed through with him. Jacks was crouched low with his chest heaving; his face was streaked with dirt. Saunders gripped his rifle, eyes darting back towards the field. Webb was sprawled on his back, gasping heavily and trying to catch his breath. Matthews had blood smeared down one sleeve, but he was moving.

That was four.

Pritchard stumbled through next, dropping to one knee, rifle still clutched tightly in his hands. Wilson followed, his uniform torn, and sweat streaking through the dirt on his face.

Six.

Evans should have been right behind them. Archer turned, scanning the broken line of men, his chest tightening. No sign of him.

Then O'Hara crashed through the hedgerow, rolling onto his side with a grunt. He pushed himself up, wincing and with one hand clutching his ribs.

Seven.

Brookes followed, barely slowing as he ducked low and threw himself down beside the others.

Eight.

Another burst of gunfire raked the field behind them, forcing Archer to duck instinctively. The Germans were still covering the open ground, but no more men came through.

Finch hadn't made it. Button was gone. And still—no Pembroke, no Mallory, no Evans. Hastings, and Wade were missing too. Whether they had been hit, captured, or simply lost in the mayhem, Archer didn't know. There had been no time to look. There was no time to wait. The retreat had scattered them all. His mind reeled, grasping at fragments, faces, shouts, the last glimpses of men diving for cover or not getting up at all. He tried to piece it together, to make sense of who might still be out there, who might already be dead. But the bedlam gave no answers. His thoughts skidded between fury and guilt, panic and purpose. He couldn't afford to stop. Not now. Not while others might still be fighting, still alive, counting on him to lead. He took a shaky breath, forcing it past the tightness in his throat. Focus. One step, then another. That's how you survive. That's how you get them home, that's how he gets home.

Eight men. That was all he had left.

They crouched behind the hedgerow, sucking in lungfuls of air, faces slick with sweat and grime. No one spoke at first, the reality of their losses sinking in for all of them. The gunfire behind them had started to fade, but the Germans weren't far behind. They couldn't stay here.

Jacks shifted beside him, gripping his rifle tight, his knuckles white. "We can't stay here."

Wilson checked his ammo, jaw tight. He didn't look up. "They might still be out there."

Saunders let out a breath, shaking his head. "Bloody hell."

Pritchard's eyes flicked over the field back through the tangled bushes and searched for movement. His jaw was clenched so tight it looked like he might crack a tooth, but he didn't say a word.

Matthews wiped a hand across his face and then checked the wound on his arm. He exhaled sharply, but still—no one asked the question they were all thinking.

Archer swallowed hard and forced his mind to steady. Pembroke. Mallory. Finch. Evans. Were they wounded? Dead or worse, captured? His gut twisted. The retreat had been ordered, and now five men were unaccounted for. Rage burnt under his skin, frustration at the Germans, at the chaos of it all. But he couldn't let it take hold. He couldn't think about it. Not now. The men still here needed him. They had to move.

Jacks shifted beside Archer, gripping his rifle tight. He had barely moved since they'd made it through the hedgerow. His breathing was heavy, shallow. Mallory was gone.

They had fought beside each other for weeks. They'd relied on each other and covered each other's backs. And now, just like that, he was missing. Maybe dead. Maybe lying wounded somewhere out there.

And Jacks hadn't been there for him.

His fists clenched as he stared at the ground, and his rifle trembled slightly in his grip. He had seen men go before— Richards, Hawkins, Townsend, Davies—but Mallory? That wasn't supposed to happen. Mallory was the constant. The steady hand. He wasn't supposed to be one of them.

Jacks drew in a sharp breath, shoulders tight, jaw working. For a moment, he looked like he might speak, then he just shook his head, blinking hard, eyes glinting with the threat of tears he refused to let fall. Jacks forced himself to steady. No time for this. They were exposed and low on numbers. Thinking about it wouldn't bring Mallory back.

But the thought wouldn't leave him.

Archer took one last glance over the field, his chest aching: not just from the run, but from the number who were missing. Where was Pembroke? Mallory? Where were the rest?

The realisation landed like a stone settling on his shoulders. He turned to the men with him. This was it.

"We move. Now." Archer's voice was firm, giving nothing away of the weakness he felt inside.

No one argued. There was no time to mourn. Not yet.

Meanwhile, deeper in the woods, three men remained behind: hidden, trapped, and waiting for darkness to fall. The woods were alive with movement as branches snapped, boots pounded against the damp earth, and the harsh bark of German orders cut through the darkness.

Mallory crouched low, his breath coming in tight, controlled gasps. His fingers clenched around the strap of Pembroke's webbing, holding him steady as Evans adjusted his grip under the captain's arm. Pembroke was deadweight between them. His head lolled forwards, and his breaths were shallow. The mortar blast had taken him out cold.

They had tried to move, tried to follow the others, but the chaos had turned against them. The Germans had pushed in too fast, too aggressively, forcing them to break for cover before they could reach the field. Now, they were trapped and pinned down in the thick undergrowth as enemy soldiers swept through the trees, chasing Archer's group down.

Mallory pressed himself lower into the damp earth, feeling the weight of Pembroke sag against him. Evans did the same, his eyes anxiously darting towards the shadowed shapes moving between the trees.

A squad of Germans passed barely ten feet away with their rifles raised. They were so close that Mallory could see their breath misting in the cool air, and their eyes scanning the darkness. One of them slowed, his head tilting slightly, listening. Mallory froze. His heartbeat thudded against his ribs, deafening in his own ears.

The German soldier took another slow step forwards, boots sinking into the soft earth. The muzzle of his rifle shifted, sweeping towards them.

Mallory didn't move. He didn't breathe. Evans remained completely still beside him. His rifle was slung over his shoulder, so his hands were free to support Pembroke's weight. Mallory kept his rifle ready. His grip was firm, but he made no move to raise it. Pembroke lay motionless between them.

The German hesitated. For a moment, it seemed he had sensed something—some shift in the shadows that didn't belong. Then, from deeper in the woods, a distant shout. A call from one of his own. The soldier lingered a second longer, then turned away, moving towards the voice.

Mallory allowed a slow breath to escape. The Germans weren't done searching—not yet. But for now, they had passed. He exchanged a look with Evans, a silent understanding between them.

They couldn't stay here.

But moving meant making noise. And noise meant death.

So, for now, they remained still, barely daring to breathe, waiting for the darkness to swallow them whole.

But the Germans weren't leaving.

Mallory pressed himself deeper into the damp earth. Every instinct screamed at him to move, to run, to fight—but he couldn't. Not with Evans beside him. Not with Pembroke still deadweight between them.

They could hear the enemy moving: deliberate now, no longer chasing, but searching.

A shout. A discovery.

Mallory didn't move, but his stomach twisted. They had found someone. Then came the sound he dreaded. A weak, ragged groan.

Finch.

The soldier coughed. It was a wet, sickly sound that sent a fresh wave of nausea through Mallory's gut. He was still alive. Barely.

Footsteps crunched closer, boots shuffling over the dirt. Voices murmured in German. One of them chuckled.

Mallory forced himself to remain still, though every muscle in his body coiled like a spring. Beside him, Evans' breathing had changed, no longer slow and controlled but tight, laboured.

Finch made a noise—not words, but a hoarse, broken whisper.

A German's voice answered, mocking, dismissive. Mallory couldn't see their faces, but he could picture the smirk, the casual indifference.

A click.

Mallory's blood turned to ice. A pistol being unholstered.

Finch must have seen it too, must have known what was coming, because he made one last, desperate sound, barely more than a whimper.

A pause. A heavy breath. Then—Pop.

A single shot. Small. Precise. A bullet to the head. Finch twitched once, then went limp.

Mallory felt Evans tremble beside him, felt his barely

restrained fury. He wanted to scream. To move. To raise his rifle and cut them all down. But if they did, if they fired, they were dead men.

The Germans didn't leave immediately. Mallory heard a thud as one of them kicked Finch's body over, Evans flinched at the sound of cloth tearing — one of the Germans was going through Finch's pockets. A muttered remark followed, offhand and amused. Mallory clenched his teeth.

Then, laughter.

That was what did it.

Mallory's fingers dug into the stock of his rifle so tightly his knuckles ached. He wasn't aware of how hard he was grinding his teeth until his jaw began to throb. Evans' whole body was rigid, trembling. Hs breath came in tight bursts as he fought the same instinct.

They lay there, completely powerless, their hatred burning like a slow, smouldering ember.

Someday, this moment would resurface. Someday, there would be payback.

But not today.

For now, they could do nothing but remain still and listen as the men who had just executed Finch, laughed and walked away.

The Germans moved through the trees in slow, deliberate sweeps, their boots crunching over fallen branches. They weren't in a hurry anymore. The chase had ended. Now, they were clearing the battlefield.

Mallory lay beside Evans, pulse hammering, face pressed into the dirt. Time had stretched unbearably long. Neither of them had moved.

A German soldier stopped barely five feet away, muttering something under his breath. He was close enough that Mallory could hear the creak of his leather belt, the rustle of his uniform as he adjusted his grip on his rifle. For one agonising moment, he turned towards them.

Mallory held his breath. If the German saw them, they were dead.

Then, from deeper in the woods, a voice called out—a sharp order. The soldier hesitated, then turned away, moving towards his unit.

A few minutes later, Evans watched as the Germans withdrew. Their voices grew fainter as they regrouped. Mallory didn't move until the last traces of their presence had faded into the distance.

Only then did he shift slightly, glancing at Evans. "You alright?" he whispered.

Evans gave a stiff nod; his face was still tense with fury.

A low groan between them made both of them freeze. Then Pembroke stirred, his breath ragged, his head shifting slightly.

Mallory moved quickly and gripped his shoulder. "Sir, keep quiet."

Pembroke blinked groggily. "Where...?"

"We'll explain later."

The sky had darkened. The woods were silent now. It was time to move.

"Stay here," Mallory instructed both Evans and the awakening Pembroke.

Mallory pulled his rifle into his shoulder, and his eyes strained through the darkness. The Germans were gone.

He crept forwards and knelt beside Finch. The uniform was ruffled, buttons undone, pockets turned inside out. Papers and scattered belongings lay around him, discarded — just like his life. Mallory reached down, pulled the open battledress back together, and where the buttons still remained, gently pushed them back into place. Then, with a steady hand, he closed

Finch's eyes. The lad didn't deserve to be left like this — exposed to the dirt and the boot prints of men who'd treated him like a stain in the dirt—wiped out and walked on without pause. A photograph lay half-buried in the mud beside him, creased and smudged. Mallory picked it up, wiped it clean on his sleeve. A young woman. A child. He didn't know who they were, but Finch had carried them close. Mallory slipped the photo back into the breast pocket, pressing it flat. One final gesture. One small mercy.

Mallory adjusted his rifle, then stepped over to Pembroke and Evans.

"Sir, if you're able, I suggest we move."

Pembroke gave a weak nod. He wasn't in a position to argue.

Mallory slung his rifle, took one last look back at Finch, and without a word, he melted into the darkness.

The hedgerow was gone, swallowed by the deepening dusk, but they knew the direction they needed to head.

Archer moved at the front, leading the men away from the battlefield, and his eyes adjusted to the shifting gloom. The air was thick with the lingering stench of smoke and gunpowder, but the guns had fallen silent. Too silent.

As they moved out as one, no one spoke. The only sounds were the steady crunch of boots on damp earth and the soft rustle of uniforms brushing against the undergrowth, every man mindful that a single noise could give them away.

They were tired but not broken. The brief rest in the woods had given them time to catch their breath, to still their hands and steady their minds, but it hadn't erased the weight of the days gone by. The strain of battle still clung to them—aching muscles, bruised bodies, the dull throb of exhaustion sitting just beneath the surface.

They moved in silence, step by careful step, but Archer could feel it in the men around him. Not just fatigue, but doubt was creeping in, slow and insidious. The kind that came when men had seen too much, lost too many, and weren't sure what was waiting for them on the other side of the darkness. He picked up his pace, just a fraction, enough to be noticed. A silent signal. Forwards. Purpose. He didn't look back, but he hoped they'd follow — not just his footsteps, but his will to keep going.

They had been moving for what felt like hours, heading north, hoping to reach British lines before dawn. But the land was empty. No friendly patrols, no distant rifle fire, no sign of life.

Then, on the horizon, a faint orange glow flickered against the night sky.

At first, it could have been the last traces of sunset, but Archer knew better. Dunkirk was burning. Even from here, miles away, he could see the telltale glow of fire consuming the port city. The sky above it was a haze of smoke and destruction.

Jacks shifted beside him, his voice barely more than a whisper.

"Is that Dunkirk?" he asked as he stared at the glow on the horizon. "We must be getting close to British lines by now?"

Archer didn't answer immediately. He wasn't sure. He checked his compass, adjusting their course slightly, but even that didn't offer much reassurance. Archer turned to Jacks.

"Yes, that's Dunkirk." There was no relief in his voice.

Jacks kept his eyes scanning the terrain: silent, watchful, hopeful. Behind them, the others followed with their heads down, conserving their strength. No one complained, but Archer could feel the burden pressing down on them all.

A flare went up in the distance. A faint greenish glow hovered in the night sky before fading. British? German? No way to tell. A resigned nod passed between Archer and Jacks.

They kept moving. There was no other choice.

One foot in front of the other. Keep going. Survive the night. Reach the lines.

No one spoke. They just walked, deeper into the dark.

Pritchard appeared out of the darkness, moving swiftly but carefully. Archer spotted him first, stepping out to meet him as the others instinctively crouched lower, rifles ready.

"What is it?" Archer kept his voice low, scanning Pritchard's face for any sign of immediate danger.

"British," Pritchard murmured. "Not far. In a small hamlet. A group—ambulances, trucks, some carriers." He took a steadying breath. "I can't make out what unit they are, but they're definitely British. It's difficult to say, but looking at the vehicles, I'd guess there's about thirty or so."

Archer exhaled slowly, assessing the situation.

Behind him, Jacks muttered, "Are they laid up for the night?"

"From what I saw, I guess they could be," Pritchard admitted though there was hesitation in his voice.

Archer was silent. Once again, he found himself needing to approach a British unit in the dark. They would be nervous, tense, and probably terrified. Waltzing up and saying hello wasn't exactly an option.

"Pritchard, Jacks—approach carefully. Let them know we're out here and want to come in."

Archer knew it was better to send them instead of leading the approach himself. Pritchard and Jacks would be more discreet, less likely to spook the sentries than if all eight of them moved in at once.

A low whistle signalled the all-clear. Pritchard and Jacks had done their job, no shouting, no gunfire. Just a quiet approach, a clear word to the sentries then a simple signal back to Archer to bring them in. Archer moved forward with the others, boots soft on the earth as they crossed into the hamlet.

The hamlet was little more than a cluster of farmhouses, their stone walls dark against the night. A few outbuildings sat nestled among trees, their roofs sagging under years of neglect. Faint candlelight flickered behind shuttered windows. It was barely visible against the glow of Dunkirk burning on the horizon.

Scattered between the buildings were military trucks, ambulances, and a few Bren carriers. Their faded paint was streaked with mud and dust from the long retreat. Some had makeshift repairs—canvas covering shattered windscreens, sides hastily patched with whatever they could find. Others bore bullet holes along their frames, scars from enemy fire, but the vehicles were still running and that was all that mattered.

A few of the men worked by lantern light, checking engines, tightening straps, shifting supplies in the backs of trucks. Their wooden decks were stained dark with the blood of the wounded.

Even in the dim light, it was clear the group was a patchwork of survivors. Some men wore the dirty khaki of frontline infantry, their helmets dented, uniforms torn. Others had the blue-grey coveralls of RAF ground crew: men who were more used to turning spanners than firing rifles. Among them were gunners from an artillery regiment, their once-pristine tunics now caked with mud. Their weapons were obviously lost somewhere in the retreat. Engineers, mechanics and supply handlers moved among the wounded and vehicles alike.

A group of signallers clustered around a Bren carrier. They were hunched over a Wireless Set No. 11, its dials glowing faintly in the dark. One man tapped at the receiver, adjusting the frequency, while another fiddled with the long whip antenna jutting out from the back of the vehicle. Occasionally, a burst of static crackled through the set, but no voices followed. The way they sat told Archer everything—no one was answering.

This wasn't an organised fighting force. This was what was left.

A lone figure stepped out of the shadows near an ambulance and wiped blood from his hands onto a tattered cloth. Archer tensed, instinctively expecting an officer—but as the man stepped closer, the flickering lantern light caught his face.

The padre.

Reverend James Cartwright looked as exhausted as the men around him. His uniform was stained with dirt and dried blood, and his sleeves were rolled up as though he had just finished tending to the wounded. His usual air of calm was still there, but his eyes were shadowed with fatigue. Lines of worry etched deeper into his face than the last time Archer had seen him.

Archer stepped forwards.

Before Archer could speak, another man emerged from the gloom, walking with the steady, deliberate gait of a career soldier. His uniform was in better shape than most although it was streaked with mud, and his worn boots and the steady set of his jaw marked him as a man used to being in command.

RSM George Jennings.

Archer didn't recognise him, but the brass crown and wreath insignia on his sleeve left no doubt who he was. An RSM...and not one from his own brigade.

Jennings stopped beside the padre, his sharp gaze flicking over Archer and his men before settling on him with the quiet authority only a Regimental Sergeant Major could carry.

"Lieutenant," Jennings said, his tone firm but measured. "Looks like you had a hell of a time getting here."

Padre Cartwright let out a slow breath, his tired eyes flicking over Archer and the men behind him. Relief crossed his face. It wasn't just at seeing a familiar face, but at knowing another officer had arrived.

"Tom," he exhaled, his voice carrying quiet gratitude. "I wasn't sure I'd see you again."

Archer gave a small nod. "There seems to be a bit of that going around."

Cartwright offered a weary half-smile. He glanced towards the trucks and wounded men. "We've been dragging this lot along, trying to keep them moving. No officers left. Just me and Jennings, and..." he sighed, rubbing a hand across his face. "I'm not exactly military."

There was something unspoken in his tone, but Archer could hear the relief at having someone else to share the load.

Archer glanced at the men around them: the patchwork of soldiers, the wounded, the worn-out signallers still hunched over their silent radio.

"Alright, Padre. What's happening? Where's the rest of the battalion?"

Cartwright exhaled heavily. His eyes were shadowed with exhaustion. "I linked up with Battalion HQ just before the final push. I'd been moving between companies, tending to the wounded, giving last rites—doing what I could. When the order came to break out, I stuck with the wounded at the aid post. Figured they'd need me more than anyone."

He shook his head, gaze unfocused. "It was chaos, Tom. Some got out in dribs and drabs, but every time a group slipped through, Jerry was waiting. We tried moving under cover of darkness—kept getting bounced. Gunfire. Flares lighting up the night. Mortars landing in the fields. I saw entire sections wiped out trying to cross a road. Those that made it were scattered. By the time I lost sight of Major Ellis, there was no battalion left, just pockets of survivors running for their lives."

Cartwright exhaled, glancing over at the huddled men. His voice was lower now, hesitant. "Tom...I won't lie to you. The wounded can't take much more. They've got nothing left in them: no strength, no hope. I've done what I can, but I'm not a miracle worker."

He let the words settle before continuing, his expression tight. "I know what surrender means. I know what Jerry's

233

capable of. But I also know that if we keep dragging these poor souls through much more, they'll die anyway. Maybe they'd be better off in German hands."

There was a heavy silence between them for a moment. The distant crackle of gunfire somewhere to the east broke it.

Jennings walked over to the two men, clearing his throat. The old RSM had been standing nearby, listening in, his face unreadable in the dim light.

"Padre's not wrong," he said finally, his voice gruff but steady. "Some of them are in a bad way. I've seen it before—another night or two, and they'll be dead on their feet. We're not exactly flush with options. I was just saying to the padre—either we leave 'em behind with a white flag for Jerry to pick up, or we keep moving and more than likely end up in the bag ourselves."

Cartwright nodded. His voice was quiet but firm. "I was going to ask for volunteers to stay behind with me. They shouldn't be left unattended."

Jacks came over, his tired feet dragging softly through the dirt. "I've split the lads, Sir—half on guard, the rest bedded down."

"Thanks, Corporal." Archer heard the words but barely registered them. His mind was still on the padre. He turned back. "How many volunteers to stay behind?"

Jacks shifted uncomfortably, his jaw tightening. "Sir?"

Archer met his gaze. "The Padre is considering staying behind with the wounded and surrendering to Jerry."

Jacks froze. A muscle twitched in his cheek. Then he spoke. "With all due respect, Sir—fuck off."

"Corporal!" Jennings barked, his voice bristling with

indignation. A lifetime in the British Army had ingrained discipline in him, and he'd never imagined hearing such an outburst especially in front of officers.

"Sorry, Sir!" Jacks shot back sharply, but he was clearly unrepentant as he addressed all three senior ranks. "But we don't leave our own behind. I haven't spent the last two weeks being chased, blown up, and watching my mates die just to end it like this!" His fists clenched at his sides, but his eyes flicked to the wounded men, betraying the conflict within him.

"I can't accept that we just hand British soldiers over to the enemy especially when there's still fight left in us!"

Jennings' voice cut through the tension like a blade. "You'll do as you're bloody well told, Corporal."

Archer kept silent, then felt the unnerving weight of every gaze shifting towards him. They were waiting—for him. But why? The padre was the senior officer. Why weren't they looking to him?

The realisation struck hard, and a sudden weight pressed down on his chest. His knees almost buckled under it. He had made countless decisions in the past weeks—life-and-death calls as well as split-second choices in the heat of battle. But those had been instinctive, immediate choices he could justify to himself later.

This one was different. This one lingered.

His first thought was cold and pragmatic. If they left the wounded behind, the group would move faster, increasing their chances of survival. But his second thought, the one that gnawed at him, was with Jacks. What had been the point of everything—the fighting, the losses, the sacrifices—if, at the final stretch, they abandoned their own? If they took the easy way out?

Archer exhaled, steadying himself. He knew what he had to do.

Chapter 13

The air was thick with the scent of damp earth and petrol. A low mist clung to the ground, curling around the hulking shapes of the vehicles mustered on the hamlet's edge. It was 05.00 hrs, and the night was on the verge of breaking—a faint, greyish hue barely visible on the eastern horizon.

Archer stood near the lead truck, watching as the last of the men climbed aboard. There were thirty-eight men in total—thirty stragglers from various units, plus himself and the last eight from D Company. He had insisted they stay together. So space was a premium, and anything that wasn't essential was being thrown away.

A pair of Royal Signals men stood beside their battered wireless set; their faces were drawn as they took one last look at the thing before heaving it onto the roadside.

"Hasn't worked for days," one of them muttered, half to himself. "Should've ditched it sooner."

Archer barely acknowledged them. He was watching Jennings and Cartwright oversee the loading of the wounded. He noticed at least six men who were unable to walk, and whose stretchers were carefully wedged into the backs of two battered ambulances. Another four or five were walking wounded, limping, or nursing bandaged wounds but still fit enough to move under their own steam.

"We'll have to cram them in," Jennings grumbled, tightening the straps on a stretcher. "If we break down or take a hit, God help us."

Archer nodded but said nothing. They didn't have a choice.

Nearby, Pritchard and some of the RAF ground crew were tossing aside crates of plane parts, clearing every inch of space in the trucks.

"Nothing but what we carry," Archer had ordered.

They were down to the bare essentials—bullets, a few bandages. Even the stretchers had been stripped of blankets, leaving only the bare canvas.

Archer glanced at his watch. 0516 hours. They had to move.

He stepped onto the running board of the lead truck, turning to face the men.

"We're going hell for leather to the coast," he said, his voice carrying through the still morning air. He had briefed everyone earlier.

"If Dunkirk still stands, we've probably got four or five miles before we reach our lines. If we get split up, don't stop—just keep moving north until you see the water."

A murmur of acknowledgement rippled through the men. They were exhausted, weakened, running on adrenaline and sheer bloody-mindedness. But they were still here. Still fighting.

Archer hauled himself into the truck's cab, settling beside Pritchard. The airman driver at the wheel clenched his jaw, and his hands gripped the wheel tight enough to turn his knuckles white.

Archer took one last look at the darkened hamlet behind them, then nodded.

"Go."

The engines roared to life.

The convoy lurched forwards, tyres spitting mud and gravel as they surged into the night, leaving the wreckage of Cassel behind them.

The convoy hurtled down the damaged road, engines growling as they bounced over potholes and craters left behind by days of bombardment. The cold pre-dawn air bit at exposed skin, but no one spoke of it. They gripped their rifles, eyes scanning the darkened landscape as the vehicles rumbled towards the coast.

In the cab of the lead truck, Archer leant forwards, squinting at the road ahead as the mist curled across the fields.

Pritchard rode beside him, rifle in hand. The night had been their ally by cloaking their escape in darkness. But dawn was creeping in, stretching long fingers of pale light across the land. With it came the growing risk of discovery.

Archer's gut twisted. Every instinct screamed to keep under cover of darkness, to move only when the shadows were long. But they didn't have that luxury. If they stopped now, they'd never reach Dunkirk in time. Their best chance—maybe their only chance—was to keep going. Daylight be damned.

An itch of unease crawled along Archer's spine. The countryside had teemed with Germans just a day ago—vehicle after vehicle had thundered down the road—yet now, there was nothing: no distant engines, no patrols, no movement on the ridgelines. They pressed on as the road narrowed, winding through a ruined village where skeletal houses lined the street like broken teeth. They passed burnt-out vehicles and twisted wrecks scattered along the way, and as they moved farther north, the sight of abandoned British trucks—a remnant of a hasty retreat—deepened the unsettling silence that gripped Archer and his men.

Inside the cramped cab, Archer's tension was laced with an unnerving excitement. They were making good time, and every bump of the convoy set his heart racing. The small stream of vehicles bounced and crashed along the uneven road. The Bedford trucks rattled with each impact, their springs cracking and groaning under the strain while the Bren carriers barely faltered. Their tracks sank effortlessly into potholes and small craters as if they were devouring the shattered pavement. The relentless clatter of metal and the rhythmic, jarring movements amplified the unspoken question among the men: were they really going to make it? This mechanical symphony of strain and speed drove home the precarious nature of their retreat, leaving Archer and his companions on edge as they hurtled north towards an uncertain fate.

In the cramped, rattling interior of an ambulance, Padre Cartwright gripped his satchel with white-knuckled determination as the vehicle lurched over broken cobblestones. Each jolt and knock drew a string of curses from his weathered lips, and the vibrations made it nearly impossible to steady his hands. Amid the mingled stench of antiseptic and cordite, he knelt by a wounded soldier, frantically adjusting a bandage to a deep gash while the ambulance shuddered around him. Every bump seemed to amplify the havoc of the battlefield, yet with each profane remark, Cartwright's focus sharpened—his care for the injured was a small but fierce defiance against the relentless violence outside.

In the open truck under a clearing sky, Jacks and RSM Jennings shared a cigarette as the engine's steady drone mingled with the quiet tension of the retreat. Jacks exhaled a slow plume of smoke while Jennings muttered a low curse at each jolt that rocked the truck along the shattered road. For a few stolen moments, their eyes wandered over the desolate landscape until both men caught sight of two looming silhouettes in the sky: two Messerschmitts. Their dark forms cut sharply against the brightening daylight. In that silent exchange, the simple act of sharing a cigarette became a wordless acknowledgement: even in brief reprieves, the threat of the enemy was never far away. Almost instantly, their shared gaze hardened into resolve as they sprang into action, ready to counter the sudden intrusion.

Both men immediately began shouting warnings. Jacks pounded on the cab roof, trying to alert its occupants while Jennings waved his arms frantically at the truck behind, signalling it to pull off the road. Pritchard was seated next to Archer and leant out of the window to see what the commotion was.

"Plane! Get off the road!" Jacks screamed at him.

"Get off the road!" Pritchard yelled, turning directly to the airman driving the truck.

The airman looked at him as if the command were unintelligible. Realising the gravity of the threat, Archer bellowed, "Get off the bloody road!"

The airman swung the wheel sharply to the left. Screaming in protest, the truck grated and jolted at the sudden, violent manoeuvre. It slammed into the verge with such force that the vehicle and its contents were briefly thrown into the air; the truck swayed and rocked wildly as if caught in a stormy sea. The airman struggled desperately to regain control of the beast; his efforts were drowned out by the cacophony of metal and alarm.

The rest of the convoy, witnessing the lead truck pull off the road so suddenly, quickly realised something was wrong. One by one, vehicles began swerving off the road, scrambling into the neighbouring fields just as the two fighter planes began their dive towards the scattering convoy. The drone of the Messerschmitts grew louder and fiercer as they closed in.

"Troops out!" shouted the drivers in the trucks and carriers, and it was a cry repeated several times by Archer, Jacks, and anyone else who carried any semblance of command.

Padre Cartwright had finally steadied himself after being violently tossed about in the ambulance as it had struggled to get off the road. Leaning forwards, he reached for the handle of the back door, squinting against the bright light streaming in. Instantly, he became aware of the engines' growls, followed by the rapid zipping of the two 7.92 mm MG17 machine-guns and the thudding blast of the 20 mm cannon mounted in the nose. Then came the inevitable splutter of earth as each round tore through the ground, carving its path with relentless force.

Cartwright froze as he watched the barrage progress—first striking a carrier, then a truck parked ahead. He witnessed each round hitting the engine compartment and shattering the windscreen before a burst of flame erupted from the engine bay. An explosion roared as something struck the fuel tank, sending flames shooting skyward.

Jacks forced himself into a shallow depression in the ground as he watched the first strike hit, immediately followed by a second plane unleashing a burst of machine-gun and cannon fire. This time, the German return fire was only slightly off-target for the vehicles but not for the poor souls who had dove for cover.

Jacks watched in grim horror as each bullet and shell from the plane's guns tore through the signallers who had leapt from their carrier. He saw, in excruciating detail, how each impact split a man's back open like a butcher's knife slicing through meat, and then he witnessed one man's head explode in an instant gory mess of brain and bone.

Archer looked up, his breath catching as he took in the burning wreckage of the truck, flames licking hungrily at its frame. The second plane was already climbing, its dark exhaust trail lingering in the sky, leaving nothing but devastation.

"Stay down!" he bellowed, raw with urgency. He remained crouched, eyes tracking the aircraft as it ascended: waiting, watching, to see if it would return. The seconds stretched, each heartbeat loud in his ears. But the plane kept climbing, banking away into the haze. Archer exhaled sharply, steeling himself. The lull wouldn't last.

"On your feet!" he ordered, rising as he cast a sharp glance over his men. "Rally up. We need to get moving."

Padre Cartwright, ever determined to help, hurried towards the signallers but found all three lying lifeless. Their bodies were contorted in grotesque angles from the impact. He knelt, murmuring a short prayer, and then began to remove their dog tags. Archer approached and saw Padre Cartwright engaged in his sombre duty —a task he had become all too familiar with over the past few weeks.

Meanwhile, Jacks, feeling the searing heat from the burning Bedford lorry on his back, watched as the men clambered up into the remaining vehicles. With space at a premium in both the truck and the carrier, many were forced to stand.

Inside one of the ambulances, Padre Cartwright had returned to methodically tend to the wounded, his hands remained steady despite the grim task at hand. Archer appeared at the open door, his eyes scanning the chaos beyond. For a fleeting moment, their gazes met—a silent, shared acknowledgement of the burdens they carried. Cartwright offered a tired, rueful smile that spoke of countless similar moments while Archer's half-smile conveyed both respect and his unyielding determination.

"Is there anything you need, Padre?" Archer asked in a low, earnest tone, knowing that aside from friendship, he had little more to offer.

Cartwright shook his head slowly; his voice was soft yet firm. "Tom, you're doing all you can now. I just pray that God gives you the will to get us home and that wound stays clean." He was referring to the cut on Archer's face that he had stitched up a few days earlier.

Archer raised a hand to his face; aside from an odd stinging sensation, he had nearly forgotten about the wound. In that brief exchange, amid the relentless turmoil of war, it was clear these two men were forging a bond—a camaraderie born of hardship.

"I'll do my best, Padre," Archer said with a low smile before he turned back to the lead truck, hoping that, indeed, God would get them home.

The acrid scent of burning fuel and scorched earth still clung to the air as Archer, recalling the padre's words, gently touched the stitched wound on his cheek. The men were gathering, shaken but alive, and as the initial chaos settled, Jacks strode over, his expression grim.

"We lost five, Sir," he said without preamble. His voice was steady, but Archer could see the tension in his jaw.

"Henderson, Clark, and Wilkes—the signallers. Mercer and Fraser, two lads from the Warwicks. Caught in the truck."

Archer felt the weight of the words settle over him, heavier than the kit on his back. Five more dead under his command.

He forced it down. There were more names to write in the book.

He nodded once. "Alright. Get the lads squared away. We'll move soon."

Archer found Jennings near the carrier he had been organising a tow for. The Regimental Sergeant Major looked up as Archer approached, brushing mud from his uniform with a sharp motion before stepping forwards.

"Mr. Archer," Jennings greeted, brushing the last of the mud from his hands. "She's still good," he added with a slight nod towards the carrier. "Which is something."

Archer leant against the battered hull, letting out a breath. "Well done, RSM," he said, meaning it. Then, quieter, "Jacks just gave me the rundown. Five dead."

Jennings exhaled, rubbing a hand over his unshaven jaw. "Then we're down to thirty-three. Three stretcher cases, eight walking wounded—useless in a fight. That leaves twenty-two fit and able."

He met Archer's gaze. "It goes without saying, Sir, they're knackered."

All around, the men were reboarding the remaining trucks and carriers—some already crammed inside, others waiting their turn or helping the wounded up. A few lingered nearby with their weapons slung and uneasy voices stirred among them. Not panic but real concern he turned, following their gaze to the distant sky.

A large formation of aircraft were moving in from the east.

Archer pulled out his binoculars, scanning the sky. He counted silently at first, then aloud.

"Nineteen...twenty...twenty-one..." He trailed off as the final number settled in his mind.

The formation held steady. It was a dark swarm against the pale sky. Then, all at once, their bomb doors yawned open.

German Dorniers. The twin tails gave them away.

The rumble of distant explosions followed seconds later, rolling towards them like approaching thunder. Archer lowered the binoculars, turning sharply to Jennings.

"Jacks, over here."

Jacks came running and stood next to the RSM, exhaling hard.

"Yes, Sir?"

"Well, that tells me one thing. Dunkirk is not lost if they're still attacking it from the air!" He continued.

"The real issue is, we need to know what's ahead before we make any more moves," Archer said, straightening. "I want a recce done. If we're going to push on, we need to be sure what's ahead of us."

He glanced towards the horizon where a dark plume of smoke signalled their destination. "I can't imagine Jerry has left the door open for us."

Turning back, Archer gestured to Jacks. "Go get Pritchard and Webb. We'll take the carrier and see what's down this road."

Jacks gave a curt nod and set off to find them.

Archer turned to the RSM and spoke with a firm tone. "Mr. Jennings, take charge of the men." He pointed towards a deep hedgerow to their left. "Move the vehicles and lay up along that hedgerow as best you can. If we're not back within the hour or you run into trouble—" He hesitated, then exhaled. "Well, it's up to you. Every man for himself. Surrender, make a break for it—your call."

Jennings, almost taken aback by Archer's blunt instruction, took a moment before responding. He studied the young officer, then gave a small nod. "Sir, something tells me you'll be back."

Archer flashed a quick smile and shook the RSM's hand. "Good luck, Mr. Jennings."

Not waiting for a reply, he turned and clambered into the Bren Carrier, dropping onto the metal bench as Pritchard fired up the engine. Archer tapped Pritchard on the shoulder and said, "Let's go."

The carrier was a fast, nimble beast—lighter than a tank but just as determined. Its low-slung frame hugged the ground, and its engine growled as Pritchard pushed the throttle forwards. The treads clattered over the uneven dirt, a rhythmic clanking that underscored their urgency.

Unlike the trucks or heavier transports, the Bren Carrier could move like a scalded cat. It bounced and skidded over rough terrain, fast enough to outrun trouble but sturdy enough to punch through obstacles. The open top gave Archer an unobstructed view of the road ahead as the wind whipped him, and the machine roared forwards.

Jacks sat up front beside Pritchard. His rifle was balanced across his knees, and his eyes scanning the hedgerows ahead. "If we're walking into a mess, I'd rather be in this than on foot," he muttered, shifting slightly as the carrier jostled over the rough ground.

Behind him, Webb gripped his Bren gun tight, resting it against the side of the vehicle, ready to swing it up at a moment's notice. He exhaled and gave a mock sigh of relief.

"Well, this is a bloody revelation. All that marching, and it turns out we had these the whole time? Someone owes me a refund on my boots." Archer gave a tight smile but said nothing. His focus remained ahead with his eyes locked on the road winding towards the unknown.

The distant thump of artillery rolled towards them, low and steady. Archer tensed.

"Pritchard, get us off the road. Make for the trees—we'll move in on foot."

Pritchard didn't hesitate. The carrier lurched to the right, bumping over uneven ground as it pushed into the cover of the trees.

The carrier rolled to a halt at the edge of a tree line, its engine idling softly. Archer dismounted first, moving low through the undergrowth with his rifle at the ready. The others followed, careful not to disturb the thick foliage. They reached a small rise overlooking the road ahead where the ground sloped gently down towards the enemy position.

Archer raised his binoculars, adjusting the focus as he peered through the branches. What he saw made his stomach tighten.

A German artillery position was dug into the roadside. It was well protected by sandbags and camouflaged netting. Three field guns—likely 10.5 cm leFH 18 howitzers—were positioned to fire towards Dunkirk. Their crews moved with practiced efficiency. Two Sd.Kfz. 251 half-tracks flanked the position; each of them was equipped with a mounted MG42 covering the road. A makeshift command post—little more than a tent and a field table—sat nearby, where officers huddled around a radio.

Infantry were scattered throughout the area. Some were manning machine-gun nests while others rested near supply crates. None seemed particularly alert.

Jacks, crouched beside Archer, let out a low whistle. "Well, that's a bloody fortress."

Pritchard pointed towards the half-tracks. "Those things will shred us if we don't take them out fast."

Webb, scanning for weaknesses, noted the spacing between

the artillery crews and the infantry. "They're spread thin," he said. "If we hit them hard and fast, they might not recover in time."

Crawling back to the carrier, Archer and Jacks moved swiftly through the undergrowth, their breath tight in their chests. The close thump of artillery shook the ground beneath them. It was a steady drumbeat of destruction rolling towards Dunkirk.

By the time they reached the convoy, the men had settled into a makeshift defensive position. Some clutched their weapons tightly, others hovered near the trucks and ambulances, shifting uneasily. Tension thickened the air, every man waiting for the next decision.

Eyes turned as the carrier rumbled in, and Archer and Jacks leapt out before it had even stopped. They strode towards RSM Jennings, who emerged from the hedgerow where he'd taken position, his expression unreadable.

"We don't have much time. Jacks, get the padre," Archer ordered, scanning the lorries and ambulances.

The padre arrived quickly. His face mirrored the exhaustion they all felt. He gave Archer a nod, understanding without words that something was coming.

Archer wasted no time, briefing Jennings and the padre on what they had seen at the German artillery position. When he finished, he took a steadying breath.

"As I see it, we've got three choices," he said, his voice low but firm. "We surrender to the guns and hope for the best. We split up, every man for himself. Or..." he exhaled sharply. "We break through."

Silence stretched between them, the weight of the decision settling. Archer's gaze flicked between the three men—waiting, testing.

Jennings was the first to speak. "If we want to get the wounded through, we need to break through. That's my thinking, Sir."

Jacks nodded with unwavering loyalty. "If that's your call, Sir, I'm with you."

Archer turned to the padre. "Padre?"

Cartwright met his gaze without hesitation. "Tom, you're the soldier. I'll follow your lead."

Archer knelt in the turf, one knee pressing into the cold earth as he gathered the remaining men of D Company around him. There were only nine of them left. Once, they'd been a full fighting force. Now, they were a handful of survivors, bruised, bloodied, and running out of luck—but still standing. Still fighting.

He swept his gaze over them. These were the men who would make or break this desperate charge.

Jacks knelt beside him, rolling his shoulders, his usual easy smirk absent. He'd been Archer's shadow from the start, always ready, always steady. No need to ask if he was in; Jacks was there.

Wilson and Saunders crouched together, rifles resting across their knees. Wilson, a wiry man with sharp eyes and a sharp tongue, had been with them from the beginning. Saunders the quiet youngster, was a man who had overcome great fear to be one of the bravest men, but he clearly missed the fatherly figure of Mallory.

A little farther off, Pritchard checked his rifle, methodical as ever. As the best shot in the battalion, he never spoke more than necessary, but when he did, his words carried weight. His poacher's eye had saved them more than once, and it would need to again.

Beside him, O'Hara tightened his grip on his kit, a flicker of tension in his jaw, still holding onto the edge of fear, but it hadn't stopped him from stepping up when it counted. He'd been a solid hand from the start and had never let Jacks down.

Webb sat back on his haunches with the Bren gun resting across his lap. His fingers drummed against the barrel. The man lived for the noise of battle, always eager for a fight, but he knew when to take it seriously. He fiddled with one of his ammunition pouches.

At the edge of the group, Brookes was knelt...not a D company man, but he had volunteered to defend Cassel to the last when D Company were given the task. He had been a quiet man and wasn't one to waste words. But when it came down to it, he could be counted on to hold his ground.

And finally, Matthews who shifted his weight and was streaked with dirt. He was an engineer, their fixer, the man who could make things work when everything was falling apart. He'd patched up trucks, bridges, and men alike. And now, he'd help patch together their one last shot at getting out.

Archer drew a rough map in the dirt with his bayonet. "This is how we do it—fast and hard." His voice was steady, but the weight of what was coming pressed down on every man.

"Matthews, Saunders, Webb—you're with me in the first Bren Carrier." His eyes flicked towards the stragglers. Jennings had gathered men from broken units, and now they were being thrown into one last fight. Archer focused on two of them, both wearing the insignia of the Royal Sussex Regiment.

"Holloway, Corporal Adams—you're with us. Stay close and follow my lead."

Holloway, a lean, sharp-faced rifleman, gave a quick nod, while Adams, slightly older, adjusted the sling on his Lee-Enfield. Neither hesitated. They'd lost their units, but they still had a fight to finish.

His gaze shifted to Jacks. "Jacks, you take Wilson, O'Hara, Pritchard, and McBride, he's one of the lads Jennings' picked up, and take them in the second carrier. We hit the guns first, disrupt them, cause hell—hopefully giving the RSM the chance he needs."

Archer turned to Jennings. "Mr. Jennings, you lead the convoy. Keep the trucks moving and have every man ready to fight. If any of us stop, we're finished."

He pulled his binoculars from inside his battledress and passed them over. "You'll have to pick your moment. Watch the roadblock. When we hit them hard and you see your chance, you move."

Jennings took them without hesitation, adjusting the focus as he scanned the horizon. "If you cause enough noise, we should make it."

Archer turned to Webb and Pritchard, lowering his voice. "You two set up here, along the treeline." Archer dragged his bayonet through the dirt, marking the line.

"Webb, you provide covering fire with your Bren—expending everything you have. No point in saving anything now." He allowed himself a brief, grim smile before adding, "Pritchard, you do what you do best. Focus on their machine-guns if you can."

A sullen pause followed before Archer added, "You two will be on your own up there."

Webb adjusted the Bren across his knee. "Wouldn't be the first time, Sir."

Archer acknowledged the remark with a glance but pressed on. "As soon as we hit the guns, get down there fast. Once you're with us, we get back in the carriers, and we get the hell out!"

Pritchard gave a slow nod, calm as ever. "We'll provide cover until you're in position. Trust me, Sir—we'll be right with you."

Archer exhaled. "Right. No second chances. We break through, or we don't get through at all."

Jennings tucked the binoculars under his arm. "You take care of the guns. We'll punch through the gap."

Almost out of nowhere, the calm and familiar voice of the padre cut through the tension. "Lieutenant...and what shall I do?"

The small group turned as one; some looked him in quiet bewilderment while others were just impressed that the padre was asking.

Archer looked at him with respect and, without missing a beat, replied, "Sir, you can pray for us—and hold the fuck on!"

The grin that broke across Archer's face was contagious. Laughter rippled through the men, some patting the padre on the back as they turned towards their positions. The moment of levity cut through the tension like a blade. In another world, it might have been a joke that lasted longer. But in this one, they had a battle to fight.

Chapter 14

In the distance, the sky over Dunkirk was on fire.

Thick, black plumes of smoke clawed at the heavens, twisting like grotesque fingers as the inferno of burning ships and shattered dockyards raged beyond the horizon. The air, which was thick with the acrid stench of fuel and scorched wood, was being carried inland by the same wind that carried the dull, distant rumble of bombs falling on the beaches.

The British Expeditionary Force was dying by inches—holding the last line and bleeding to buy time for those still scrambling to escape. But Archer wasn't there. He wasn't on the beaches, and there was no warship waiting for him.

The war was still here. Right in front of him.

Archer wasn't looking at Dunkirk. He barely even registered the drone of Luftwaffe bombers prowling high above the beaches. None of it mattered.

The war was right in front of him.

He crouched low in the carrier which stood just short of the treeline, and his fingers gripped its cold, metal side. In his other hand, he clutched his rifle. The bayonet was fixed. One final scan.

Webb and Pritchard were already in position—somewhere up ahead, crouched low behind a fallen tree, the Bren gun loaded and ready.

Across the field, nestled in a shallow depression, lay the German artillery position.

The three field guns stood in a staggered line, their long barrels angled skyward, belching fire and destruction towards the sea. The crews worked in rhythm, shovelling shells into place: loading, firing, and reloading again—fast, mechanical, relentless.

Straddling the road, two half-tracks sat idle just beyond the guns. Their crews were alert but still at ease—watching, waiting.

They weren't expecting trouble. They thought the British were finished. They were about to be very, very wrong.

Archer glanced over his shoulder towards the other carrier where he could see Jacks twisting his hand on the steel armour with his fingers drumming against the surface. The engines were growling now, revving like caged animals, but their noise was covered by the relentless explosions from the guns. Inside the armoured hulls, his men clung to whatever they could, each one steeling themselves for the madness about to unfold.

Webb knelt behind the fallen tree, the Bren's bipod resting on the damp, slowly decomposing bark. Three yards to his left, Pritchard lay prone. His breathing was steady, slow, controlled. His cheek pressed against the stock of his rifle as he adjusted the iron sight to 200 yards to focus a German soldier smoking a cigarette with one hand resting on the machine-gun, and the other leaning against the armoured hull of a half-track.

The gunner wasn't paying attention. He was watching the artillery crews and probably admiring their precision as the field guns belched fire with spent brass casings tumbling to the ground while another round slid smoothly into the breech. A lanyard was yanked hard—and with a sudden burst of flame and thunder, the shell screamed skywards.

Webb licked his lips. His grip tightened.

"You set, Prit?"

A barely audible, "Yes" came in response. Pritchard never shifted his aim.

Webb exhaled calmly as if he were taking an afternoon stroll through the park.

"Fire."

Crack. The German machine-gunner dropped immediately and folded over the weapon.

Archer's mouth was dry. He swallowed hard and gave the only order that mattered.

"Go!"

The world exploded into motion

The Bren gun was roaring to life. Webb's first burst raked across the nearest gun crew. The lead German artilleryman was ripped from his feet, and his body jerked as rounds tore into his chest. The others dived for cover, but there was no time.

255

Another burst clattered into the stack of shells beside the gun, sending shrapnel flying in all directions.

Pritchard was already training on the machine-gun of the second half-track. Crack. Pritchard saw the bullet ricochet vertically off the armour, and he immediately reloaded, adjusted and crack. This time he made certain and watched the machine-gunner twist as he fell back.

Then came the charge.

The carriers lunged forwards, tracks churning up dirt and grass. Their engines howled as they hurtled down the incline towards the enemy position. Clinging to the metal frames, the men had their rifles clenched in white-knuckled grips, and their teeth bared as the vehicles lurched violently over the uneven ground.

Archer could barely hear himself think: the deafening roar of engines, the hammering of the Bren, and the rising screams of Germans all merged into one chaotic symphony of battle.

Suddenly, the MG42 opened up.

A hidden machine-gun position—set precisely to defend the artillery—erupted in a stream of fire, sending a blistering line of rounds towards the onrushing carriers.

Bullets shrieked against the armour. Sparks flew as the driver hunched lower, instinctively trying to avoid catching a stray round.

"Hold on!" Archer bellowed.

Another burst. A second, harder impact.

This time, the rounds didn't just ping harmlessly away.

Corporal Adams jerked violently. He'd been hit twice in the chest. Slumping against the armour, his rifle slipped from his grasp, and his eyes were wide but already unfocused.

Archer saw it: the life left him in an instant. But there was no time—no way to stop, no way to mourn. Adams was gone.

The target was now only yards away.

Then. Impact.

The first carrier, Jacks' carrier, smashed into the nearest gun crew.

A German barely had time to turn before the treads ground him into the dirt, the hull slamming into a stack of wooden ammunition crates. Splinters and brass shells exploded outwards as the carrier ploughed through.

With his rifle raised, Archer didn't even register the full impact before he was moving—leaping from his carrier as it skidded to a halt

A flash of movement. He fired.

A German crumpled, clutching his throat.

Saunders was already there with his bayonet thrusting deep into the belly of a gunner whose hand was on the lanyard. The man had no idea. One second, he was about to fire—the next, he was staring down at the British steel buried in his gut.

Immediately ripping the blade free, Saunders turned, fired—his Lee-Enfield kicking against his shoulder as a second German fell. A red mist sprayed the sandbags behind him.

Holloway and Matthews were already charging towards the third gun. Both men had only one thought: get to that gun.

Jacks and his men bailed out of the carrier. Their boots hit the ground hard as they scrambled over splintered ammunition crates and charged towards the gun crew. Bayonets gleamed relentlessly in the midday light. Jacks had already dropped one German before his feet even hit the ground—his first rifle shot punched clean through the chest of a gunner who had barely begun to turn.

To his right, Wilson and O'Hara smashed into the second

gun crew. Their bayonets drove deep into the first men they reached. A group of German infantry, who were scattered behind the guns and sandbag emplacements, frantically tried to organise themselves, scrambling for cover and weapons, desperate to stem the oncoming assault.

Jacks didn't give them the chance.

He sprinted through the gun smoke. His rifle was slung up, and the bayonet was ready as the nearest German officer fumbled for his sidearm. Jacks lunged—his bayonet punching up under the ribs. The German let out a strangled gasp, and his pistol clattered uselessly onto the dirt. Jacks ripped the blade free, blood spraying onto his uniform. He barely noticed.

To his left, Wilson took aim from a crouch. He fired one, two, three well-placed shots, dropping another German just as he reached for the gun's breach to take cover. The man crumpled. His blood smeared across the hot metal.

"Move up! Take the bastards out!" Jacks roared. His voice was raw with brutality, but there was no triumph in it—only necessity. The clash was savage, fought in breathless gasps and bayonet thrusts, where hesitation meant death. Every blow landed at arm's length. Every scream was close enough to feel. It was a fight they hadn't asked for, but one they couldn't back away from.

Wilson barrelled into another German. His bayonet struck high into the man's collarbone, but the enemy was still fighting.

The German lashed out with a boot, sending Wilson stumbling back before swinging wildly with the butt of his Kar98k rifle. O'Hara fired from the hip, his round punching through the German's throat to cut off his battle cry in an instant.

Jacks glanced back. McBride was reloading, fumbling slightly as he worked the bolt, but the fight at the guns was over.

Then the gunfire changed.

The infantry had regrouped.

Jacks barely had a second to take it in before bullets snapped past him. The sharp crack of Kar98k rifles and the rattling bursts of MP40 submachine-guns forced them into cover.

The Germans were organised and fighting back—hard.

The charge was over. Now, it was a gunfight.

Jacks drove forwards with Wilson was beside him, and both men hunched low as they sprinted to the sandbags.

Jacks reached the nearest German who was crouched behind cover. His rifle swung in a savage arc before the butt cracked into the man's face, splintering bone. The German toppled backwards, groaning in pain.

Jacks didn't finish him off. No time.

He and Wilson threw themselves behind the sandbags, pressing low as bullets ripped through the air. The two sides were locked in a brutal exchange of fire.

The gunfight had barely begun when the half-tracks finally reacted. For a moment, it was just rifle fire snapping through the smoke with men firing from cover: the desperate, brutal exchange of a fight that could go either way.

Jacks and Wilson fought to keep the Germans pinned. Their backs pressed into the sandbags as rounds bit into the earth around them, but it was clear—they weren't breaking the enemy fast enough. Then came the roar of the MG42s.

A sudden burst of fire from the nearest half-track ripped through the British position, stitching a line of devastation across the sandbags. McBride was still running for cover behind one of the guns when the rounds caught him. He never stood a chance. The MG42 chewed through him, his body jerking violently, and he collapsed hard against the base of the gun, lifeless. The British dived for cover.

Then—the second half-track opened fire. The combined fire was murderous. O'Hara popped up to take a shot—and in the same instant, the second MG42 spat a burst of lead straight into him. His rifle flew from his hands as he crashed backwards, dead before he hit the ground.

Holloway crouched beside him and flinched as blood sprayed across his sleeve, but there was no time to process it. More fire ripped into their position. Sandbags exploded into the air. Bullets tore through them like paper, rounds whizzing so close that Jacks could feel them tug the air past his face.

Archer saw it all. From where he knelt behind the first gun, he saw McBride drop. He saw Jacks and Wilson barely keeping their heads down. He saw the half-tracks repositioning, their gunners sweeping the field, locking down the British advance. And that's when it hit him.

They were losing momentum. The charge had stalled, and in seconds, the Germans would have full control of the fight. The firefight had turned against them. The half-tracks were the problem. Their combined fire was like a scythe, cutting down anyone who moved, and Archer's men's rifles weren't enough to suppress them. Unless they found a way to disable the Germans' MG42s, they were going to be pinned down and picked apart. Archer's heart pounded against his ribs. This wasn't how they were going to die.

Not here. Not now.

The gunfire raged across the battlefield. Tracer rounds streaked through the light smoke as the MG42s from the half-tracks continued to tear into the British position. In the treeline, Webb gritted his teeth, watching the chaos unfold.

"Come on, Prit," he said urgently, yanking the Bren's bipod from the fallen tree. "We should've gone by now. We need to get to Archer!" He turned to move, but Pritchard didn't follow.

Webb stopped, glancing back. Pritchard was still prone, rifle steady, breath slow and controlled, eyes locked on the half-tracks. He wasn't moving.

"Prit?" Webb frowned.

Pritchard exhaled. His cheek pressed against the rifle stock. It was a movement he'd done hundreds of times, both in civilian life and now in war.

"You go," he said, his voice calm, steady. "I'll be right behind you."

Webb stared at him, and the gunfire around them faded for a second. "Prit, don't be daft. Let's go!"

Pritchard didn't move. His finger settled near the trigger. He repeated the words, quieter this time. "I'll be right behind you. Just go."

Webb froze, torn between orders and instinct. He could see it now—the way Pritchard was lying, the way his eyes didn't leave his sights. This wasn't hesitation. This was a decision. Webb's jaw clenched. He wanted to argue, to drag Pritchard away if he had to, but there wasn't time. He forced himself to nod.

"Alright, Prit. I'll see you down there."

With that, Webb turned and ran, sprinting down the rise towards the mayhem at the guns.

Pritchard adjusted his rifle with minute precision. His sight moved to the gunner on the first half-track. His expression never changed. t was just the solid stare of a man who had made his decision. He released his breath slowly. The stock was firm in his shoulder with the familiar pressure of the trigger against his finger.

The nearest half-track's mounted MG42 swept back and forth, ripping into the British position. Wilson was pinned and forced low against the sandbags with his rifle useless against the sheer weight of bullets tearing through his cover. And just beyond him—Archer.

Pritchard could see the lieutenant yelling, gesturing, trying to rally the men, but the battle was slipping out of his hands. He tightened his grip, steadied his breathing, and lined up the shot.

The German gunner was oblivious, focused entirely on pouring fire into the British position. His hands gripped the MG42 firmly, and his face twisted in the thrill of destruction.

Exhale.

Pritchard squeezed the trigger.

The rifle cracked. The recoil slammed into his shoulder.

Through the scope, he saw the round punch clean through the German's throat. The man jerked back violently, and his hands spasmed off the MG42; the gun tilted uselessly before he slumped forwards into the hull.

One half-track was momentarily silenced.

Pritchard worked the bolt, ejected the smoking casing, and immediately shifted his aim.

The gunner on the second half-track had seen what had happened. He shouted to his driver, ordering him to swing the vehicle around. The half-track lurched, grinding into a ninety-degree turn, and its turret-mounted MG42 swivelled towards the treeline. Pritchard could see the gunner searching for him, but the man's eyes had locked onto something else: Webb. The gunner saw the lone soldier sprinting down the rise, clearly mistaking him for the sniper. He took aim. The first burst of fire ripped into the dirt, kicking up a spray of mud and earth in front of Webb.

Pritchard didn't hesitate. The second burst never came.

A British .303 bullet punched clean through the gunner's skull, scrambling his brain in an instant. His body crumpled sideways, hitting the cold steel of the armour before sliding lifelessly to the ground.

Pritchard worked the bolt, chambered another round, and swung his rifle back to the first half-track. The newly-manned MG42 was just coming to life—another German had scrambled to replace his fallen comrade. Pritchard took his time.

He fired. The man jerked violently. Another poor victim to

Pritchard's expertise with a rifle at two hundred yards.

From his position in the treeline, Pritchard was single-handedly dismantling the German half-tracks. His skill with a rifle at 200 yards had turned the tide of the battle. Each shot was measured, precise. A deliberate execution. The first gunner never saw it coming. Neither did the second.

Now, the field had changed. The machine-guns that had held the British pinned were silent. Their operators were dead, and the hulking vehicles were suddenly vulnerable. Yet Pritchard wasn't finished. He chambered another round, steadied his heartbeat and fixed his eyes on the battlefield. There were still threats, still Germans scrambling to recover, and he was going to keep them down as long as he could.

A few hundred yards back, RSM Jennings stood rigid with his binoculars pressed to his eyes and locked on the distant battlefield. He couldn't see Pritchard working his rifle, but he could see the results. The half-tracks had been distracted. Their gunners had shifted focus, no longer guarding the road but turning to deal with the British assault on the guns.

The convoy had been waiting with engines idling, and the men's rifles were at the ready as they watched the gunfire erupt ahead. The plan had always been to charge forwards once Archer and Jacks caused the distraction.

Jennings clenched his jaw. The second half-track was moving, crossing the road. This was the moment. He leant forwards and banged on the lorry cab's roof.

"Move!"

Spinning to the lorry behind him, he snapped his arm forwards, repeating the order. Turning back, he slammed a fist on the cab once more and roared, "Come on! Let's go!"

The truck lurched into motion, the driver slamming his boot onto the accelerator, shifting gears hard into second. The wheels hit the ruts in the road, bouncing violently as the truck gained speed. Its suspension groaned under the strain. Jennings and another soldier leant over the cab with their rifles braced, pointing forwards and scanning ahead. In the back, the men who could still fight held their rifles ready, covering every direction.

The convoy was rolling now, two lorries and the ambulances crashing over the uneven road, jolting as they hit every pothole and ridge. Every man was focused on what lay ahead, hoping—praying—this was going to work.

In the last vehicle, Padre Cartwright sat rigid in the ambulance's passenger seat, gripping the dashboard to steady himself against the relentless bouncing. The old soldier behind the wheel barely flinched. His eyes were on the road, and his hands were tight on the wheel. Cartwright swallowed, then bowed his head for the briefest of moments, murmuring a silent prayer.

Not for himself. For the men around him—the able and the wounded alike. For all of them. He hoped this was going to work.

The trucks continued to roar forwards, bouncing violently over the rutted road. Jennings gritted his teeth and braced himself against the lorry cab with his rifle at the ready. The convoy wasn't slowing down. Ahead, the battlefield was a swirling chaos of smoke, fire, and gunfire, but Archer's assault on the guns had done exactly what they needed.

The Germans were too distracted to notice the convoy. The enemy's focus was locked on Archer's men, their officers were shouting, scrambling to recover from the shock of the attack. Some Germans turned as the convoy thundered through. Snapping off wild, ineffective shots they had no time to properly react.

A few bullets clattered off the lorries. A round shattered a side mirror, and another punched through the canvas of the rear truck, but nothing stopped the momentum. Jennings didn't flinch.

"Keep moving!" he bellowed over the roar of the engines.

The convoy wasn't stopping. Padre Cartwright ducked instinctively as a round whined past the ambulance, but the driver beside him didn't even blink; his hands remained tight on the wheel, driving straight through the storm of chaos ahead.

Jennings glanced over his shoulder, checking the other lorries: they were still moving, and the men in the back had their rifles gripped tightly. Their eyes were darting over the battlefield, waiting for something to stop them.

Nothing did. Then—they were through.

The worst of the fire faded behind them. The shouts of German officers grew distant as the convoy tore down the open road beyond the killing field. Jennings exhaled sharply but didn't relax. They had made it through the first gauntlet, but they weren't safe yet. He turned, looking ahead towards the route to Dunkirk. They still had miles to go.

But for now—they were still alive.

Archer watched the convoy tearing through and slammed another round into his rifle. He pressed low behind the German artillery piece, and his breath was ragged with exertion. The fight had descended into a brutal, desperate exchange of fire, and for the past few minutes, it had felt like they were on the verge of losing it.

But something had changed. He frowned, scanning the battlefield. The ringing in his ears did little to drown out the crack of rifles, and the distant echoes of German voices barking orders. The machine-guns had stopped.

For the first time since the charge, there was a lull. Not silence, not yet, but a shift. The MG42s were no longer shredding everything in sight.

This wasn't victory; it was opportunity. Archer turned to Jacks, who was crouched behind a sandbagged wall, reloading. "Jacks!"

Jacks was still catching his breath, but he wiped the sweat and dirt from his face and managed to respond, "Sir!"

Archer glanced up again, squinting through the smoke and haze. He could still see enemy movement, but something was off. The Germans were less aggressive, more hesitant.

"Those machine-guns..." Archer muttered. "They're down."

Jacks frowned, quickly peering over the sandbags. "Not for long I bet!"

Archer nodded knowing several things. Firstly, he didn't have the men or the ammunition to win this fight. He looked around at his men—Wilson, Holloway, Saunders—all waiting for the next move, all knowing they couldn't hold this position forever.

Suddenly, there was movement from the ridge. Archer caught a glimpse of a lone figure darting down towards them. Webb.

He was breathless, covered in dirt, and his Bren gun was swinging left to right. But he was alive.

Chapter 15

The Bren Carrier lurched forwards, its tracks grinding over loose gravel as Wilson pushed the throttle hard. The engine roared, belching black smoke as they sped towards the convoy. Jennings' trucks were barely visible through the lingering dust and haze of battle ahead. Archer gritted his teeth with one hand braced against the hull, and his rifle clutched tight in the other. Every instinct told him to keep his head low, but his eyes remained locked on the road ahead.

Archer could see the lorries were still intact with their engines idling as the first shapes of British troops came into view. Men were crouched behind their vehicles, rifles at the ready and eyes scanning the battlefield for movement. They had seen Archer's carrier coming, but no one had relaxed. No one knew if Germans were right behind them.

Jennings stood beside the lead truck, binoculars in hand, face set in grim determination. At the sight of the carrier, he lowered them sharply and strode forwards, his heavy boots crunching over dirt and stone.

Archer barely waited for the carrier to roll to a stop before vaulting off the side, hitting the ground running. The air was thick with the smell of smoke, sweat, and exhaustion.

"Mr Jennings get them off the road!" Archer's voice was sharp, urgent. "We're too exposed here!"

Jennings gave a curt nod, already thinking the same. He turned and bellowed over his shoulder, "Get those trucks off the bloody road! Into the tree line! Now!"

The order sent the convoy into frantic motion. Drivers threw their trucks into gear, and engines growled as they swerved towards the nearest tree line—a thin strip of cover running parallel to the road. It wasn't much, but it would get them out of immediate sight. Archer signalled to Wilson in the carrier to follow.

Archer climbed into the cab of Jennings' lorry and turned

to him. "Everyone make it?"

"Sir, yes, Sir!" Jennings replied, the gratitude obvious in his response.

"Good," Archer continued. "The guns must have been supporting troops ahead. We can't be that far from our lines now—probably a mile or two at most."

He paused as the lorry pulled into the tree line, looking up at the sky before checking his watch. 12.19 hrs.

"The roads are out of the question." He jerked a thumb back the way they had come. "That racket we just kicked up—you can bet Jerry's got every roadblock manned and everyone ahead on alert."

Archer felt they had stretched their luck as far as it would go. The roads were likely death traps now. The Germans knew they were out here, and Archer realised his men weren't just escaping now—they were likely being hunted.

He glanced back at the vehicles and at the dozen or so men still able to fight, standing among the wounded and weary. But it was the stretcher cases that worried him most. They had already carried them through miles of hell, and some weren't going to make it much farther without the help they desperately needed.

He pinched the bridge of his nose, thinking through their options.

Staying with the vehicles and pushing through? No. Too loud, too exposed. The roads would be crawling with Germans.

Abandon the wounded and move fast? Not a chance. He wouldn't leave men behind. If it cost them time, so be it.

That left only one choice: move on foot, stick to cover, avoid the roads.

He looked at Jennings, who was watching him, waiting for the final order. Padre Cartwright was already tending to Brookes' wound. The RSM was speaking in low, steady tones, but Archer could see the worry in his face. They all knew what this meant.

It couldn't be too far to go now, but they'd probably have to take a winding route...hours of carrying men through open country in daylight when the Germans would be everywhere.

Archer ran a hand through his hair and took another deep breath. No other choice.

He turned back to Jennings and the others within earshot, his voice firm. "We'll go on foot from here. Get the men ready to move. We'll rotate stretcher bearers."

Jennings didn't hesitate. He just nodded.

But from the group, a voice spoke up. "What's the point, Sir?"

Archer turned. Lance Corporal Rawson stood there, helmet askew, face pale with exhaustion. His rifle hung loose in his grip, and his shoulders slumped.

"We're done for, aren't we? We don't even know if there's anyone left to reach."

A murmur of unease rippled through the men. Someone shifted their weight, and another rubbed a hand over their face. The thought was there, unspoken, in all of them.

Archer met the corporal's gaze. He felt it too: the exhaustion, the creeping doubt. But if he let it take hold, it would spread like rot.

"Corporal, you raise a valid point. What is the point?" Archer met the man's gaze, his voice measured but firm. "Well, here's how I see it." He paused to make sure he had their attention.

"Three weeks ago, my battalion was over three hundred strong. Today, it's what you see here." He gestured towards Jacks and the others, his jaw tightening. "Every one of us has lost men—mates. And I, for one, can't accept that what they gave was for nothing."

His temper flared as the faces of the dead flashed through his mind. He forced a breath, steadying himself.

"I get it—we're all tired. We're all scared. But if there's one way to honour the men we've lost, it's to keep going." He paused, then let the words come, raw and unfiltered.

"I... we will come back. And when we do, we'll take our vengeance on these bastards. That's why we keep going."

Archer held his gaze on the lance corporal who was clearly beginning to squirm under the direct stare.

"Well, that's that then." RSM Jennings cut through the moment, his voice brisk. "Jacks, get your lads up and moving. Corporal Rawson, with me. Let's get these stretchers sorted."

He turned to the rest of the group. "You all heard the lieutenant. We can't be sitting here all day. Let's get a wriggle on!"

The men began slinging rifles, shifting their gear as they got ready to move. Archer glanced towards Padre Cartwright, catching his eye. The padre, busy organising the wounded, looked up and gave the smallest, approving smile before returning to his work.

The sun had climbed higher. The overcast sky had given way to the warmth of a summer afternoon. As the remaining men moved onwards, fields stretched ahead in rolling waves of dark-green, brown, and pale green, crisscrossed by irrigation ditches, dirt tracks, and sunken lanes. They moved in silence: heads low, rifles ready, each step measured and deliberate.

Archer led from the front with Jennings beside him. The group stayed close to the hedgerows, and their boots were muffled by soft soil and tangled roots. Every open stretch was a risk. They moved in bursts—crouching low, sprinting in small groups of three or four, then pressing flat against the earth. Everyone held their breath, waiting for the zip of a machine-gun or the crack of a rifle.

The wounded struggled. The stretcher bearers rotated

every fifteen minutes, sweat trickling down their faces. The men carrying the worst of the wounded stared into the abyss, exhaustion pressing heavier with every step.

No one spoke—not unless they had to. At times, the low moans of the wounded broke the silence. Considering their pain and suffering, this was to be expected. Archer paused, acknowledging not just their endurance, but that these men were of an outstanding character, resilient beyond measure.

They moved through the signs of past battles. At one point, there was a burnt-out French truck lying half-buried in a ditch, its cab melted to slag. Bullet holes pockmarked the metal, and blackened corpses were still inside. It was a reminder of what happened to those caught in the open and at the mercy of the Luftwaffe.

They pushed on.

A hedgerow ahead loomed thick and unforgiving. It was a tangled mass of brambles, twisted roots, and dense undergrowth. There was no easy way through. Archer ran a hand over the foliage, feeling the tangle of thorns and branches. No gaps. No clear openings.

Jennings exhaled sharply. "No way through here. We need a break in the hedge, or we're crawling through on our bellies."

"That's not happening with the stretchers," Jacks muttered, dropping to one knee and scanning the view for potential threats.

The men spread out along the hedgerow, searching for a weak spot. Minutes dragged by. Then, after nearly ten minutes, Wilson came up alongside Archer. "Might have something here, Sir!"

Archer moved up along the hedgerow with Wilson and Jennings, their boots crunching softly over the soil. The hedge was a dense, living wall: a mix of gnarled hawthorn, thick blackberry brambles, and twisted branches fused together over decades. The break Wilson had found was barely a yard wide, but it was still a snarled mess of thorns, tangled vines and mud-caked roots. Low-hanging branches arched overhead. Their skeletal limbs clawed at the air while below, a thicket of nettles and brambles lay woven together like barbed wire.

Jennings inspected the small break, pushing some of the brambles back with his rifle, but some branches barely moved.

"It's not as thick, but it's still a bastard," he muttered.

Wilson pressed a boot forwards, trying to push through, but the brambles lashed at his legs, thorns scraping against his trousers with a snag. He recoiled, muttering a curse.

Archer stepped closer to assess it. The branches were old and brittle in places, but the brambles were fresh—new growth that tangled everything together. At the base, roots curled out like grasping fingers, caked in dry, crumbling dirt. He pulled up his collar, folding his arms across his chest. No finesse. o slow peeling back of branches. Just brute force. He hunched his shoulders, leant in and rushed forwards.

The first shove barely made a dent. The brambles clawed at his uniform, thorns caught on fabric and snapped free with a whip-like crack as he forced his way forwards. He gritted his teeth and pushed harder. The hedgerow creaked and shuddered, the thick mesh of branches resisting him at every inch. Thorns raked across his arms, his chest, his thighs—and then one found his face.

"Shit!" Archer spat, wincing as a thorn scraped against his still-healing wound.

He tried to force himself forwards, but his legs tangled in the undergrowth, and his arms were wedged at his sides. He was stuck.

Behind him, Jacks let out a breath. "Oh, for Christ's sake. Hang on, Sir."

Jacks placed his rifle on the ground, braced himself, and threw his weight forwards—both hands against Archer's front.

"One, two—"

With a grunt of effort, Jacks shoved.

Archer lurched forwards, the brambles snapping and cracking around him and sharp twigs whipped at his face. He burst through the other side, stumbling into a crouch. His sleeves and trousers were torn, and his breath was ragged.

"Bloody hedgerows," he muttered, wiping sweat and droplets of blood from his forehead.

Jennings, watching from the other side, immediately saw the opportunity. Archer had crushed a weak spot in the brush, leaving a small gap where the branches were loosened.

"Right, that works," Jennings said, stepping up. Instead of going through Archer's gap, he leant in just beside it. He folded his arms, hunched his shoulders, and forced himself through with sheer strength. The hedgerow groaned again, but the woven branches broke apart as Jennings muscled his way through. The hole was getting bigger.

"That's it! Push through! Use your weight!" Archer called.

One by one, the men followed suit, pressing into the weakened break, and branches cracked under their combined force. The brambles tore at their sleeves, but they were through, breathless and scratched to hell. Behind them, the hedgerow stood gnarled and broken, but a narrow passage had been forced open by sheer determination.

Archer rolled his shoulders, and picking thorns from his clothing. He exhaled and glanced back at Jacks with a wry smile on his face. "Right, get the fit men through first," Archer ordered. "Then we'll push the wounded through."

The first few men squeezed through, pulling branches aside, boots tripping on roots as they passed through.

Then came the real struggle.

The first stretcher team approached. Branches snagged at the fabric, and thorns tore at sleeves. The man on the stretcher winced as the movement jostled his injuries.

"Steady, steady—don't tip him!" one of the bearers hissed.

But they continued to press forwards, forcing their way through. The brambles clawed at their uniforms, and for a moment, one stretcher tilted dangerously, one bearer nearly losing his grip.

Archer lunged forwards, grabbing the frame just before it tipped.

"Got it. Keep moving!"

The bearers gritted their teeth, pushing on as the men on the other side grabbed hold and dragged them through the last tangle of brush.

One by one, they cleared the obstacle, breathless and covered in scratches. A few men wiped blood from their hands where the thorns had bitten deep, but most of them were unscathed

Archer glanced back the way they'd come. No movement. No sign they'd been spotted. For now, they were still ghosts in the landscape.

But the hardest part was yet to come. Padre Cartwright stepped through the gap, his expression grim.

Archer saw it immediately. Something was wrong.

"What's up, Padre?" he asked, already bracing for bad news.

Cartwright exhaled, the breath escaping in a low, weary sigh as he gently placed the stretcher down. His hands trembled slightly, sweat darkening the collar of his uniform, the weight of the day's burdens etched across his face. Archer could see one of the men on the stretchers was slipping away. The lad lay flat on his back, his breath ragged, and his eyes half-lidded. Sweat slicked his skin, and his uniform was damp with fever and blood. Archer could see the bandages across his torso were soaked through. He couldn't have been more than twenty. His face was gaunt, and his lips lay cracked and dry.

The padre knelt beside him, murmuring something soft with his hand resting lightly on the boy's chest. There was a faint twitch of fingers, reaching for something unseen. His lips moved, but no words came.

Then—a slow, shuddering exhale.

And that was it.

No last words. No cries for home. Just silence.

The men nearby looked on, hollow-eyed, and then turned away. There was nothing else to do.

Archer crouched beside the boy. He swallowed hard, then reached down, gently placing a hand on the lad's head, his fingers lingering, unwilling to let go so soon. Both he and the padre murmured a small prayer, their voices low and hollow in the stillness. When it was done, Archer looked up into the padre's wet eyes—both men sharing a silent, searing disgust at the waste of it all. The padre's hand came to rest on Archer's shoulder, wordless and warm. Another life snuffed out in a war that showed no mercy.

There was no time for ceremony or grief. Archer stood up, turned to the men, and with a small level of hatred in his voice, "Come on. Let's get moving!"

The late afternoon light stretched long across the fields. The sky was tinged with hazy gold and deepening blue while the air was heavy, warm, but thick with the scent of turned earth, crushed grass, and distant smoke.

Archer exhaled slowly as he took note of the time slipping away. He paused and arched his back, bones clicking softly beneath the webbing. They had been moving for hours, the weight of exhaustion pressing down, but they had made progress—good progress. And, more importantly, they hadn't encountered the enemy.

He had half-expected German patrols or stragglers, or even

a scout car prowling the backroads, or maybe a low-flying reconnaissance plane. But so far, the fields had remained empty, and it seemed as though the countryside was indifferent to the war tearing across it.

As far as he could tell, they were still ghosts in the landscape, slipping through the cracks.

Still, the war was never far.

The low, distant thunder of artillery had been growing louder. It was a constant, grinding reminder of the battle raging to the north. Every so often, the wind carried the dull crack of rifle fire, or the angry rattle of machine-guns, or occasionally the distant wail of aircraft engines.

Dunkirk was burning. They could all see the plumes of smoke rising over the port. It was a constant reminder to Archer: a beacon and a warning. It meant a way out. A destination. An end to the burden he carried and continued to carry. His mind was fixed on the north.

But he also knew he would be catching up with the war soon enough.

It was late afternoon when Archer called a halt.

The sun cast long shadows over the landscape. Its fading light filtered through the tangled hedgerows that lined the ridgeline. Below them, sprawled across the shallow valley, was the German front: a hastily established but well-manned position.

It was clear to Archer that the enemy hadn't been here long, but they had wasted no time fortifying key locations. Using binoculars, he could see the checkpoint dominated the narrow road at the valley's base; a simple wooden barrier flanked by sandbags and a pair of machine-gun posts. German soldiers loitered nearby, and some leant against the open-topped Kübelwagens parked at the roadside with their rifles slung casually over their shoulders.

Slowly moving the vision through the binoculars to beyond the checkpoint, Archer could see signs of a more developed defensive effort. A few slit trenches had been dug along the fields. They were shallow furrows in the earth, and their occupants were barely visible beneath the camouflage of scattered brush and broken branches. They weren't a prepared defensive line. They weren't a fully established defensive line, but they were enough to slow down any assault.

Machine-guns were positioned at key points with their barrels trained on likely approach routes, ready to cut down anything that moved. Archer noted that the Germans had repurposed the remnants of farm buildings for cover, stacking crates and debris into makeshift firing positions. A half-track sat near one of the buildings. Its crew chatting idly though the mounted MG34 on its pintle mount remained ominously manned. Its barrel tracked left and right as if expecting trouble.

Archer crouched low behind the hedgerow, his rifle resting against his knee. The distant rumble of battle drifted toward them, carried on the evening breeze. Jacks slipped in beside him, silent, and reached out for the binoculars. Archer handed them over without a word, his eyes fixed on the horizon. Jacks scanned the ridge slowly, then gave a faint nod. No words were needed. They both understood trouble was building beyond that ridge.

Beyond the valley, mortars thumped in a steady rhythm, each dull crump followed by a distant explosion. The sound rolled over them like a warning. Around Archer and Jacks, the others stiffened, no one spoke, but every man heard it. Felt it. Something was shifting out there, and whatever it was, it wasn't far off. Machine-guns rattled sporadically, their sharp bursts echoing between the hills. Mixed into the noise was the faint drone of engines. Tanks or transport lorries, Archer couldn't tell.

Binoculars raised again, he saw the German soldiers who moved between positions, their figures shifting in the fading light. Some crouched near their weapons, others hurried between their positions and the roadblock, lugging ammunition crates or conferring with officers.

More worryingly, he spotted a mortar team working methodically behind the checkpoint, their movements practised and unhurried. He watched as a round thumped skyward, followed by a puff of smoke and the distant arc of its flight. Further ahead, muzzle flashes flickered along the horizon, and the tremors of distant blasts rolled back toward them. Jacks edged closer beside Archer. Around them, the rest of the platoon sank lower into the hedgerow, rifles resting in hand, eyes fixed on the skyline. No one spoke. But they all heard it. Felt it.

The Germans weren't firing blindly. Their mortars landed in tight groups, hammering an unseen target beyond the valley. Archer couldn't see the British positions, but the Germans could. They were aiming at something.

The Germans weren't standing idle. They were keeping up the pressure.

They were in strength, but their focus was elsewhere. Archer exhaled slowly and ran through his options. If he waited until nightfall, the risk of confusion with men getting lost, or worse, someone making a noise at the wrong moment. Whereas in daylight, the risk of being seen was high, but so was their ability to move quickly and keep together. They'd have to use the terrain, picking their way along the hedgerows and low ground to stay out of sight. The valley was dangerous, but it wasn't impassable.

Archer studied the valley. His eyes scanned the ground ahead. The hedgerows offered some cover, running like twisted green scars along the slope, but the open ground between them was the real problem. They would have to move in short bursts, keeping to the shadows where they could. He traced the path in his mind: down the slope, along the sunken track that ran parallel to the road, then across the lower ground where the Germans had left a gap between their mortar crews and the roadblock. It wasn't perfect, but it was their best chance.

He turned across to Jennings and Jacks. "We move in three groups. First section Jacks. You and the lads." They all understood the reference to the remnants of D Company. "The second section takes the stretchers and the wounded, following close behind. The last group covers. No bunching up. If they see us, we'll be caught in the open."

Jennings gave a sharp nod. "You expecting trouble?"

Archer glanced towards the distant flashes of battle. "If the Germans don't spot us, no. If they do..." He gave a small grin and exhaled. "Then we run like hell."

Archer waited and crouched low while the first two groups began to move. Jacks and his men slipped away first, sticking to the hedgerows as they worked their way down the slope. They moved well: experienced infantrymen used to this kind of careful advance.

The second group, with Jennings leading the wounded and stretcher bearers, followed a minute later. Their progress was slower, more deliberate. The muted shuffling of boots, and the occasional grunt of effort as they carried the injured, made Archer's stomach tighten. He knew that group was their biggest liability. If they were spotted, there would be no running. No sudden dive into cover.

He glanced at the men with him, the last group, and he felt the stark contrast to the disciplined units ahead. He had a mixed bag of stragglers. None of them were truly his men, but their lives depended on him all the same.

Cartwright was the only familiar face. The padre had no

weapon only his medical satchel and an unshakable sense of duty. He'd already done more than expected of a non-combatant, but the strain was showing.

Archer didn't know them, not really. Doyle and Anderson had been with the padre when Archer found them back at the ruined barn. They'd fallen in with the group naturally, quietly. No fuss, no need for introductions. Just two more men trying to survive. Looking at them now, Archer saw how young they both were, perhaps the same age as himself. But he was the one they looked to. Young and tense. Perhaps even a little scared? Who could blame them.

These RAF airmen, Leading Aircraftmen Doyle and Anderson now had the look of men who hadn't slept in days. Their uniforms were dirtied from the retreat, their eyes flicking constantly toward the valley as if expecting to be caught at any moment.

Parker and Slater were older, but not by much. Men from the Sussex Regiment, from what he'd gathered, they had shown discipline and resourcefulness. Archer didn't know their full stories, but they'd pulled their weight. They moved more on instinct than drill, rough around the edges, perhaps but steady when it mattered. They'd stayed with the group because it was their best chance, and that counted for something.

Archer knew better than to judge a man by how he got here. He was learning that in this war, everyone was adapting, one way or another.

A fresh burst of machine-gun fire rattled from beyond the valley, followed by the distant crump of a mortar impact. The battle raged on; it was a constant backdrop to their escape. It was also a blessing and a curse—a distraction that kept German eyes ahead. But it was also a reminder of what lay behind them.

Archer crouched lower as he watched the second group disappear into the hedgerows. Jennings and the stretcher bearers were slow but controlled. Every movement was deliberate, and the wounded shifted only when necessary. The occasional stumble made Archer's breath hitch, but no cries of pain escaped, no sudden noises to give them away.

So far, so good.

His own group was next.

He turned his head slightly, catching Cartwright's eye. The padre gave a firm nod, gripping the strap of his satchel as if bracing himself. Doyle and Anderson lingered just behind him, shifting anxiously. Parker and Slater kept their heads down. Their movements were sharp, but Archer still wasn't sure whether it was discipline or desperation guiding them.

A burst of machine-gun fire cracked across the valley, tearing through the air. Archer froze, his heart hammering.

Not at them. Further ahead.

He exhaled slowly, motioning to the others. Time to go.

They moved in short bursts, staying low, stepping carefully. The ground sloped unevenly beneath them, loose stones shifting under their boots. Every step felt agonisingly slow.

Ahead, the sunken track stretched like a lifeline, running parallel to the road where the Germans were still focused forwards. If they could reach it, they would have some degree of cover.

Archer risked a glance down towards the valley.

A German mortar team was still working methodically, their helmets bobbing as they dropped fresh rounds into the tubes. Two officers stood nearby, conferring over a map. One gestured towards the distant British line.

Then. Movement.

A motorbike with a sidecar roared up the road, kicking up dust as it skidded to a stop near the checkpoint.

The officer turned sharply, striding towards the new arrival. More Germans moved towards the roadblock and focused on whatever message had just arrived.

Archer clenched his jaw.

A distraction? But for how long?

Archer and his men reached the track. One by one, the men dropped into it, pressing low against the embankment. Doyle exhaled sharply. His nerves were barely under control. Cartwright steadied him with a firm hand on the shoulder.

So far, they were still unseen.

Archer motioned for them to keep moving. The stretchers were farther ahead and almost lost in the hedgerows. The first group—Jacks' men—had already disappeared beyond sight.

Archer swallowed hard.

Halfway there.

He kept his head down and fixed his eyes on the ground ahead as they moved in staggered bursts. Every step felt like a test of patience. Every slight noise was an imagined betrayal of their presence.

Ahead, the hedgerows and uneven dips in the terrain provided enough cover to keep them concealed. For now. The distant rattle of machine-gun fire and the steady thump of mortars masked their movements, but the sound did little to settle Archer's nerves. This wasn't silence. It was uncertainty.

He glanced over his shoulder. Cartwright, Doyle, Anderson, Parker and Slater were keeping pace though Doyle's breathing was growing more ragged with each step. The young RAF man wasn't used to moving like this, but he gritted his teeth and kept going.

A movement ahead caught Archer's eye. He froze, holding up an open hand. The group dropped instantly, pressing low against the embankment. Archer scanned ahead, heart hammering.

For a second, nothing. Then he sighted movement just beyond the next hedgerow. A German patrol of five men, who moved steadily along the valley's edge. With their rifles held across their bodies, it was clear they were alert. They weren't looking in Archer's direction, not yet, but they were close...too close. Archer barely breathed. If one of them glanced to their left, if one of them noticed the slightest shift in the hedgerow's movement, it would be over.

He slowly and carefully turned his head towards Cartwright and the others. A silent signal. Wait.

The Germans stopped. One of them muttered something and gestured towards the roadblock.

Archer's fingers curled around the stock of his rifle. If they turned this way... if they came just a few steps closer...

The seconds stretched. The waiting was worse than the running.

Then one of the Germans shrugged, adjusted his helmet, and kept moving. The others followed, and their boots crunched softly as they passed beyond the tree line.

Archer forced himself to breathe.

He turned back to his group, making eye contact with each man. They weren't safe—not yet—but they had just passed through a noose without it tightening.

He gestured forwards. Keep moving.

They were getting closer now. He could feel it.

The problem was, so could the Germans.

Archer had just motioned his men forwards when a sharp bark of German cut through the air.

His stomach dropped.

The patrol had stopped, heads turning towards the valley floor—towards Jennings and the wounded. One of the Germans raised a hand, gesturing sharply to his men. Another raised his rifle, stepping forwards for a clearer look.

For a split second, there was a chance they might move on. Maybe they weren't sure what they had seen. Maybe—A German shouted an order.

Crack!

The first shot rang out. One of the stretcher bearers jerked backwards, a rifle round punching through his chest. His partner—the other stretcher bearer—let out a strangled curse as the stretcher fell from his grasp, The sound of his curse was lost beneath the scream of the wounded man as the stretcher hit the ground.

Then the valley exploded into gunfire.

Archer didn't hesitate. His rifle was up before he even registered moving. He squeezed the trigger, and the shot punched into the nearest German's chest, sending him sprawling into the dirt.

"Go!" Archer bellowed, his voice raw. "Move! Now!"

The German patrol scattered for cover, and their shouts rang through the air. More rifles snapped up—bullets cracked overhead, punching into the dirt, snapping branches loose.

Jennings and the wounded were caught in the open.

Archer fired again, barely aiming—just enough to force the Germans down for a second. Then he was moving, hauling Doyle forwards, shoving the RAF man towards the slope.

Ahead, Jennings dropped to a knee, his rifle kicking against his shoulder as he fired at the patrol. One of the wounded men, with his arm in a sling and a bandaged head, ran past Jennings but was hit in the chest. His face contorted with pain as the impact sent him slumping sideways, blood spilling into the dirt. Jennings roared at his group to move. His voice was hoarse.

The Germans were pressing harder. More troops poured into the fight, their fire hammering down. The open ground ahead was no more than thirty yards, but it had suddenly become a passage of death.

Archer's rifle snapped up again, the sight barely settling before he squeezed the trigger. The shot clipped a German in the shoulder, spinning him sideways. It wasn't enough. There were too many.

Jennings, still crouched, kept firing. His rifle jerked with every shot. The wounded staggered forwards, some half-dragging themselves, but others were frozen in the open, too terrified to run.

Archer had been joined by both of the Sussex men. All three of them fired measured shots into the Germans. They knew it was a feeble effort against the coming onslaught as the machine-guns began their relentless back-and-forth. Another man went down. Archer didn't see it—just heard the sickening thud as the round struck flesh and bone. That sound was becoming all too familiar.

Then from his peripheral vision, Archer saw Cartwright moving forwards; his uniform flashed between bursts of gunfire as he ran. The padre wasn't running away. He was running towards the wounded.

"Padre, get down!" Archer bellowed, but his voice was swallowed in the sudden madness.

Cartwright dropped to his knees beside the fallen man. Realising there was nothing he could do for the man, he grabbed the stretcher and turned to the soldier at the other end who had already unslung his rifle and was firing back at the enemy—defending the wounded like it was the only thing that mattered.

"C'mon. Let's get out of here!" Cartwright bellowed, his voice straining over the gunfire.

A sudden burst of rifle fire tore into the Germans, forcing them into cover. Archer's head snapped towards the tree line where figures moved through the hedgerows, rifles cracking in quick succession.

Jacks and the last men of D Company had arrived. Hearing the commotion, they had returned, pushing through the hedgerow and opening fire in unison. Saunders had dropped prone, taking a steady aim. He exhaled, pulled the trigger smoothly, and watched as his target spun violently, the bullet ripping through his ribcage.

Matthews was crouched deeper in the hedge, working his bolt fast, firing round after round in quick succession. The others were frantically chambering and firing. Their shots snapped through the air, forcing the Germans to hesitate.

It wasn't enough to turn the tide, but it bought the men caught in the open a few precious seconds.

Cartwright dragged the stretcher forwards with the man behind him struggling to keep pace. They were nearing the hedgerow, closing the gap to safety. The other men from Jennings' group had already passed through, collapsing just beyond Jacks and his men. Some knelt while others were bent over, gasping for breath. Jennings, the last man through, staggered to a halt.

Jacks, despite being the junior rank, turned to him and gave the only order that mattered.

"Keep going."

He barely waited for Jennings' nod before looking to Wilson.

"Tug! Go with the RSM!" Wilson immediately pulled back from his position in the hedge, heading towards Jennings. He knew instinctively that his job was to lead the group forwards.

As he moved past the exhausted survivors, he took in their hollow faces, their drained expressions. They had been wounded for days, and their blood loss and fatigue was carved into every movement.

"Don't worry, lads. We're on the last stretch now!" Wilson had no idea if that was true, but he had to say something.

Passing Cartwright, he gave a quick, informal salute—more a tap to his helmet than anything else.

"Padre," he said simply. "C'mon. We're going."

Archer had pushed farther down the lane, reaching the opening where Jennings' group had been caught. With Jacks' men laying down fire from the other side, it gave Archer, and the few men who remained, the opportunity to make a run for it. He pushed forwards, rifle clenched in one hand.

"Let's move!"

One after another, the men sprinted forwards, crouching and wincing as bullets whizzed overhead, kicking up dirt around them. The rate of fire was incredible; it was a relentless hammering of rounds tearing through the air.

Then—the all-too-familiar zip of a machine-gun.

Beside Archer, young Doyle jerked mid-stride and went down hard, crashing onto his side. No scream, no sound. Just a sudden, brutal collapse.

As he ran on, Archer glanced back, instincts screaming to grab Doyle, but there was no time. The Germans were already shifting, their fire intensifying.

The second airman, Anderson, hesitated. Just for a second.

"Leave him! Move!"

Parker shoved Anderson forwards, snapping him out of it.

They ran.

Chapter 16

The hedgerow ahead exploded with gunfire as Archer and his group barrelled onwards towards Jacks' position, bullets kicking up dirt around them sharp and close. Exhaustion burnt deep in their legs as their desperate sprint became a mad scramble. They dodged, stumbled and half-threw themselves forwards, every step feeling like it could be their last.

Anderson, the RAF airman, lagged behind. His breath was coming in short, panicked gasps. Not trained for this. Not ready for this. His uniform was soaked through with sweat, clinging to his skin as he crouched low, pushing himself onwards, trying to make himself as small a target as possible.

Ahead, Parker and Slater pushed hard, their faces set in grim determination. Slater, his rifle clutched tightly in one hand, threw glances over his shoulder, spitting curses between ragged breaths as he ran.

"Keep moving!" Archer snapped.

Parker had dropped to one knee beside a body, the stretcher bearer who'd gone down minutes earlier. glancing up to see Slater still in the open. His eyes locked on the rifle still slung across the dead man's back. Dropping to his knees, he wrestled it free, yanked at the sling, and then tore open the soldier's ammunition pouches. His fingers found three charger clips— fifteen rounds of .303. He tightened his grip on the rifle and clenched his jaw. Then, without hesitation, he set off again, a rifle in each hand, sprinting to catch up.

The gunfire intensified. The Germans had adjusted their aim, their shots stitching closer to the retreating men. Archer saw bullets tear through the earth just feet ahead which sent up sprays of dirt and grit. The hedgerow loomed ahead, Jacks' men were firing from cover, trying to suppress the enemy long enough for Archer's group to reach safety.

"Move, move, move!" Archer bellowed, forcing himself forwards, his rifle swinging across his chest, adding to his momentum as he ran.

Parker reached Jacks first, dropping into cover, his rifle snapping up as he turned. Archer vaulted into the hedgerow next just as Anderson stumbled in behind him, collapsing onto his hands and knees, gasping for air. Slater hit the dirt hard, rolling to a stop before springing up onto one knee.

Behind them, the Germans were closing in.

Jacks was already shouting orders as Archer slid to a stop beside him, his breath coming in ragged gasps.

"Took your bloody time!" Jacks barked, half-grinning despite the lunacy that surrounded them.

Archer barely spared a reply. "Get ready to move—this isn't stopping."

Slater, having adjusted himself, turned to Anderson.

"Here." He shoved the rifle he had picked up towards Anderson.

Anderson stared at it like it might bite him. "I—I'm not a bloody infantryman."

"You are now." The Sussex man gave a grim smile. "Keep your head down and pull the trigger when you have to."

Anderson swallowed hard but took the rifle. His hands shook, but he set himself. He'd come this far; he was determined to make it home. He opened the bolt, checking the rifle instinctively.

"Here." Slater pressed two of the charging strips into his hand. "We're going to need everyone."

Noting that the airman wasn't unfamiliar with the rifle, Slater patted his shoulder. "You'll be okay."

Archer scanned the retreat path, his breath ragged. From beyond the hedgerow, he could see the land stretched in rolling waves—fields of trampled crops, scarred earth, and winding ditches carving through the landscape like old battle wounds. Another line of dense hedgerows loomed in the distance, tangled and thorned, their gnarled branches swaying in the wind.

It would have to do.

Gunfire snapped overhead, vicious and unrelenting, cutting through the air with splintering cracks. Bullets whipped past, some thudding into the open mud around them, flinging sharp sprays of dirt into faces and eyes. There was no real cover—just a shallow dip in the field, barely enough to hide in. The air reeked of burning powder, sweat, and the raw churn of earth beneath boots and bodies.

Behind them and somewhere to the right, a machine-gun opened up. Its relentless hammering drowned out the distant roar of battle. A fresh volley of rounds ripped into the ground just feet away. The impacts were hollow and brutal. The enemy wasn't firing blind anymore—they were adjusting. They were closer.

The wind carried the distant wail of artillery. Its low, rolling thunder was slightly muffled by the tree line ahead. Far on the horizon, thick columns of smoke curled black against the grey sky. Their edges were blurred by the shifting breeze. Yet, the acrid stench of charred wood and burning fuel clung to the air as a grim reminder of the battle raging miles away.

But Archer had no time to dwell on that. The battle was coming to them. Here.

Gunfire snapped through the hedgerows, and bullets continued to whip past in lethal bursts, tearing into the dirt just feet away. A fresh volley cracked overhead. Branches shattered. Leaves spun wildly in the air. The Germans weren't just firing now—they were close.

Archer gritted his teeth. They had to move.

Archer scanned the retreat path one last time, his mind racing. The terrain offered little cover—just open ground, ditches, and the next hedgerow ahead. They had to move fast, but they couldn't just run blind. Somehow, they had to control the retreat, covering each other in bounds.

His men were exhausted, running low on ammunition, and the Germans weren't letting up. If they tried to fallback all at once, they'd be cut down before they made it twenty yards.

He turned to Jacks. "We move in bounds! Hold a position, cover the next lot moving, then fallback! Keep your spacing. Don't bunch up! Stay sharp!"

Jacks gave a curt nod, already signalling to his group.

"Jacks, Matthews, Anderson, Slater—you're up first! Move now!"

Jacks and his men pushed off the ground and sprinted, their boots thudding heavily against the churned-up dirt. The hedgerow ahead seemed an eternity away; the open space between them and safety would be a killing zone if the Germans adjusted their fire.

As they ran, Archer dropped to one knee, rifle snapping to his shoulder, and his finger tightened on the trigger.

"Covering fire!"

Parker and Saunders hit the dirt beside him. Their rifles barked in sharp, controlled bursts. Bullets whipped past, ripping into the hedgerow and ground, sending shattered leaves and splinters raining down.

A German machine-gun raked the field. It was a long, scything burst that tore into the earth, kicking up sprays of dirt and debris just behind Jacks' group.

Archer grimaced. Come on. Move faster.

Jacks and his men reached the next hedgerow, and threw themselves into cover, their own rifles immediately snapping up.

Through the gunfire, Archer heard Jacks' voice shouting, "Fire!"

Now it was their turn. The chase was on.

Archer sucked in a breath, and his muscles coiled like a spring.

"Go! Go!"

293

He launched forwards. His boots hammered against the dirt, legs burning with every stride. Parker and Saunders bolted beside him. Their gear rattled and breaths cam in sharp, ragged gasps.

"Watch your spacing!" Archer called out, forcing the words past his exhaustion.

The open ground stretched before them. Each step was a gamble. The space between them and the hedgerow felt impossibly vast. The weight of their rifles and gear dragged at them, but they forced themselves forwards, driven by nothing but instinct and survival.

Gunfire whipped past, and the air snapped as bullets tore through it, kicking up dirt and shredded grass. The ground shook with impacts, and the heavy thud of rounds found earth just behind their heels.

Saunders cursed through clenched teeth, his breath rasping. "Bloody hell!"

Parker staggered mid-stride as a round ripped through the air inches from his shoulder. The shockwave slammed into him like a shove. He didn't stop. He couldn't. His boots pounded forwards, faster, as if the bullet had given him new urgency.

Archer's lungs burnt. Desperately sucking in air that was thick with dust and cordite, his throat was raw. Each breath was fire, and his heartbeat was a frantic drum against his ribs.

A crack. A hiss of breath beside him.

Saunders stumbled, cursing, his leg buckling for half a second before he threw himself forwards again.

The hedgerow loomed closer. Just a few more strides.

Archer could hear the relentless German gunfire still chasing them as bullets tore through the air. The sharp crack of Mausers mixed with the hammering bursts of the MG34. He felt the heat of each passing round, and the way they carved the air just behind them.

His legs screamed in protest, but he didn't let up.

With a final lunging step, Archer threw himself headfirst into cover, hitting the dirt hard before rolling onto his side as leaves and loose earth scattered around him.

Parker tumbled in beside him a heartbeat later, twisting mid-air, landing with a grunt as he pulled his rifle in tightly.

Saunders crashed down beside them, clutching his leg but already shifting into a firing position. His face twisted in pain, but his hands were steady.

The moment they were down, Archer whipped around, dragging his rifle up. He sucked in a sharp breath, vision tunnelling for a second as adrenaline surged through his veins.

"Saunders! You hit?!" Archer yelled between breaths, not daring to slow.

"Grazed!" came the reply, strained but defiant. "Keep moving!"

They'd made it. But just barely.

Archer made his way to Jacks, signalling for him to move. Ahead of them, there was a small wall. It wasn't much but it was a solid line of stone running across the rise and only broken in places by creeping ivy and years of weathering. It wasn't much, but it was the next step.

"Go! Go!" Jacks called out to his group.

They picked themselves up and drove forwards, muscles screaming in protest, lungs dragging in air thick with smoke and dust. The ground trembled beneath their boots. Each step fought against the churned-up mud.

Behind them, the snapping crack of rifle fire mixed with the furious chatter of machine-guns. German rounds sliced through the air, ripping into the ground in sharp, violent bursts. Clumps of earth and shattered grass spat upwards, raining back down on them as they ran.

Slater hit the wall first, slamming against it, chest heaving as he dropped low. Jacks threw himself down beside him, his rifle snapping up, already searching for targets.

Anderson vaulted the last few feet, his boots skidding in the mud before he slammed a shoulder into the rough stone. He sucked in ragged breaths, but there was no hesitation. Whether it was adrenaline or instinct, he'd found his rhythm. Matthews followed close behind, diving hard into cover. His breath came sharp and shallow, chest rising and falling in ragged bursts, but his hands were steady on the rifle. Dirt clung to his sweat-slicked skin, and there was a raw intensity in his eyes, fear and focus battling for control. He'd made it to the wall, but he wasn't safe yet, and he knew it.

The moment he steadied himself, he was in the fight. Pressing against the wall, rifle firm in his grip, he picked his shots and fired. He was no longer a nervous, reluctant airman. Now, he was a full-fledged combatant.

Archer knew it was their turn. The wall wasn't far, but it felt like miles.

The ground ahead sloped gently upwards: a broad, open rise that offered no real cover. The grass was short and sparse, dry in places where the sun had baked the soil hard while patches of exposed earth showed where boots had torn through the turf. A few scattered wild shrubs and tufts of taller grass dotted the incline, but there was nothing that could stop a bullet.

A few yards ahead, Archer spotted an old split-rail fence, half-collapsed and barely standing. Its wooden beams were chewed and splintered from earlier fire—no real protection, but maybe just enough to break a line of sight. He didn't slow. Every instinct told him to keep moving. Beyond it, the stone wall stood firm at the crest, the last line of defence before the land dipped away into the unknown.

But he knew the real danger wasn't the terrain. It was the

open stretch between them and the wall.

The Germans had every advantage. They'd be positioned lower down with clear firing lanes. The machine-guns had already found their range, and the sharp crack of rifle fire snapped through the air with their bullets seeking anything that moved.

Archer felt the weight of his rifle, the heat in his lungs. The ground ahead wasn't an obstacle. It was a killing field.

He set his jaw, adjusted his grip.

"Now! Go!"

He broke into a sprint. Saunders was right beside him with Parker just behind. The ground blurred beneath them. Their boots hammered through the mud. Their hearts raced.

Gunfire ripped through the air.

A sharp crack. Then a strangled noise behind him.

Archer felt it before he saw it. He turned his head just enough to see Parker stumble. His momentum had gone in an instant, and a dark stain spread across his chest.

Parker hit the dirt hard.

Archer skidded—half-turning. "Parker!"

Parker's mouth moved, but no sound came. His hand twitched towards his rifle, but his body wouldn't move.

A second burst of fire shred the ground around him.

No time.

Archer's stomach twisted, but he ran. He had to. They dove behind the wall, heart pounding, hands shaking. Archer pressed himself against the stone, staring at the ground in contempt and disbelief.

Parker was gone.

Archer had no time for reflection. Jacks had come over, and his expression was unreadable.

"You? How you doing, Sir?" Archer just looked at him. It was a look that spoke of days upon days of battle, of exhaustion clawing at his bones, of hope thinning with every moment.

Jacks studied him for a second and then pressed on.

"Well, Sir... you may want to see this."

Archer sighed, pushing himself up to take in the vista.

The first thing he saw was Jennings' group two hundred yards ahead, moving steadily. Jennings and Cartwright were leading the wounded forwards, putting distance between them and the fight.

Archer exhaled, relieved. At least one thing was going right.

"What is it, Jacks?" His voice was tight, edged with frustration: not at Jacks, but at the sheer relentlessness of it all.

Jacks didn't answer right away. Instead, his voice turned solemn.

"Have a look over there, Sir."

Archer followed the line of Jacks' pointing hand—off to their left, across a shallow rise, and he felt his stomach drop.

A full German armoured battalion.

Rows of tanks. Troop carriers. Infantry swarming between them like ants. A force so vast, so overwhelming, that for a moment, Archer's mind refused to process it.

Then Jacks spoke again.

"And if you look over here, Sir..."

Archer turned—this time to the right. Another ridgeline. Another mass of armour. A second battalion. Positioned almost in parallel, like bookends closing around them.

A second armoured battalion.

Another full-strength force was positioned almost as if mirroring the first.

For a beat, Archer could only stare.

Then Jacks let out a breathless, almost incredulous giggle.

"Sir...we just ran straight through the bloody middle of them!"

The two men stared at each other for the briefest moment.

Then they turned their gaze to the five others still fighting and putting the last of their ammunition into the Germans still in pursuit.

Archer watched in disbelief as Anderson, clad in his blue RAF uniform, remained locked in his firing position. He was calm and steady, adjusting his stance ever so slightly between each shot before firing again.

Archer slumped against the wall. Every part of his body was heavy with exhaustion. He was lost in the moment, still trying to process what had just happened—the sheer, unbelievable luck of it.

The thought of what could have happened instead sent a cold shiver down his spine.

"What now, Sir?" Jacks asked, his voice steady but expectant.

Archer barely had time to think.

Before he could even begin to contemplate their next move, an almighty explosion tore through the ground to his left. Then another, dead ahead.

The force and noise knocked Jacks off his feet, sending him sprawling. The men instinctively ducked, pressing themselves tight against the wall as a third explosion tore into the stone, blasting debris and razor-sharp splinters in all directions.

The blast was at least ten yards away—close, but not close enough to kill them.

Archer blinked through the dust, his ears ringing, his mind reeling.

There was no thinking now.

"RUN!"

The word tore from his throat before he even knew he was saying it. Not a direction. Not a plan. Just raw, urgent instinct.

"Run, lads!"

He was on his feet before he realised it, grabbing Jacks and yanking him upright. Both men took off. Their legs screamed in protest, and their feet pounded the earth. Another sprint. Another desperate escape. Could their bodies take any more? It didn't matter.

The world around them blurred: gunfire, the crash of explosions, the sharp sting of smoke in their lungs.

As they ran, the chaos slowly faded behind them, swallowed by distance. The sound of gunfire still echoed, but it was no longer right on top of them. The world ahead stretched wide with rolling fields, broken hedgerows, and pockets of shell-churned earth. The remnants of abandoned farms stood in the distance—some were still burning while others had been reduced to rubble from earlier bombardments. The land itself was scarred...a testament to the brutal fighting that had swept through here in the past days.

Somewhere ahead, beyond the next ridge, another group was moving.

Jennings adjusted his grip on his rifle, scanning the fields and ditches for movement. Every rustling bush, every shifting shadow, was a potential threat. Behind him, Wilson and the wounded pressed forwards as fast as they could. Cartwright moved between them, urging them on with quiet, measured words.

The first low, whining shriek cut through the air. It was a chilling sound that made Jennings' gut tighten. Then the shell slammed into the fields ahead of them, barely two hundred yards away, sending up a fountain of dirt, flame, and shattered debris. The shockwave hit a second later: a deep, concussive thump that rattled his chest.

He flinched before he snapped his head towards the explosion. Another whistling scream followed. Then another. Each round punched into the earth closer than the last.

It was an artillery barrage, rolling forwards in tight brackets, creeping towards them like a slow-moving hammer to drive everything before it into the dirt.

For a moment, the world ahead was nothing but fire and ruin. Along the ridge, half-collapsed buildings spewed smoke into the sky, and dark figures moved in the haze but were indistinct against the burning remains of what might have been a farmhouse or a derelict outpost. The flames cast flickering shadows, stretching and distorting the wreckage ahead in unnatural shapes.

Jennings squinted, trying to make sense of it. Were those British troops still holding, or Germans pushing forwards?

The answer came in the next explosion. A shell tore through what was left of the burning structure, sending flaming timbers spiralling into the air. The figures scattered, but in which direction, he couldn't tell.

Behind him, Wilson cursed under his breath, tightening his grip on the strap of a wounded man's arm. "Jesus! Whoever that is, they're taking a beating!"

Jennings didn't respond. His eyes were locked on the ridge ahead where the land dipped sharply, and he was able to occasionally glimpse the canal through the rolling haze. It was a slow-moving waterway lined with battered stone embankments on both sides.

And there, barely visible through the haze of drifting smoke, stood the bridge. Jennings took a slow, deep breaths as he looked at its single, narrow crossing. Its surface was littered with abandoned crates, sandbags, and a few motionless figures—whether dead or unconscious, he couldn't tell.

Jennings let out a breath.

Through the drifting smoke and rolling dust, the bridge came into full view. The stone surface had been weathered and worn smooth by years of foot and cart traffic. The structure arched slightly over the slow-moving canal, and its edges were lined with crumbling stone barriers, and some had been blown apart by earlier shelling.

The canal itself was murky, its stone embankments lined with overgrown reeds and uncut wild grass. Here and there, pieces of debris—twisted metal and chunks of stonework—littered the slopes. A shattered branch drifted slowly across the canal's gentle current, a surreal, almost peaceful image amid the hell unfolding around it.

Jennings found himself momentarily hypnotised by the branch's quiet journey towards the bridge. He blinked and pulled himself from the daze. To his right, on the near side of the bridge, a row of shattered trees leant at odd angles. Their branches had been sheared and splintered by the concussive force of recent artillery strikes, some reduced to bare trunks, no more than jagged telegraph poles. Smoke drifted lazily from a nearby burning truck, abandoned just short of the bridge. Its metal frame was warped by the heat, still glowing faintly in places.

The town of Bergues loomed beyond the bridge. The first few rows of its buildings were pockmarked with bullet holes and missing rooftops, leaving behind skeletal remains jutting towards the sky.

On the far side of the bridge, Jennings watched British troops moving—too fast to be a steady retreat, but too orderly to be a full rout. British engineers worked frantically. Their sweat-stained uniforms were streaked with dirt and soot as they crouched around the stone supports, carefully placing explosive charges. A Royal Engineers officer stood at the edge, checking his watch; he was clearly on edge as he barked hurried orders.

Nearby, a handful of riflemen manned a makeshift roadblock, stacking crates and sandbags across the street as they watched the tree line beyond with tired, wary eyes.

Jennings exhaled sharply, taking it all in at once. He felt his stomach tighten with anticipation as he moved forwards, and his boots struck firmer ground. The sounds of gunfire still echoed behind them, but it was distant now, swallowed by the chaos unfolding beyond the ridge behind them.

They had made it.

For the first time in what felt like days, he wasn't running for his life. As he allowed a drop of relief to penetrate his thoughts, the weight of exhaustion settled over him like a lead blanket, pressing against his shoulders, and his rifle felt heavier than ever. He let out a slow breath, tasting the thick, acrid air that clung to the canal: a mix of burning fuel, damp earth, and cordite.

"Bloody hell."

He turned to Padre Cartwright, who was keeping pace beside him. The padre's face was tight with exhaustion but steady. Then, Archer's gaze swept the bridge ahead, and he watched the British soldiers working frantically to destroy it. There was no sense of triumph in his expression. He was just filled with grim determination—and the quiet, desperate resolve of a man who knew they were pushing their luck but had no choice but to keep going. Ahead, the path dipped down toward the canal, skirting the water's edge. That track would take them to the bridge, if they could reach it in time.

Behind them, Wilson, and the wounded who were mobile, stumbled forwards, relief washing over their faces as they realised they had reached British lines. Some collapsed to their knees while others slumped against the low stone barriers lining the canal, sucking in ragged breaths as they tried to process the fact that they were still alive.

One of the younger riflemen, his uniform stained with sweat and dust, let out something between a laugh and a sob, muttering, "Jesus... we made it."

For a moment, Jennings allowed himself to believe it.

Then his expression hardened.

"We've not made anything yet, lad," he said, his voice sharp with authority. He adjusted his rifle, eyes sweeping the path ahead. "C'mon, lads! Let's get across!"

Jennings led the group forwards, boots crunching on the rough towpath running alongside the canal. The water beside them was dark and sluggish, littered with debris and the occasional lifeless shape bobbing beneath the reeds. They didn't dare look.

As they moved, Cartwright glanced over his shoulder, searching for any sign of Archer's group.

There was nothing.

The thought sent a cold lump of panic to settle in Jennings' gut, but he pressed on.

They were closing fast on the bridge when a sharp yell shattered the moment.

"Halt!"

Instinct took over. Jennings snapped his arm out, signalling the group to stop: his hand flat, fingers tense. Confused, his eyes scanned the area, searching for the source of the command.

Then it came again. Louder this time. "Who the hell are you?"

Jennings turned to his right, then froze.

Two rifles were levelled at him from a slit trench that had been dug hastily into the soft earth beside the path.

He didn't flinch. Instead, he straightened his back. His firm voice carried the evidence of experience.

"Regimental Sergeant Major Jennings. 2nd Battalion, Royal Norfolk Regiment, 4th Infantry Brigade, 2nd Division."

The words were clipped and precise to be delivered with the authority of a man who had spent a lifetime in uniform.

"We've come from Hazebrouck and Cassel. We're making for Dunkirk."

A pause. A quick scan of the trench, and the men inside.

Then, Jennings' tone sharpened.

"Who's in command here?"

The two men in the trench exchanged glances, conferring in low voices.

Then, without hesitation, one of them scrambled out and sprinted away, disappearing into the ruins.

Jennings shifted his stance, adjusting his webbing as he waited. Beside him, Padre Cartwright ran a sleeve across his brow. His breath was still heavy from the march. Neither man spoke.

Two minutes later, the sentry returned. This time he was with an officer whose dust-covered uniform was marked by the insignia of the Sherwood Foresters.

The captain's sharp eyes swept over them, taking in Jennings, Cartwright, and the weary men behind them. He exhaled.

"We weren't expecting any more British troops," he admitted, his voice edged with disbelief. Then, after a brief pause, he met Jennings' gaze and gave a curt nod.

"Well done, RSM. Getting through Hazebrouck and Cassel is no small feat."

Before the captain could say more, Cartwright stepped forwards. His uniform was still marked with blood from the wounded he had tended, but his expression remained steady.

"Captain, where's the nearest Regimental Aid Post? I've got wounded who need immediate care."

The Sherwood Foresters officer exhaled sharply, and his eyes flicking over the group. "About a mile back, near a crossroads. We've been sending walking wounded there."

"Do you have transport?" Cartwright pressed, his tone firm but controlled.

The captain shook his head, frustration flickering in his features. "Not much. Most of our trucks are either wrecked or already gone. Your best bet is getting them to that aid station on foot. If they've got anything left, they'll help you."

Cartwright set his jaw, but before he could reply, a corporal from the Foresters stepped forwards, his rifle slung over his shoulder. "Sir, there's still a truck by the field post. It's taken some damage, but it runs."

The captain's gaze snapped to the corporal. "How many can it take?"

The corporal hesitated, then glanced at the group behind Cartwright, taking in the exhausted, bloodied men. He let out a sharp breath.

"If they're stacked in," his eyes flicked back to Cartwright, assessing him for a moment. Then, with a knowing look, he continued. "With a push, we'll get them all in...if the padre can drive it."

Cartwright's expression hardened with resolve. "I can drive it."

The captain smiled. "It's yours then. Corporal, show the padre the way."

Cartwright turned to Jennings and Wilson, "You two wait for Lieutenant Archer and we can catch up at the R.A.P."

Jennings, ever the pragmatist, nodded. "Aye, Padre." Then he turned to the captain, "Captain, there's more behind us. A unit under Lieutenant Archer. He's bringing up the last of our men. They shouldn't be that far behind us."

The officer glanced over his shoulder towards a group of Royal Engineers scrambling frantically near the bridge. His jaw tightened, and his eyes flickered with urgency before turning back to Jennings and Cartwright.

"Then they'd better hurry," he said sharply. "The bridge is being set to blow in the next five or so minutes."

Jennings exchanged a tense glance with Cartwright, who gave a swift, acknowledging nod before hurrying after the corporal. Standing rooted in place, Jennings locked his eyes on the urgency ahead of him. The engineers moved quickly, with frantic movements as they worked desperately to rig charges beneath the bridge's stone supports.

From the urgency of their work, it was clear they were completing their task

A sudden silence fell across the field, chilling and heavy. Jennings tensed, and his gut tightening. Silence was never good. Not here, not now.

Then, from somewhere far behind him, came the shriek of incoming shells; it was a sound he'd heard too many times to mistake.

"Take cover!" he roared, his voice a harsh rasp.

Men dove to the dirt as the shells burst. The explosions hammered down on the far ridge. Fountains of dirt and flame rose into the sky, scattering blackened earth and debris. Jennings threw himself flat as the concussive force shook the ground beneath him. He squeezed his eyes shut against the blast and gripped his helmet tightly, gritting his teeth as the earth rattled violently beneath him.

Lifting his head a moment later, his vision was blurred by the cloud of dust and smoke. Beside him, Wilson spat dirt from his mouth, coughing harshly. His face was streaked black with soot.

"You alright, Wilson?" Jennings growled, pushing himself up onto one elbow.

"Been better, RSM." Wilson's reply was dry and humourless, and his voice was hoarse from exhaustion.

Jennings lifted his head again, peering into the haze. The engineers at the bridge had scattered for cover, and the officer stood barking urgent orders and gesturing frantically at the charges. One of them glanced nervously at his watch; his face was pale beneath grime and sweat.

Jennings swore under his breath. His gut tightened. Five minutes? He doubted they'd even have that now.

His eyes darted anxiously back towards the open ground behind them. Searching desperately through the smoke-obscured terrain, he saw nothing but swirling dust and flickering shadows.

Come on, Archer...

A strained voice broke his concentration. "RSM!"

Jennings turned sharply to his left.

The Foresters officer stared at him with narrowed eyes. His voice was edged with urgency. "Get across that bridge—now!"

Jennings hesitated just one heartbeat longer as his eyes lingered desperately on the empty fields. Then, reluctantly, he accepted reality and turned towards Wilson. With a rough, resigned voice, he said, "Come on, Corporal."

They hurried across, boots tapping sharply against the cobbled surface of the bridge. Moments later, both men dropped into cover behind the ruined wall of an old house; their breath came fast and shallow.

A figure approached swiftly; it was the corporal who had guided Cartwright to the truck. He halted beside Jennings and leant in close to be heard clearly above the distant crackle of gunfire.

"Padre says to remind you—meet him at the R.A.P."

Jennings nodded curtly, keeping his eyes fixed on the bridge. "Understood."

The corporal dashed away without another word, leaving Jennings and Wilson alone. Jennings' gaze returned to the swirling smoke behind them. His heart sank with every passing second.

Archer was still out there.

Chapter 17

The ground trembled beneath their feet as Archer and his men sprinted for the canal path, legs pumping, boots slamming into the earth. Gear clattered against their backs, every step a brutal jolt. The bridge was ahead, so close, yet impossibly far. Gunfire cracked around them. Bullets tore past with a savage hiss, snapping through the air, kicking up dirt and stone in violent bursts. The air was thick with smoke and grit, choking lungs and stinging eyes. Every man ran with the same sick certainty, that the next step might be his last. Any second now, a round would punch through someone's body, drop them mid-stride. The fear wasn't just in the mind, it was in the chest, the gut, the fingertips. It crawled under the skin like fire. There was no room for tactics now. No cover, no clever angles. Just a desperate sprint over open ground, fully exposed, fully committed. Survival meant movement. Hesitation meant death.

They didn't look back. They didn't dare.

Archer's breath came in ragged gasps, and his legs burnt as he pounded through the open fields. His rifle was gripped in one hand, swinging in rhythm with each desperate stride. The earth sank beneath his boots, and mud and dirt was kicked up by the stampede of his exhausted men.

Behind them, the thunder of German beasts drew ever closer—a relentless drumbeat of death. The deep growl of engines was punctuated by the crack of machine-gun fire and the whistle of mortar and artillery shells overhead. Archer didn't dare look back. He didn't need to. He knew what was there: two armoured battalions, intact, pushing forwards. This force couldn't be hunting them alone, but the feeling of being chased down like prey was impossible to shake.

Yet the fact they were advancing gave him a sliver of hope... a twisted, desperate kind of hope. The Germans weren't trying to finish them off. Their fire was mostly directed ahead, targeting something beyond them, driving hard toward the British lines.

Which meant, if they could just keep running, just stay ahead of the storm a little longer, they might make it. And it was on him to get them there.

Jacks and Webb ran beside him, their faces streaked with sweat and grime. Their boots pounded the earth in rhythm with Archer's.

As the group reached halfway between the hedgerow and the ridge ahead, Saunders stumbled, panting hard. His leg was dragging, the earlier graze throbbing with each step, and his hands clawed at the straps of his webbing as though loosening them might make him lighter.

Anderson was faltering. His breath was ragged, but Matthews was right there, giving a constant stream of orders and encouragement, half dragging, half pushing the airman forwards.

Slater was bounding ahead even though his movements were awkward. He was driven only by instinct and fear, and every jolt of exertion sent pain lancing through his body.

Ahead, a hedgerow erupted in a fireball.

A German high-explosive shell slammed into the embankment, blowing mud, stone, and branches into the sky. The blast flung Saunders off his feet. He landed hard with a sickening crack. Jacks and Archer grabbed him under the arms, dragging him upright.

"Move, you bugger! Move!" Jacks barked.

More shells ripped through the fields, smashing into trees, turning them into jagged splinters. The earth trembled with each impact, and mud and debris rained down over the retreating British troops. The Germans were closing in.

Behind Archer, dark shapes moved through the rising smoke—infantry advancing in waves, hunched low as they picked their way through the ruined fields and shattered hedgerows.

The tanks rumbled behind them. Panzers and half-tracks ground forwards, their turrets scanning for targets while the thud-

thud-thud of heavy machine-gun fire rattled over the battlefield.

Then—the British guns opened up.

A 2-pounder anti-tank gun cracked like a whip. Its shell streaked across the field, catching a half-track square in the chassis. The vehicle lurched violently, flames bursting from its shattered hull as men spilt from the wreckage, writhing in the dirt.

Another 2-pounder fired. This time, it aimed at a Panzer just cresting a rise. The round slammed into its turret, and sparks sprayed from the impact. The tank kept moving, but its gun remained frozen, the shot jamming the turret ring.

The Vickers machine-guns erupted. Their deep, stuttering roar cut through the smoke. Tracer rounds laced the battlefield, kicking up dirt and blood, and forcing the German infantry to dive for cover.

The few remaining British mortar teams scrambled, desperately adjusting their range, lobbing explosives into the advancing ranks. A shell landed dead centre, and the explosion sent bodies flying, limbs and dirt raining down in a grotesque spray.

But the German artillery was already responding.

A fresh wave of high-explosive shells screamed down from above to slam into the British positions with brutal precision.

Archer and his men hit a final hedgerow, bursting through it at a full sprint.

"Get down!" Archer bellowed.

They threw themselves to the ground, and their bodies slammed into the dirt. Archer sucked in deep, ragged breaths, his chest heaving as he tried to regain control.

Jacks was already checking Saunders over. "You good?" Saunders groaned, shaking his head with a grimace, then gave a half-smile. "Just a scratch—nothing worth fussing over." No real wound—just a shallow graze and a bit of a shake from hitting the ground hard.

Behind them, the German spearhead advanced relentlessly with tanks and infantry rolling forwards; their roar was a deafening thunder, and gunfire cracked through the air like whips.

Archer took stock of their situation, reality crashing down like a hammer blow. Two hundred yards behind them was the unstoppable machine of the German advance. Ahead, the last desperate stand of the British defenders.

He turned, meeting the eyes of his men. To a man, they were looking at him; all of them were breathless and waiting.

Waiting for his next move.

Archer sucked in a lungful of air. The burn in his legs dulled under the wave of exhaustion. His heart slammed against his ribs, and his entire body screaming for rest. But rest meant death.

He forced himself to think.

Looking back two hundred yards behind him, the Germans weren't slowing down—tanks, infantry, machine-guns, all rolling forwards like an unstoppable tide.

Ahead—the bridge. The last way across.

The British were dug in on the far side of it with their machine-guns and anti-tank crews ready to destroy anything that moved. To them, he and his men were just silhouettes in the smoke—no different from the enemy bearing down on them.

For a second, his instincts screamed at him to drop, to disappear, to find cover. But there was no cover. Just open ground and the bridge.

Stay, and they die. Run, and they might live. His mind flashed back to the first time he had ever stood before a superior officer as a fresh-faced lieutenant in a crisp uniform. His instructor's voice had rung in his ears:

"A good officer weighs his options. A great officer knows

313

when to stop thinking and act."

Now was that time.

He turned and met the eyes of his men. They were waiting. Breathless. Trusting him to lead.

No more time. No more second-guessing.

"Jacks!" His voice was hoarse but firm. "Stay here! Wait for my signal!"

Before Jacks could protest, Archer pushed off before his own mind could betray him.

Bullets snapped past his ears.

He ran.

Archer stared at the bridge, then back at the British lines on the far side.

"Christ!" he thought. "This is utter madness. One wrong move, they'll gun me down!"

His run turned into a sprint. His legs pumped as fast as they could go.

"I'm British! Hold your fire!"

His voice tore through the chaos, but it wasn't enough.

Archer threw his rifle high in the air, arms spread wide, swinging them back and forth in an X-shape, desperate to make himself seen.

"I'm British, damn it! Hold your fire!"

Wilson squinted through the smoke as he scanned the far side of the bridge. He could see a shape moving through the haze—running figures, chaos.

"Christ, they're moving fast!" he thought, his grip tightening.

Then—something caught his eye.

A lone figure, sprinting like hell, arms waving wildly. A rifle thrown high in the air.

Wilson's stomach lurched. No—no, it can't be...

Then he heard the voice.

"I'm British! Hold your fire!"

Wilson's breath hitched. "It's Archer!" he yelled. "Jennings! It's bloody Archer!"

314

Jennings, standing near the sandbag line, snapped his head around. His sharp eyes locked onto the sprinting figure, and then the flashing movement of his waving arms. The hoarse voice carried over the chaos.

Recognition hit like a punch to the gut.

"Hold your bloody fire!" Jennings bellowed, spinning towards the nearest gun crew. "Friendlies! Friendlies!"

The soldiers hesitated, fingers tight on the triggers. The pause was a breath away from disaster.

"Hold your bloody fire, damn it! Jennings roared again, shoving past Wilson and sprinting towards the bridge.

Around them, men stared in disbelief. The enemy was to their front, closing fast, their fire hammering into the British positions—yet here were two men screaming for a ceasefire.

Then Jennings saw it.

The last Royal Engineers were pulling back, their kit rattling as they ran for cover. The officer in charge was already reaching for the detonator.

Jennings' heart slammed into his ribs. No. Not yet!

He lunged forwards, shoving past a stunned private, boots pounding against stone.

"Hold it!" he bellowed, his voice cutting through the danger. "There's still men out there!"

Startled, the engineer officer turned. His gloved hand hovered over the plunger. His face twisted in frustration.

"Orders are orders, Sergeant Major!" the officer snapped, his fingers tensing over the trigger.

"Not while they're still on the bloody bridge!" Jennings snarled, gripping the man's arm.

A moment's hesitation.

Ahead of them, the thunder of German machine-guns grew

closer.

Jennings locked eyes with the officer.

"Give them time."

Archer hit the bridge at full tilt, boots slamming against the stone as he reached Jennings who had crossed over the bridge to meet him.

The bridge trembled beneath him, vibrating from the relentless impact of German machine-gun fire. Bullets snapped past his ears, ricochetting off stone parapets and chipping shards of stone into the air like razor-sharp shrapnel. A mortar round whistled overhead and slammed into the far embankment with a deafening crack, sending a plume of dirt and debris skywards.

Ahead of Archer, Jennings was already turning towards him. His face set with urgency, but his voice was lost in the din of battle.

Another artillery shell screamed down, exploding just beyond the canal. The shockwave rippled across the bridge, and the concussive force nearly knocked Archer off his feet. The air reeked of burning cordite, and thick smoke curled around them like grasping fingers.

Archer whirled towards Jacks and the others, cupping his hands to his mouth. He bellowed, "Move!" He threw his arm up, beckoning them urgently.

Jacks didn't hesitate. He spun to the others. "Let's go!"

As one, Saunders, Slater, and Matthews staggered forwards, legs burning, stumbling but forcing themselves onwards. They ran for the bridge, ducking as bullets whipped past. Their bodies were silhouetted against the hellish glow of fire and smoke.

Then—the British defenders understood.

Jennings and Wilson weren't raving mad; they were trying to save their own men.

Without hesitation, the British lines erupted with fresh fire, machine-guns and rifles hammering into the advancing

Germans, throwing up plumes of dirt and blood. The Vickers chattered in fury. Its tracers sliced through the thick smoke, forcing the enemy to hit the ground.

The race for the bridge had become a fight for survival.

Tracer rounds laced the air, carving fiery lines through the thick haze, punching into the advancing Germans. Somewhere beyond the bridge, the Vickers machine-gun rattled, sending a sustained burst into the grey-clad figures attempting to push forwards.

Archer barely had time to process it before another round of high-explosive shells crashed down along the canal bank. The blast sent German soldiers hurtling into the air. Their bodies twisted mid-air before hitting the ground. The enemy's advance faltered for just a moment, but the relentless crack of Mausers and MG34s answered. Bullets whined off the stone ruins.

Archer stood firm at the bridge's edge, his breath ragged, his heart hammering in his chest. His boots felt welded to the stone as he watched the last of his men racing towards him through the swirling smoke and fire.

Jacks led the way, sprinting hard, his rifle clutched tightly in each hand. Behind him, Saunders and Slater ran side by side, their movements ragged with exhaustion. Matthews who was limping but determined, lagged a few paces behind, his face twisted in pain.

Wilson was waiting.

Through the haze, he stood near the sandbags, waving his arm high above his head, shouting hoarsely, "Come on! Over here!"

The British lines were erupting, covering their dash with a wave of machine-gun fire. The air was alive with whizzing tracers and the brutal, stuttering roar of the Vickers. A German mortar shell slammed into the far bank, sending up a geyser of mud and water, but the men kept running towards the bridge.

Jacks was first across, his boots hitting stone as he dived behind cover, gasping for breath.

Matthews and Slater followed, but were stumbling onto the bridge, half-dragging each other the final yards before hurling themselves over the sandbags.

Saunders was seconds behind them, still a little dazed and sore from the graze in his leg.

Then Wilson, realising Saunders was struggling, surged forwards, grabbed Saunders under the arm, and half-hauled, half-shoved him the last few feet.

Archer exhaled sharply, and his grip on his rifle loosened for the first time. They'd made it.

But it wasn't over.

He turned. Jennings was already moving, grabbing Archer's arm and hauling him towards the Engineers' trench.

"Come on, Sir! No time to stand about!" Jennings barked; his voice was raw with urgency.

Archer threw one last glance at the assaulting Germans beyond the canal, then turned and ran.

They scrambled into the trench where the engineers huddled around the detonator. Their faces were streaked with sweat and grime.

The officer in charge looked up with his hand already hovering over the plunger. His eyes flashed with impatience.

"We can't wait any longer, Lieutenant!" he snapped.

Archer raised a hand. "Not yet, Sir."

The engineer's brow furrowed in frustration. "What? We don't have—"

"Wait, Sir. Please," Archer cut in, his voice like steel. "Let them get closer."

Jennings glanced at him sharply, understanding dawning in his eyes.

They needed this to be decisive. To hit the Germans at the

perfect moment.

Archer turned back towards the bridge. His knuckles tightened on the trench's edge.

The Germans were coming.

And when they were on it, when they were fully committed to the crossing...

Then they'd blow the bloody thing to hell.

The first wave of Germans surged forwards. Dark shapes cut through the morning haze. They moved in short, controlled bursts, trained by experience and doctrine to advance under cover. Their rifles snapped quick, disciplined fire towards the British positions.

Then the Vickers opened up.

The first squad was instantly ripped apart. Bodies were flung backwards as .303 rounds from a crossfire of two Vickers and rifles tore into them. Men dived for cover, throwing themselves behind the bridge's stone parapet, but there was nowhere to hide.

The second wave pushed forwards, sprinting for the halfway point. A German officer waved his men on, pistol raised.

Crack!

His head snapped back. A rifle round had found its mark. The bridge was turning into a killing zone.

Bodies clogged the crossing, and lifeless figures draped over the twisted wreckage of their fallen. The assault slowed with hesitation creeping in as the British firepower refused to let up.

Then—the German mortars came. The first round struck short, exploding against the embankment with a thudding roar. Dirt and stone erupted into the air.

The second was dead on.

A mortar shell screamed down. Its whistle rose above the chaos for a fleeting second—then impact. The round hit dead centre in a forward-facing British slit trench.

The explosion was instant. In such a confined space, the blast was amplified which turned the trench into a death trap. A

319

violent shockwave ripped through the narrow walls, sending an eruption of dirt, blood, and shattered bone skywards. The two men inside never stood a chance.

Tearing through flesh, uniform and bone, the first soldier closest to the impact, was obliterated outright. His rifle was flung clear, cartwheeling into the dirt ten yards away. The second man, who was caught on the edge of the blast, was hurled backwards like a ragdoll, and his body slammed against the trench wall. He crumpled in a twisted heap as his arms flailed weakly, and his body became peppered with shrapnel wounds. The air reeked of burnt flesh, gunpowder, and churned-up earth. When the dust settled, all that remained was a gaping hole, filled with blood, broken kit, and the lifeless remains of what had been two men seconds earlier.

Farther down the line, men scrambled away from the devastation, throwing themselves into the dirt as more mortar rounds rained in.

"Stretcher bearer! Stretcher bearer!"

More explosions followed, hammering the British line. Archer ducked low, wiping dirt from his face.

"They're zeroing in!"

Jennings snapped his head up just as the first tank appeared through the haze. It clanked forwards, its turret swinging slowly, the stubby barrel of its 37mm gun lowering towards the defenders.

Then came the first burst from its coaxial machine-gun.

Bullets ripped through the air, slamming into sandbags and shredding the upper floors of the British-held buildings. A second tank appeared. This one rolled forwards with less caution, its turret already firing high explosive rounds into the ruins.

Boom!

A British position vanished in a fireball, the rifle pit collapsing inward with a dull, concussive thump. From the smoke, a few figures staggered away—one crawling, his uniform smoking. Then—one of the Vickers teams went silent.

Archer snapped his head left, spotting the gun lying on its side, the crew sprawled across the sandbags. The tank had found its mark.

"We've lost the Vickers!" someone bellowed.

Then—THUMP.

The hard crack of a two-pounder firing.

The round struck the lead tank, bouncing off the angled armour with a metallic clang.

A second shot followed almost immediately.

This time, it punched through.

The hatch burst open, and the commander clawed his way out as his uniform smouldered, and his body twisted in pain.

Before he could even scream, British rifle fire ripped into him, rounds slamming into his torso. His body convulsed, twisted, and then tumbled off the side of the tank.

But behind him, the second tank was already moving.

It rumbled forwards with its guns roaring and blasting in blind fury at the British line.

The machine-gun spat fire. Tracers whipped through the air while the 37mm gun recoiled back, chambering another round.

Inside the tight, metal coffin, the German loader worked frantically, slamming fresh shells into place. His hands were slick with sweat and cordite. Barking orders with a raw voice, the commander ordered the driver to force the steel behemoth forwards, and it rolled over the wreckage of the earlier charge.

Bodies—German—lay sprawled across the bridge, some motionless, others twisted into unnatural angles. The tracks of the tank crushed them beneath its weight; bones snapped, and flesh mangled into the steel treads.

321

Then—

BANG!

Archer's knuckles tightened against the trench's edge, and his eyes locked on the enemy pushing forwards. The second German tank was halfway across. Its machine-gun was still blazing into the British line. More infantry followed in its wake, clambering over the wreckage with their boots pounding on the shattered stones of the bridge.

It was time.

Archer turned sharply to the engineer officer.

"Now!"

The officer didn't hesitate. His fist slammed down on the detonator.

For a split second—nothing.

Then—

Hell was unleashed.

A deep, guttural boom erupted from beneath the bridge. A violent roar swallowed the battlefield. As a column of fire and stone exploded skywards, the ground bucked, and the force ripped the very air apart. One moment the bridge was a solid structure, the next second it had disintegrated into a maelstrom of splintered stone, and shattered bodies. Rolling out like a thunderclap, the shockwave knocked men flat. Archer felt himself hurled backwards, dirt and debris raining down as if the earth itself had been torn open.

German infantry caught on the bridge were instantly vaporised—the ones near the edges were flung like ragdolls, their bodies cartwheeling through the air before smashing into the canal.

The first tank, crippled by the 2-pounder, was perched at the bridge's entrance when the charges blew. The force of the explosion sent a fireball through its shattered hull, and flames now burst from every hatch before the wreck started popping and it eventually exploded.

But the second tank—the one still advancing—never had a chance. The blast erupted directly beneath it, and a massive fireball engulfed the steel behemoth. Shockwaves ripped through its underside, sending its turret flying as the hull lifted from the bridge in a cloud of fire and debris.

30-tons of machine twisted violently in midair; its frame was wrenched apart as the collapsing bridge gave way beneath it. For a split second, the burning wreck seemed to hover in the firestorm. Then it plunged straight down, vanishing into the churning, firelit water below.

A deep, thunderous groan echoed across the battlefield: the dying breath of the bridge. For a split second, cracks spread like veins through the ancient stone, spiderwebbing across the arches and supports, loosened mortar crumbling away. Slowly, with a sickening roar, the entire central span gave way.

Massive blocks of stone—some the size of small vehicles—sheared away from the structure, tumbling into the canal below. A great cloud of dust and debris exploded outwards as the centuries-old foundations crumbled under the force of the charges. The iron railings twisted and snapped. Sections of reinforced framework tore free and plummeted alongside the shattered masonry.

The shockwave surged through the water, sending violent ripples across the canal's surface as half-submerged wreckage bobbed and spun in the turbulent current.

The German tank caught in the explosion was lost in an instant. It was hurled sideways in the violent collapse, its blackened hull flipping end over end before vanishing into the boiling, firelit water. The remains of the bridge followed, falling in chunks, some vanishing beneath the waves, others jutting out like broken teeth from the riverbed. What had been a direct path across the canal seconds ago, was now nothing but a shattered ruin with stone, steel and bodies sinking into the depths.

This assault had been stopped, but there was no time to celebrate. The echo of the explosion faded, leaving behind a haunting quiet. The kind that never lasted long.

For a few seconds, nothing moved. Smoke billowed over the ruins of the bridge, curling into the morning sky like a funeral shroud. The canal churned with debris, shattered stone and twisted steel bobbing alongside lifeless bodies. The air stank of cordite, burning fuel and blood.

Then, from beyond the smoke, came the thunder of new artillery. The ground trembled. A fresh barrage rained down, hammering the far end of the British line.

The Germans were regrouping. Archer wiped dust from his mouth, and his jaw tightened.

The fight wasn't over yet.

Archer lowered his arm from his face, the shockwave still ringing in his ears. Smoke coiled through the air, thick with burning fuel, pulverised stone and the acrid stench of death. The canal was an inferno of wreckage, and the twisted steel of the bridge jutted from the water like broken ribs.

He turned to the engineer officer who was wiping sweat and dust from his face. His hand was still rested on the detonator box as if ensuring the job was done.

Archer straightened, swallowed, and extended his hand. "Hell of a job, Sir."

The officer blinked at him, surprised at first. Archer was only a lieutenant, after all. But after a beat, he grasped Archer's hand firmly.

"Just doing my job, Lieutenant." The man exhaled sharply, rolling the tension from his shoulders. "But I'll take that. Bloody fine timing on your part, too."

A rare grin flickered across the engineer's exhausted face before he glanced towards the smoke still rising. "You'd best get moving. I reckon Jerry's not done yet."

Archer took the hint.

"Right. Jennings, let's move."

They moved fast, keeping low, ducking over the shell-shattered road and across ruins where dust and smoke still hung thick in the air.

The artillery hadn't stopped and was not stopping.

A fresh barrage screamed overhead. The sharp whine of incoming shells split the air before crashing into the British line, sending plumes of fire and stone skywards. Archer flinched as a round smashed into a nearby building, the impact punching through brick like paper. A section of the upper wall collapsed and cascaded down in a rain of rubble.

Jennings yanked him forwards, his voice rough over the chaos. "Move, Sir!"

They half-ran, half-stumbled towards the British positions, past hunched figures coughing through the dust, and men bent double as they reloaded weapons with shaking hands. Farther down the line, a sergeant bellowed orders. His voice was barely cutting through the clamour of rifle fire and the chattering of a surviving Bren gun.

A wounded soldier clutched at his bloodied arm as his teeth bared in pain while a medic worked frantically. Both men flinched every time another explosion rattled the ground.

A fresh crack of a German sniper round punched through a wooden beam only inches from Archer's shoulder.

"Snipers!" someone yelled.

Jennings and Archer threw themselves into cover, pressing against the shell-ridden remains of a shop front. Dust rained down around them, and the ground vibrating with the constant hammering of German machine-guns. Archer glanced ahead. Wilson and the others were hunkered down, waiting for them with weapons raised and ready.

They weren't out of this yet.

When they reached Wilson and the others, Matthews was the first to break the silence.

"Jesus Christ." Matthews exhaled, shaking his head. He glanced back towards the blackened ruins of the bridge, the shattered remains still smouldering. "Now that was a proper demolition."

Archer raised an eyebrow. "Professional opinion?"

Matthews snorted, rubbing the dirt from his face. "Aye, Sir. Bang on, that was. Never seen one go up so clean."

Jacks let out a rough laugh, shaking his head as he spat dust from his mouth.

"Oh, piss off, Matthews. You said the same thing about the last bridge we blew up."

Matthews grinned, flicking a bit of rubble from his sleeve.

"Aye, well. I suppose I've got a thing for bridges."

Jacks rolled his eyes, muttering, "At least this one didn't nearly take us with it."

Archer hid a smirk, but before anyone could respond, a fresh burst of German machine-gun fire tore through the rubble nearby, kicking up stone and dust.

The moment was over.

Jacks stepped forwards. His mood had changed from being playful, and he set his face to a grim but focused determination.

"We need to talk, Sir." He lowered his voice. "We're out. Of bloody everything."

Archer's stomach tightened. "Ammunition?"

Jacks shook his head. "Nearly all gone. The lads have maybe two rounds each—if that. We're down to bayonets and strong language."

Archer glanced around, assessing the men. He could see it in their eyes: exhaustion, but also the cold, settled knowledge that there was nothing left to fight with.

Before he could speak, Wilson stepped in.

"Cartwright went to the R.A.P., Sir."

Archer looked up sharply.

"With the wounded?"

"Yes, Sir. He managed to scrounge a truck and got them away."

Archer lifted his chin, processing everything that was happening.

Somewhere in the distance, the last echoes of artillery fire faded. The ceaseless hammering that had rattled their bones for what felt like hours was gone, leaving behind only the crackling of distant fires and the low groans of the wounded.

For the first time since the bridge blew, there was a pause—a brief, uneasy silence that felt almost unnatural.

Men who had been hunched low, bracing against every impact, now dared to lift their heads. A few soldiers blinked into the smoke as if waiting for the next barrage that hadn't come.

Even the distant German guns seemed to have gone quiet.

Archer exhaled. His muscles were still tense and unwilling to believe it was over.

Then, before he could decide what to do next, a sharp voice cut through the haze.

"You lot look like hell."

Archer turned—a Captain from the Sherwood Foresters stood nearby, his uniform dirt-streaked but posture still clipped and proper.

His eyes swept over Archer's men, taking in their tattered state, the empty rifles, the haunted expressions.

"So, where've you come from?"

Archer turned, still brushing dust from his tattered uniform, meeting the captain's gaze evenly.

"Sir, we're what's left of D Company, 9th Battalion, Greenmoors. Assigned to 145th Brigade, 48th Division." His voice steady but tired. "We were the rearguard for the brigade's withdrawal from Cassel."

The captain exhaled sharply through his nose, then rested his hands on his hips, his voice carrying a hard, knowing edge.

"I'm going to assume you're out of ammunition, your men are spent, and you've got no orders beyond 'hold until the last bloody second'?"

Archer gritted his teeth. "That about covers it, Sir."

The captain huffed, shaking his head. "Seems to be a lot of that going around." His tone was stark and edged with dry sarcasm.

Chapter 18

The ruins of an old shop slumped against the shattered street. Its façade had long ago been blasted away, leaving only jagged fragments of brick and timber clawing at the sky. The first floor was exposed. It was nothing more than a shell with charred beams overhead, and its shattered walls barely offered shelter from the elements. Dust and debris coated the ground, and what little remained of the interior had been stripped away—only splintered shelves and broken counters hinted at what the place had once been.

Scattered amongst the wreckage, a handful of Sherwood Forester men moved with quiet purpose. Some stacked rubble to reinforce a makeshift barricade near the doorway while others checked their rifles with practiced motions, almost mechanical. A soldier crouched by a small cooking tin, stirring something that smelled like tea though no one paid it much attention.

Outside, the sky hung heavy and grey, thick with the distant drone of engines and the occasional thud of far-off explosions. Somewhere beyond the horizon, Dunkirk was burning. The Luftwaffe's latest raid had sent columns of smoke curling into the sky like funeral pyres. The air carried the acrid stench of cordite and charred wood which clung to everything. The war had hollowed out this place, and yet, for now, it still held.

It was amongst this wreckage that Archer and his men had regrouped and met the captain from the Foresters.

Markham pushed himself upright, rolling his shoulders as he took in the group properly. His expression was weary but steady, and his Midlands accent carried through the ruined space with a quiet authority.

"Captain Edward Markham, Sherwood Foresters," he said, offering a hand in greeting.

Archer took it with a firm shake. "Lieutenant Tom Archer, Greenmoors." He glanced around the defensive position. "Appreciate you holding on to let us cross."

Markham huffed a tired chuckle, rubbing a hand across his jaw. "Not like I had much of a say in it." His eyes flicked over the men behind Archer, noting their ragged state, and the silent way they held themselves. "Looks like you've been through it."

Archer exhaled, glancing at Jacks, Jennings, and the others. "We have. Just trying to get what's left of us to Dunkirk."

Markham gave a wry smile. "You and the whole bloody British Army!" He gestured towards the ruined street where a few of his men worked quietly to reinforce barricades of rubble and sandbags. "Well, this lovely place is called Bergues. We're the last line now."

There was a finality in his voice, and Archer recognised it immediately. Markham had already made peace with his fate.

Markham let out a breath, rolling his shoulders as if the weight of it all sat heavy upon them. "What's left of us—131st Brigade: the Queen's Own Royal West Kents, the Sussex boys—we're holding the canal line. Our job's simple: buy time. As you've seen, the bastards are pushing in hard from the south, trying to break through the perimeter. If we break here, it's over."

His eyes flicked back to Archer, and though his tone remained level, he jabbed a finger towards the horizon where thick plumes of smoke from Dunkirk's latest air raid curled into the sky. "Ten miles between us and the beaches. We hold, more men get out. We fall, and the whole bloody thing caves in."

A silence settled between them, broken only by the distant hum of aircraft and the occasional crack of gunfire.

Markham turned back to Archer, and his face was grim but resigned. "So that's it, really. We're here until we've got no bullets left. The colonel's adamant—we'll make them pay for every inch."

Archer looked solemnly at Markham. For a brief moment, his fingers hesitated as he reached into his breast pocket, pulling out the metal flask Pembroke had given him at the start of all this. How long ago had that been? It felt like another lifetime.

Was Pembroke even still alive? Archer had no way of knowing. There'd been no word, no sign. His last glimpse of

Pembroke had been in the bitter retreat, swallowed up by smoke, gunfire and the bodies of the fallen. Dead? Captured? Still out there somewhere, fighting to survive? The thought of a man who had become a friend through all this settled in his gut like a stone.

He gave the flask a shake before offering it to the captain. Pembroke lingered in his mind.

Markham eyed it, and a faint smile broke through the exhaustion. He took the flask, tilted it back, and let a quick sip burn its way down his throat. The warmth settled in his chest: a brief, welcome comfort.

"Thank you. I think I needed that," he murmured, passing the flask back. Then, straightening, he continued, "Well, Archer, this isn't going to get us anywhere. Can I ask you to pop over to our Company HQ? I'll meet you there. It's just across the street—baker's shop, other side of that row." He gestured in the general direction.

"Of course, Sir." Archer's response was swift and respectful.

Markham gave a final nod before turning and jogging off towards the command post.

Archer watched him go before snapping back into command mode. "Jacks, Jennings—get the lads together. We're moving."

"Yes, Sir!" Both men responded almost in unison.

Relief washed across the faces of the men—exhausted, hollow-eyed, but grateful with the realisation they weren't getting tied up in this fight. They were moving on.

Archer stepped into the small bakery through a battered

opening which had once been the main door where locals would have entered, perhaps a bell ringing to announce their arrival. Now, there was no door, no bell—just the ruin of a once-proud shop.

Once, this place had been an essential place to meet, to talk, to buy bread. Now, it was a place where men planned how to keep hell at bay.

"Ah, Archer! Good man!" Captain Markham's voice carried an excitable tone. "Can I ask you for a favour?"

Archer stared at him, a flicker of bemusement crossing his face. *Christ, he's not going to give me a mission, is he?*

His expression must have given him away because Markham chuckled.

"Calm down, Lieutenant. I'm not sending you forwards or anything like that." A small smile crept onto the captain's face as he saw the relief in Archer's.

"No, old chap. It's entirely personal." Markham pulled out three or four sheets of paper which were folded in half, and he passed them to Archer, his voice dropping slightly. "When you get back to Blighty, can you see this gets to the wife?"

Archer automatically reached out, taking the papers as if they were written orders.

Markham tapped a scribbled note on one of the pages. "Address is there. I'm afraid I'll have to stiff you for a stamp, though."

Archer glanced over the address before tucking the papers into his pocket. "I'd be delighted to, Sir."

"Good man." Markham extended his hand, and Archer took it in a firm shake. "Good luck, Archer."

"Good luck to you, Sir." With that, he turned and stepped out into the grey light of the derelict street. The distant thud of artillery continued to rumble behind them as he spotted Jennings and Jacks who were already forming the men into a single file.

Their faces were set for the long march ahead.

The march began in silence. Boots scraped against broken ground, and the rhythm was steady but slow; exhaustion pressed down on every step. Somewhere far behind them, the artillery echoed as a reminder that time was against them.

No one spoke. What was there left to say?

As they pressed on, the ruins began to thin, giving way to open fields scarred by craters and the scattered wreckage of war: burnt-out vehicles, a shattered gun carriage, the skeletal remains of a farmhouse that had taken a direct hit.

Then came the smell.

Even before the Regimental Aid Point came into view, it was in the air. The cloying, metallic tang of blood and the sharp sting of antiseptic failed to mask the rot of the dying. There was a low murmur of voices that carried on the wind, punctuated by groans, ragged breaths, and the occasional choked sob.

The Regimental Aid Post was little more than a makeshift clearing nestled behind a collapsed barn where the skeletal remains of its charred beams jutted out like broken ribs. Tents sagged under the pressure of pain, and death flapped weakly in the breeze. Their canvases were stained with dried blood and filth. Stretchers rested on trestles, and their occupants groaned or lay unnervingly still while others—too many—were simply sprawled on the dirt, waiting their turn to be seen under the open sky.

Stretcher bearers moved with grim efficiency, picking their way through the wounded. Their uniforms were dark with sweat and grime. Meanwhile, orderlies worked with desperate urgency; their hands were slick with blood as they bound wounds and administered what medicines they still had, or whispered reassurances to men who were barely clinging on.

Archer noticed a young private, face streaked with dirt,

gripped another man's hand as a padre murmured a hurried prayer beside him. Barely masking the underlying rot of too many untreated wounds, the sharp stench of iodine and antiseptic made Archer's nose tingle.

A steady chorus of pain filled the clearing: low moans, occasional sharp cries, the rattling breaths of the dying. Nearby, an orderly cursed under his breath as he fumbled with a bandage while another barked for more dressings. The distant sounds of battle seemed muffled against the suffering here. Yet there was no need for a reminder that the war raged on—not when another ambulance pulled up in a cloud of dust, its brakes squealing. The driver and an orderly leapt out, swinging open the rear doors and climbing in. Moments later, they emerged, struggling under the weight of another stretcher, another poor soul groaning as he was lifted down into the mayhem.

Archer and his men were thankful they were not among these poor souls, but they were all too aware it was only the grace of luck that had kept them from it.

An orderly, sleeves rolled up and uniform stained dark, barked orders at a subordinate who scrambled to comply. A surgeon, his hands slick with blood, worked frantically beneath a tattered canvas sheet, the dull glint of a scalpel just visible in the dim light.

Archer felt the hopelessness of the scene pressing down on him. This wasn't a place for men to be saved. It was a place for them to stop dying. A place where time and medicine could do no more, and mercy came not from the hands of the living, but from the slow embrace of silence. Here, pain was measured in gasps, hope in dwindling heartbeats, and death in the quiet surrender of a man who no longer had the strength to hold on.

His gaze drifted across the ruined aid post, past the orderlies working with mechanical urgency and past the wounded writhing on stretchers until it landed on a familiar figure.

Padre Cartwright stood apart from the others. He was slumped against the shattered remains of a wall; his eyes were hollow, and his uniform was streaked with mud and dried blood. The weight of his calling—the burden of offering comfort in a place where none could be found—had etched deep lines into his face.

Forlorn and exhausted, the padre's hands clutched a small leather-bound book against his chest. His fingers tightened and loosened around it as if searching for words that would never come. He exhaled sharply, running a hand through his matted hair, and for the first time since Archer had known him, he looked truly lost.

Archer took a step forwards.

Cartwright didn't notice him at first. His head was bowed, and his lips moved in a soundless prayer—or perhaps just a desperate, whispered plea. When he finally looked up, his eyes were dark hollows. Helplessness bore down on him, relentless and crushing.

"They're not taking them," he said, his voice barely above a whisper.

Archer frowned. "What?"

"The stretcher cases." Cartwright exhaled sharply, shaking his head. "Orders came down. Only the walking wounded are being taken. Take up too much space on the ships." He looked away, staring out over the stretchers laid out in the dirt. "Three of our wounded men...they were walking when we got here, but now..." His throat worked, but the words caught. "They're in no condition to move."

Archer's jaw tightened. He scanned the aid post. His stomach twisted as he took in the gaunt faces, the shivering bodies barely clinging to consciousness. These men had made it this far. They should have been safe. But now they were being left behind.

"Who gave the order?" Archer demanded.

Cartwright's voice was hoarse. "The order's come down—stretcher cases are to remain behind."

Archer stared at him. "But who the hell gave that order?"

"High Command." Cartwright exhaled sharply, looking over the wounded. He tried to explain. "They're prioritising the walking wounded. They are only taking men who can make it on their own."

His eyes flicked to a stretcher near them where a young soldier barely out of his teens lay motionless. His face was pallid, and his breaths were shallow. Cartwright swallowed hard. "The order's clear, Tom. We're to leave them."

Archer's jaw clenched. "And what? We just..." He stopped himself, dragging a hand down his face. He already knew the answer.

Cartwright hesitated, his fingers tightening around the small Bible in his grip. "The medical officers and orderlies...they've drawn lots."

Archer's head snapped up. "What?"

Cartwright's voice carried the heavy loss within it. "Someone stays with the wounded. That's how it's done." His gaze drifted across the broken bodies lining the aid post. "We won't leave them alone, so...we drew lots."

A cold weight settled in Archer's chest. He studied Cartwright, suddenly uneasy.

"We?"

Cartwright didn't answer at first. He exhaled sharply as his gaze flicked towards the wounded laid out around them. When he finally spoke, his voice was quieter and edged with something Archer couldn't quite place.

"I was prepared to stay," he admitted. "But I lost the draw."

The padre gave a small, weary shrug. "Suppose it wasn't my

time."

Cartwright let out a breath. It was half a sigh and half a bitter chuckle, and then he managed a faint, tired smile. "Well, it would have been a good test of my faith."

Archer studied him for a moment. "Test?" he echoed, surprise flickering in his voice. "Padre, you can't be doubting your faith, surely."

Cartwright hesitated, as if weighing the question. Then, slowly, he exhaled. "Looking around here, it's hard to imagine..."

Archer didn't let him finish. "Padre, I won't pretend to understand matters of faith," he said firmly. "But if there's ever a time you need it, it's now. Question Him if you must, but don't turn away—not now."

Cartwright glanced at him, something unreadable in his tired eyes. Then, after a long pause, he nodded. "Perhaps you're right, Tom," he murmured, his voice steadier than before.

Archer gave a small, firm nod. "Right now, I have to be. Because if we've got anything left to get us out of this, it's faith." He glanced around at the haggard faces still with them—the men who had made it this far but still had a long way to go. "If not for you and me, then for them. They're going to need it."

A flicker of something—resolve maybe—passed through Cartwright's eyes. He straightened slightly, squaring his shoulders, and the weary slump eased just a little.

Archer offered a faint smirk. "Besides, you might've lost the draw, but that doesn't mean you're off the hook, Padre. We still need you."

Cartwright let out a quiet chuckle, shaking his head. "God help you, then."

Archer clapped him on the shoulder and grinned. "Reckon He already has."

With that, Archer called out, "RSM, get the lads ready. We

338

move in five."

Jennings gave a sharp "yes Sir," and was already turning to round up the men.

As the group stirred into action, Jacks appeared at Archer's side, lifting his shoulders as he pulled the sling of his rifle higher. "Y'know, Sir, if we push hard, we could make it before dark," he said, his voice carrying a hint of quiet hope. "Eight miles to the beaches, give or take. Tough slog, but we've done worse."

Archer exhaled, considering the distance. Eight miles. After everything they'd been through, it felt like an impossible journey—but Jacks was right. They'd pushed through worse. "That's assuming Jerry doesn't have other ideas," he muttered, scanning the tree line ahead.

Nearby, Cartwright let out a weary sigh, rubbing the bridge of his nose. "I still have the truck," he said finally.

Archer turned to him, brow raised. "You what?"

Cartwright gestured vaguely towards the road. "Parked up just beyond that hedge."

Archer stared at him for a beat, then smirked. "And you're the one questioning your faith." He turned back to Jacks. "Pass the word—the padre's just saved us a few miles on foot."

Jacks grinned. "Sir."

There was no need for further discussion. Within minutes, they were packed in the truck, and the engine coughed to life as Cartwright took the wheel.

The Bedford's worn suspension groaned under the sudden weight of eighteen exhausted men whose bodies were crammed shoulder to shoulder in the narrow bed. The truck, built for carrying supplies rather than men, left little room for comfort. Rifles and boots tangled together, elbows jostled against ribs, and the sharp edges of ammunition pouches dug into flesh. The wooden slats along the sides, once meant for securing cargo, now served as handholds for those forced to stand, and who gripped tightly as the vehicle lurched forwards.

Archer had managed to wedge himself near the tailgate. His knees were bent awkwardly, and his back was pressed against the hard wooden panel. Next to him, Jennings perched on an overturned supply crate with his normal unreadable expression; the usual authority in his bearing had been dulled by exhaustion.

The three walking wounded had been placed in the centre where they could lean against one another for support. Their bandages, hastily attended to at the aid post, were already dark with sweat, dirt and blood. One man had his head slumped forwards. His breathing came shallow but steady while another clutched his side and gritted his teeth as the truck jostled over uneven ground.

Saunders, Slater, and Matthews had found places along the sides with their backs to the wooden panels, and their rifles resting across their laps. Anderson, the RAF airman, sat hunched between two infantrymen. His grip was tight around the rifle he had barely learnt to use

At the front, just behind the cab, Wilson and Jacks had secured a standing position, and their knuckles whitened as they braced against the roof of the cab for balance. The air inside was thick with the mingled scents of unwashed bodies, blood, and the lingering acrid bite of cordite. It was always lingering as a reminder of the fight they had barely escaped.

Outside, the road stretched ahead. Silently, the men watched as they passed the remnants of a retreating army: abandoned trucks, scattered equipment, and the occasional motionless figure half-hidden in the roadside ditches. Witnessing the realities of what had been experienced, quietened them.

The rhythmic growl of the engine was the only constant sound, save for the occasional cough or murmured curse at the truck bouncing over another rut in the road.

Cartwright gripped the wheel tightly and kept his eyes

forwards. His hands were steady despite the weight of exhaustion pressing down on all of them. No one spoke. There was nothing left to say.

They were still moving. And for now, that was enough.

As they moved ever forwards, the road became a grinding procession of men, machines, and misery. The truck rattled along at a slow, laboured pace, threading through the remnants of a retreating army.

They passed long columns of trudging soldiers with their faces hollow-eyed with exhaustion, and uniforms stained with sweat and filth. Some turned at the sound of the engine, hope flickering in their gazes—only to fade when they realised the truck was full. One man raised a hand as if to wave them down, then let it fall limply to his side, knowing better.

Becoming more frequent were abandoned vehicles lining the roadside like the carcasses of a broken war machine. Trucks had been left where they had run dry; their engines were cold and silent, and their cargoes of discarded kit and scattered rations had been spilt onto the road. Wrecked Bren carriers sat with their abandoned equipment smouldering and blackened by fire while a Matilda tank lay motionless in a ditch with its turret split open like a cracked eggshell. Its crew long since gone.

Here and there, the retreat had turned chaotic. A dead horse lay tangled in the harness of an overturned supply wagon. Its bloated body had swollen in the warm air, and the stench rolled across the road in sickly waves. A few broken rifles and shattered helmets littered the roadside, cast aside by men too exhausted to carry them farther.

The farther they travelled, the thicker the congestion became. Lorries moved in fits and starts, motorcycles weaved through the gaps and officers barked orders that no one had the energy to follow. The road ahead was still open but barely.

Then a military policeman stepped into their path, standing

in the middle of the road with one arm raised. His white gaiters and webbing were stained with the grime of sweat and filth, and his face was hollow with exhaustion.

Cartwright braked hard, and the truck shuddered to a stop. The MP strode to the driver's side, slapping a hand on the door. His voice was sharp, carrying over the din of engines and weary footfalls.

"Pull over into the field ahead. Leave the lorry. Orders are to dump it, drain the oil and leave the engine running and move on foot."

The engine sputtered as Cartwright rolled the Bedford to a final, weary halt in the field. The moment the wheels stopped turning, men began clambering out, boots hitting the dry earth with dull thuds.

Not being mechanically minded, Cartwright looked a little confused, "The corporal said to drain the oil and let leave the engine running?"

Without another word, Jacks dropped to his knees. "Not to worry, Padre. I've got this!" He crawled under the truck towards the engine with his fingers running along the underside of the sump. "Oil plug should be under here..." he muttered. Then— "Got it," he grunted, trying to twist it loose. No luck. It was seized tight. Jacks exhaled sharply and reached for his bayonet. He tried a quick, sharp stab—nothing. The tip merely scraped along the metal, leaving a shallow groove.

Frowning, he shifted his position, lying fully beneath the sump. He braced the bayonet against his shoulder, adjusted his grip, then drove it upwards with everything he had.

Teeth gritted, and his whole body strained against the resistance. His muscles were taut as his hands wrapped tightly around the hilt. The metal groaned, buckled slightly—then, with a screech of tearing steel, the blade punched through.

Thick, black oil spilt down the bayonet, trickling towards

the handle before running over Jacks' fingers. Warm and slick, it coated the backs of his hands. With one smooth, practiced motion, Jacks yanked the bayonet free and rolled out from under the truck, wiping his hands on his uniform.

"She's done," he muttered, casting a satisfied glance at the dark puddle pooling beneath the truck like spreading blood. Jacks picked himself up. "She'll be metal scrap in ten minutes."

Nearby, Saunders and Slater went to work on the tyres, their bayonets stabbing deep into the thick rubber. The blades slid in with a dull hiss, and air escaped in violent bursts as the truck settled lower onto its axles.

One tyre down. Another. A third.

Saunders grunted, unfixing his bayonet. "That'll stop them rolling out in a hurry."

Meanwhile, Jennings spotted a pickaxe resting against an abandoned lorry. He grabbed it, strode over to the front of the Bedford, and with a grunt of effort, swung it hard into the radiator grille.

Metal crunched. Coolant sprayed outward, splattering across the engine block and the dirt below. Steam hissed violently from the ruptured system, curling into the air like smoke from a dying fire.

"Reckon that's done it," Jennings muttered, stepping back to admire his handiwork.

Archer cast a final glance over the Bedford. The oil was draining, the tyres lay punctured and sagging, the radiator was a twisted wreck, and the engine—still idling—was only minutes from grinding itself into oblivion.

"That'll do," he said at last.

The truck shuddered as something inside the engine gave a metallic clunk: a death rattle of twisted parts and failing pistons. Smoke curled from beneath the hood and gave the last breath of a machine that had carried them.

"Right," Archer called, slinging his rifle over his shoulder. "Let's move."

343

The men turned away, leaving the dying Bedford behind as they trudged back towards the road, boots crunching in the dirt.

A few minutes later, with one final groan of metal, the Bedford's engine seized completely, locking itself into a silent, lifeless husk. Just another wreck in the long, broken trail to Dunkirk.

Chapter 19

Dunkirk was a ghost of itself: a city stripped bare and left to burn.

Shattered glass and broken timbers littered the cobbles. It had become a town that had long since stopped functioning. Shops stood gutted, their windows were smashed and signs hung askew from twisted metal brackets. Furniture, discarded kit, and overturned crates were strewn across the roads, left behind in the urgency and panic of retreat. Flyers that had been dropped by the Luftwaffe and other papers fluttered in the breeze, catching in gutters already clogged with ash and filth.

A rancid cocktail of smoke, sewage, and rot clung to the air. The stench of burnt flesh clung to everything. It was an inescapable, sickly-sweet reek that turned the stomach. Somewhere nearby, something smouldered—rubber, wood, maybe bodies—to create a foul, choking haze over the ruins.

As Archer and his group moved through the beleaguered Dunkirk, their steps slow and languished, they witnessed gutters clogged with filth, a slick mix of blood, stagnant water, and refuse that had been trampled into a foul paste by thousands of desperate boots. Flies swarmed in thick clusters, drawn to the carrion stench of the fallen and had the men gagging as they moved through the streets. A man lay nearby, half-covered by rubble, and his uniform was stained black with dried blood. His face was slack-jawed and bloated.

A few yards ahead, a dead horse lay sprawled across the road. Its belly had burst open, exposing a dark, wet tangle of organs that glistened in the fading light. The stench of decay poured from it in a rancid wave that made the men instinctively turn away.

Something crunched under Archer's boot. He glanced down. A shard of bone, pale against the dirt. Archer immediately aware of the horrors that had occurred and were continuing to occur in the hell that was Dunkirk. It lay among the broken glass, splintered wood, and spent shell casings: just another fragment of the battlefield scattered through the ruins. He exhaled slowly, breathing deeply out of his mouth. It barely helped.

As they walked amongst the bodies of the fallen which lay where they had dropped, some were sprawled in the open-abandoned in their final moments. Others had been covered with greatcoats by passing men who'd had a brief second to spare. A few remained slumped in doorways with their expressions frozen in exhaustion as if they had simply sat down and never stood up again. Archer felt the silence pressing in. The air seemed to thrum with the pressure of it, no gunfire now, no shouted orders, only the low murmur of boots crunching on rubble, the occasional clatter of shifting debris, and the ragged breaths of men who had seen too much.

It wasn't just the sight of the bodies that gnawed at them; it was the small details. A boot lying half off a foot, the twisted fingers of a man who had reached for his rifle too late, the dull gleam of a wedding ring on a hand now caked with dirt. The men kept their eyes forwards, but their faces were pale, jaws clenched tight. Each man walked as if the ghosts might reach out and pull him down too.

The roads of Dunkirk crisscrossed like a spider's web, weaving through the shattered town. They were littered with abandoned vehicles, trucks shoved aside in the chaos, their doors flung open, contents scattered across the tarmac. Artillery had chewed through the wreckage, splintering wood and steel alike. Here and there, the twisted hulks of burned-out cars and lorries marked the frantic, hopeless flight of those who were trying to escape.

Bren carriers, some burnt-out and others with shattered tracks, had been left to rust in the streets. A Renault AHN lay on its side, half-buried in rubble where a building had collapsed onto it. Its driver's seat was empty, but the windscreen was riddled with bullet holes.

Among the wreckage, stretcher bearers weaved through the devastation, their uniforms streaked with grime and old blood, and their boots kicked up flecks of dust as they hauled the latest casualties towards what passed for medical stations. The wounded lay sprawled wherever there was space: against shattered walls, slumped in doorways, or propped up against abandoned crates. Their faces were pale with hollow eyes; every movement they made was sluggish.

An orderly knelt beside a man with a roughly bandaged thigh, whispering something meant to comfort, though the soldier's vacant stare suggested he wasn't hearing a word of it. Nearby, another was being hauled from a cart, tunic cut open to reveal a hastily packed wound, his breath rattling in short, shallow bursts. Archer and his men moved past it all with their eyes fixed ahead, the horror of it lingering in the air, impossible to shake.

Behind them, in the shadow of a half-collapsed building, a doctor worked with quiet urgency. Archer could see his hands were steady despite the carnage. His face was drawn and streaked with exhaustion, and his shirt sleeves were rolled to the elbows. But unlike the frenzied field stations Archer had seen before, there was no shouting, no barking orders: just weary determination.

A man groaned from the ground to their left, and they all felt something different as his trembling hand reached for his canteen, but no one was left to help him. The ones who could still move would have to wait their turn. The ones who couldn't... would have to wait for something else. The sickening feeling of total helplessness passed through every one of Archer's small group as they continued to move onwards.

348

Everywhere, men moved with the same haunted, hollow-eyed exhaustion. These were soldiers who had fought their way back to Dunkirk only to find the end still out of reach.

Ahead of them, the road sloped downwards towards the harbour. The sky beyond was an eerie mix of thick, black smoke and flickering orange flames where warehouses burnt unchecked, throwing a dim glow over the water.

Dunkirk was dying. But for now, it still held.

The rumble of distant guns was constant: a dull, rhythmic hammering that never ceased. As Archer and his men moved deeper into Dunkirk, the sounds of the town under fire grew louder—no longer distant but a chaotic roar that filled every shattered street.

A sharp whistling tore through the sky.

"Down!" Archer bellowed.

The men dove for cover as a German shell crashed into a row of buildings ahead. The explosion sent a towering plume of fire and debris into the air with glass shattering and bricks flying like deadly shrapnel. A deafening boom rolled through the narrow streets and pressed against their chests with concussive force. When the dust settled, what had once been a cluster of shops had become a smoking ruin with flames licking hungrily at the wreckage.

"Jesus," Jacks muttered, pushing himself up and coughing through the thick smoke. "They're hammering the bloody place to the ground."

Ahead, more explosions ripped through the streets of Dunkirk, setting fire to warehouses and sending waves of men scrambling for safety. The fires burnt ferociously. Their glow reflected off the broken windows of buildings that had already been half-destroyed by earlier bombardments. The heat was suffocating. Thick, choking, black smoke clogged their throats and stung their eyes.

Suddenly from above them, the unmistakable shriek of Luftwaffe Stukas cut through the sky. The terrifying siren wail of the dive-bombers sent a fresh wave of panic through the streets. Archer's instincts screamed at him to move—anywhere but here.

"Go, go, go!" he shouted, waving the men forwards.

The Stukas swooped down, their machine-guns spitting lethal streams of bullets into the packed streets. Soldiers dived into doorways and behind the wrecks of abandoned trucks, pressing their faces into the dust as the bullets raked the ground. Some weren't fast enough. Men collapsed, torn apart mid-stride, and their cries were quickly drowned beneath the roar of the engines.

Archer threw himself behind an overturned truck as a plane swept low. Its rounds tore through a group of men still in the open. The bodies jerked violently before crumpling to the ground. No one screamed. No one had the breath to. The noise of the war was too loud, too consuming.

The Stukas pulled up, and their engines roared as they prepared for another pass.

Archer stole a glance down towards the waterfront. Columns of men were moving in the same direction—towards the beaches, towards the escape. The queue. The final hope.

The sight was staggering.

Ahead of them, thousands of men stretched in an unbroken line towards the coast. No shouting, no arguing: just silence and the occasional shuffle of boots on cobble. The line was too long for Archer to see its end. It wound down towards the water, men with heads bowed, not from fear, but from the heavy quiet of having given everything. Slumped shoulders, faces hollow and unseeing. There was no talk, no glances exchanged—just the slow, mechanical movement of men who had nothing left but to follow the one in front, step by step, as if on a long and final march.

Jacks let out a low whistle. "Christ." He shifted his rifle, and his eyes remained wide as he took in the sight. "That's it, then. We're just...waiting."

A shell landed in the distance, followed by a dull roar as another section of Dunkirk crumbled. The queue barely reacted. No one turned to run. No one broke from the line. They just stood there, waiting for their turn. Surrendering to the situation.

Some men were half-asleep on their feet, swaying slightly as exhaustion took its toll. Others stared ahead with blank expressions as if they had already left this place in their minds, and their bodies were simply waiting for their turn to follow.

As the men headed to the end of the seemingly endless queue, Archer spotted a British officer—a captain—standing nearby, scanning the line with a practiced eye. Seizing the opportunity to gather information, Archer approached and offered a salute.

"Sir, Second Lieutenant Archer, 9th Battalion Greenmoors. Can you tell me what the situation is here?"

The captain returned the salute, his face etched with fatigue but his eyes sharp. "At ease, Lieutenant. We're organising the evacuation via the East Mole. It's a makeshift pier stretching nearly a mile out to sea. The beaches are being used too. The Navy's got anything that floats out in the channel." He strained his gaze along the long line of soldiers. "Just stay in line, and you'll likely end up at the Mole."

Archer glanced towards the sea. "Any idea how long this queue will take to clear, Sir?"

The captain sighed, running a hand over his unshaven chin. "Hard to say precisely. The queue stretches back for miles, and with Jerry harassing us every step of the way, it's slow going. Some of these poor bastards have been waiting two days or more." He glanced towards the distant ships. "But we're getting there. Yesterday, they reckon we shifted around 45,000 off the mole and the beaches combined. Now that we're starting to get our act together, and that's not amounting to much, things are moving a bit better."

He gave a weary half-smile, but his eyes were sharp. "Stick with the mole, Lieutenant. It's still your best bet. The beaches are full and pretty exposed to the Luftwaffe. Just stay put and be ready when the line moves. And it will."

Archer nodded, absorbing the information. "Understood, Sir."

The captain clapped Archer on the shoulder. "I'm sure you'll get through."

Archer turned to his men. They had survived the last few weeks during the retreat—fighting their way through enemy lines with nothing but grit and determination to carry them through. And now this. Another test of patience, of endurance. As they stood in line among the ragged mass of soldiers, it was impossible to shake the crushing sense of waiting—for what, none of them knew. They had fought and bled their way to the coast only to be left waiting like cattle to be herded onto ships.

The noise of the harbour was a distant, dull murmur beneath the sounds of men shuffling their feet and murmuring in low voices. The air hung thick with smoke and the sour tang of sweat, but there was something more than just exhaustion settling over them—a quiet resignation. They had made it this far, but there was no guarantee they'd see home.

Archer glanced at Jacks whose shoulders drooped under the weight of something bigger than his rifle. Cartwright, too, looked worn, though his jaw was set with the same stubborn determination that had kept with him through every desperate hour. They'd survived the retreat—pursued, outnumbered, outgunned. Yet now, they faced a new kind of challenge: the battle to keep hope alive while they waited, trapped between the sea and the enemy.

He could feel the tension in his men, see it in the way they glanced anxiously over their shoulders at every distant rumble of artillery or the low drone of aircraft. It gnawed at him too—the thought that after all they had endured, it could still end here, stuck in this coastal town, waiting for rescue that might never come.

Forcing himself to straighten, Archer squared his shoulders against the despair clawing at him. They had made it this far. Somehow, they'd make it the rest of the way. He glanced at his men, giving them a firm nod as if that simple gesture could shore up their resolve. They couldn't afford to let the fear show, not now. He had to hold them together—just a little longer.

"Fall in," he said quietly.

The men hesitated for only a second before stepping forwards. There was no choice but to wait.

Jacks exhaled slowly, and his eyes flicked between Archer and the distant horizon. "Feels wrong, doesn't it?" he muttered. "After everything...to just stand here."

Archer nodded but said nothing. It did feel wrong. After so many days of fighting, moving, surviving, the waiting was the hardest part.

He glanced back towards the town. The fires still burnt, licking hungrily at the shattered remnants of buildings; their glow stained the sky a sickly, shifting orange. Smoke billowed in dense columns, twisting and writhing as it was pulled skywards by the relentless heat. The distant roar of collapsing masonry echoed across the town, punctuated by the sharp crack of secondary explosions as stores ignited and sent plumes of shrapnel and debris scattering like lethal confetti.

Above, the Stukas wheeled in tight, predatory circles like vultures scenting blood. Their engines howled as they banked low over the rooftops, lining up for another attack. Archer could just make out the distinctive black crosses on their wings, silhouetted against the thick haze. The piercing scream of their sirens tore through the air. They'd been designed to unnerve and break the spirit of those below. It worked. Even the most seasoned men hunched their shoulders, bracing for the inevitable dive.

Shells continued to fall in sporadic bursts, tearing into the fragments of Dunkirk with merciless precision. Each impact sent a shockwave through the ground, rattling the teeth of the men standing in line and kicking up clouds of dust and sand that settled over everything like a morbid shroud. The waterfront was already choked with bodies—some of them laid out in rough lines that were covered with tarps, but others had simply been abandoned where they had fallen. Wounded men limped along the line, some clutching at hastily applied bandages, and others dragged comrades who were too weak to walk on their own.

Archer forced himself to take it all in, to commit the devastation to memory. He could feel the tension thrumming through the men around him as their hands clenched into fists or gripped rifles so tightly their knuckles turned white.

There was no dignity in this waiting—no honour in standing idle while the town was torn apart and while men died within earshot. They could do nothing but hope the line moved forwards.

For the first time, he wondered whether they might not make it. After everything—the retreat, the battles fought, the men lost—they were still at the mercy of the enemy's firepower and the pandemonium of the evacuation. They had survived every trial, fought their way through hell, and now they were caught like rats in a trap, penned in with the sea to their front and the Germans at their backs.

He looked around, meeting the eyes of his men one by one, offering a tight nod or a reassuring word. It felt hollow, but he did it anyway. He had to keep them together. A leader couldn't afford to falter even now. Jacks gave him a faint smile though it didn't reach his eyes, and Webb just nodded once with his face set in resigned determination.

One of the young lads—Saunders who was barely more than a boy...crikey, he was a similar age to himself—looked to him. The boy's eyes were wide with fear. Archer gave him a firm nod. It always amazed him how fear sat so plainly on Saunders' face, yet when the moment came, he was one of the most reliable and bravest men Archer had ever known.

Above them, the Stukas screamed down again, and Archer tightened his grip on his rifle, forcing himself to breathe. The sound was like death itself: relentless and unforgiving. They would hold on—they had no choice. If fate had brought them this far, it wouldn't abandon them now.

The light had faded, slipping away almost unnoticed as the line crept forwards in halting inches. Men shifted on their feet, shoulders sagging with exhaustion and hunger. The air grew cooler though the glow from the fires still hung over Dunkirk like a dying ember. Archer moved with his men, staying close, keeping count. He glanced at his watch. Nearly nine.

Jacks stepped up beside him with an unreadable expression, and his eyes fixed somewhere ahead in the dark. For a moment, neither spoke.

"Still feels wrong," Jacks muttered. "Standing here like this. Feels like...we're giving up."

Archer glanced at him, but Jacks wasn't looking back. His gaze was lost somewhere out in the darkness.

"It's not giving up," Archer said, though he knew his own voice lacked conviction. "We've done all we can. To get this far." There was a slight pause. "We'll get back Jacks, I'm sure of that!"

Jacks exhaled slowly. "Mallory would have hated this.

Hated standing still, I mean. Always had to be doing something—fixing gear, checking the lads. Couldn't sit still for more than five minutes." He gave a faint smile. "He was always barking orders at me. Didn't matter that I had the stripes. Like he couldn't help himself."

He let out a low chuckle, but it was hollow; it was the kind that lingered and faded like smoke. "We'd been together since—blimey—'30. I wasn't long in, and he was a corporal. My section commander at the time." Jacks' thoughts drifted to distant times as he shuffled along in the line. "He just had that knack for it, y'know? Like he knew what was needed even when the rest of us were floundering."

Archer stayed silent, just listening. Jacks' voice softened, the words tumbling out like he'd been holding them in too long. "We'd get leave now and then. He'd drag me to his sister's pub, say it was my turn to buy but somehow end up paying anyway. Daft sod. Always looking after me even when I didn't want him to. We got into a few scraps too, like when we were in Palestine. He just knew what to do every time. Many a man owes his life to Mallory."

He paused. His gaze was fixed somewhere in the middle distance as if seeing something Archer couldn't. "Don't reckon I'll ever get used to not hearing him. Like he's just stepped away and will be back any minute, telling me I've got my kit all wrong or that I've scuffed my boots. Bloody perfectionist."

Archer glanced at Jacks, taking in the tension coiled in his shoulders, the way he was biting down on whatever grief was clawing its way to the surface. He knew the feeling well enough; he knew how it twisted inside, grinding at the edges of resolve.

Jacks took a shaky breath and looked down at his boots, scuffing one on the ground. "Didn't think it'd end like that. One minute he was right there with us, next he was just...gone. I keep thinking maybe he made it, y'know? Maybe he found somewhere to lie low, just waiting for the chance to slip through. But...hell, I don't know. Could be dead. Could be captured. Could be anything."

Jacks wiped at his eyes with the back of his hand and gave a tight nod. "Yeah. Reckon that's it. Couldn't help himself."

The line moved again, shuffling forwards by inches. Archer kept his silence, letting Jacks have the moment. A part of him felt hollow too, thinking of Pembroke and the bond they'd forged in the bedlam of the retreat. Men like Pembroke didn't break, didn't fold under pressure. But the retreat had been merciless, and the men it claimed were the kind that always seemed untouchable—indestructible—right until they weren't.

The line inched on, and the night deepened, but the sense of loss remained—thick in the air, choking and bitter, like the ash of Dunkirk.

Archer nodded, his voice calm and steady. "He just wanted to make sure things were done right. Couldn't sit still, always had to be doing something. You know Mallory—if there's a chance, he'll take it. He's too bloody stubborn to just give up. If he's out there, he's finding a way through."

Jacks glanced at him, a flicker of hope fighting to break through his guarded expression. "You reckon?"

Archer gave a tight nod, forcing himself to sound confident. "I do. Mallory's the toughest bastard I know. If anyone's got a chance of making it, it's him. He'll turn up. Probably shouting at us for leaving him behind."

That got a faint smile from Jacks—just a twitch of his lips, but it was something. Archer squeezed Jacks' shoulder briefly before they moved on. The line crept forwards inch by inch. Darkness settled deeper around them.

Silence fell between them again, broken only by the shuffle of boots on the road. A few men lit cigarettes, the glow of the embers briefly illuminating tired, haunted faces.

Archer hesitated, glancing at Jacks. It wasn't like him to voice his thoughts, but the gravity of it was dragging him down, and if anyone would understand, it was Jacks. "I keep thinking about Pembroke," he said quietly.

Jacks glanced at him, a flicker of surprise crossing his face. "Didn't know him long, did you?"

"No," Archer admitted. "But... he wasn't like the others. Didn't just see me as the fresh-faced officer straight out of training. Treated me like I was worth something. Even trusted me enough to let me make calls when it mattered."

"That's rare," Jacks said. "Most officers don't trust anyone. Especially the new lads."

Archer gave a faint smile, his gaze drifting over the line of men shuffling forwards. "Funny thing is, I met him once before. Didn't even know it till he mentioned it when I first joined the battalion. Played cricket against him when I was at school. We were just lads, and I had no idea who he was. He was this big, older bloke—already confident and sure of himself. I knocked him all over the park that afternoon. Never forgot that day was my best ever score. Just found it strange that all these years later, we ended up here—fighting side by side."

Jacks gave a low chuckle. "Reckon he must've hated you for that. He likes his cricket does Mr. Pembroke...always trying to get the lads to play."

"Looks like it," Archer said, the ghost of a smile lingering. "I didn't realise until he joked about it one evening. Told me he'd seen me somewhere before, then it came to him—'you were that cocky little batsman who knocked me all over the park.' Didn't know whether to laugh or be embarrassed. Guess it didn't matter in the end."

Jacks nodded slowly, his expression softening. "Strange how life works, eh? You think you know your path, and next thing, you're sharing rations with some bloke you gave a thrashing to on the cricket pitch years ago."

Archer nodded. "Aye. Just...makes you think. He was more than just a good officer. He was a good man."

Jacks gave a reassuring squeeze to Archer's shoulder. "He knew he could rely on you. That counts for a lot. Reckon he'd have been proud of how you've kept us together."

Archer didn't answer and just gave a small nod, letting the line move them forwards as the night pressed in tighter around them.

Jacks nodded slowly. "Stupid bastards. They wouldn't quit even when they knew it was done."

Archer let the words hang there. The line moved again, another few paces forwards, and the night closed in even tighter, swallowing the sound of distant explosions. It was a constant, repetitive pattern.

Jacks gave a bitter chuckle, rubbing at his stubbled jaw. "I'll put a bob on that their probably together working their way back Sir. I know they'll make it through somehow."

Archer looked up at the sky, the dark expanse stretching out over the sea, and the stars flickered weakly through the haze. "I hope you're right Jacks."

Silence settled over them again, but it was softer now, less raw. Jacks wiped at his eyes although he wouldn't admit it, and Archer just let him be. There wasn't much more to say.

The line was moving again: a slow but constant shuffle through the darkness. It had shifted like this for hours, inching forwards not from will, but from the numb rhythm of having nowhere else to go. Men moved in silence. Heads down. Shoulders hunched against the chill. The occasional mutter was only broken by the steady rhythm of footsteps on sand and gravel.

Archer glanced around, making sure his men stayed together, and put a hand on Jacks' shoulder, giving it a light squeeze. "We'll make it. Somehow."

Jacks just nodded. The weariness was etched deep into his face, but there was a flicker of resolve there too—something that hadn't yet been snuffed out by the weeks of retreat and bloodshed. They kept moving, surrounded by the weary, broken mass of men, stepping forwards, yard by yard towards the promise of the sea.

As darkness began to soften, the line moved forwards faster. The anxiety of the German return hung threateningly as a pale, grey light seeped into the sky, pushing back the night in slow, reluctant strokes.

Archer rubbed his gritty eyes, exhaustion pressing down on him like an anchor. He glanced at Jacks who gave him a weary nod. No words left to share, just the mutual relief that they were moving at last.

They rounded a bend in the path, and suddenly the Mole stretched out ahead of them: long, narrow, and seemingly endless, reaching out into the Channel like a lifeline to the world beyond. The sea lay calm and flat. It seemed like a mirror of dull steel reflecting the faint glow of dawn. Archer squinted towards the far end of the Mole. A ship, dark, bulky, loomed there, with smoke curling from its funnel into the pale sky. Men were already moving towards it, their figures sharp and black against the first glimmers of light.

Archer's stomach twisted at the sight. Hope, distant and fragile, flickered for a moment, but it was tempered by the gnawing thought, would they make it before the Luftwaffe returned, turning hope into despair?

Jacks exhaled slowly, the tension in his shoulders loosening just a fraction. "Blimey. Didn't think we'd make it this far."

Archer couldn't quite let himself believe it yet, even as he watched the men filing along the narrow pier, shadows hunched and silent.

There was no cheering, no celebration—just a silent, relentless push to reach the ship before the sun revealed them fully to the enemy.

Somewhere behind them, Dunkirk still burnt, black smoke clawing at the sky, but from here, it seemed almost detached—like another world, one they'd barely escaped.

The waves lapped gently against the stone supports of the Mole, hissing and whispering as if mocking the chaos that had brought them here. A few men were already on board, disappearing into the ship's dark hold while others crowded near the gangway, anxious to board before some new disaster struck. Archer counted his men—still together, still moving, still alive.

A distant rumble broke the fragile stillness, and he tensed, glancing back the way they had come. Nothing yet, just the low hum of engines far away, but it set his teeth on edge. The sky was lightening, and streaks of bruised pink and grey was beginning to thread through the smoke. Archer swallowed the knot in his throat, feeling that faint surge of hope—just a little farther. A little longer.

Jacks gave him a nudge. "You hear that? Bloody gulls."

Archer managed a thin smile as he picked up the faint, shrill cries over the lapping waves. A bizarre contrast: nature carrying on as if war had never come. He took a long breath, letting the cool, salty air fill his lungs. It didn't quite chase away the grime in his throat, but it helped.

Webb came up beside them, glancing warily at the approaching dawn. "Feels too bloody easy. Like it's a trap."

Archer didn't reply. He felt it too—that uneasy prickle along his spine: the instinct that warned him against hope. But the ship was there, solid and real, and the men kept moving towards it. He gave Webb a slight nod. It was as much reassurance as he could muster.

At the head of the line, officers were shouting orders,

guiding the men onto the ship in steady, organised groups. The hull loomed ahead: a dark, hulking shape wrapped in mist and smoke. The grey silhouette of the destroyer took shape through the drifting smoke, her lines sleek and purposeful. No name, just a pennant number H18 stencilled on her side. He'd never been so glad to see anything in his life.

He glanced at Jacks who gave him a tight smile as if daring to believe it was real. "We're almost there, Sir."

Archer just nodded, gripping his rifle sling a little tighter as they edged closer.

First light spilt over the horizon, catching the water and turning it to molten silver. For a moment, it almost looked peaceful—just men boarding a ship and heading home.

But Archer knew better.

The war wasn't done with them yet. Not until they were out on the water and away from this damned place. He kept his eyes on the ship, forcing himself to focus, to push down the creeping dread that still clawed at him.

The line moved again, and his men took the final steps of the Mole and onto the gang plank. Archer and Jacks stood to the side as they guided each man in their group on the plank. Finally, it was their turn. Jacks led, and Archer followed, the boards creaking underfoot. The smell of salt water was stronger here, and it mingled with engine fumes and the rank sweat of men.

Archer didn't look back. There was no point. They were almost there, almost out. All they had to do was board and wait for the engines to turn over and to feel the deck lurch as the ship pulled away. As Archer stepped aboard, he asked, "What's this ship called?"

"HMS Sabre, Sir," the rating replied, pride flickering through the exhaustion. "Finest destroyer in the British navy."

"Let's hope she makes it," Archer muttered.

The rating straightened, a spark of something fierce in his eyes.

"She will, Sir. This is our fifth trip. Mr Chalmers says we've got over fifteen hundred men off so far."

Archer gave a faint nod, the weight of it settling in his chest. The deck thrummed beneath his boots—steady, strong.

Behind him: fire, gunfire, France. Ahead: home. For the first time in days, he let his eyes close. Not to sleep. Not yet. Just to remember what peace might feel like.

Just a little farther. Just a little longer.

Chapter 20

The engines of HMS Sabre rumbled low as she cut through the final stretch of water, the battered ship edging closer to Ramsgate. The coastline welcomed them through the haze—blurred and indistinct at first but sharpening as they drew nearer. Archer leant against the railing, his eyes heavy, but he couldn't tear his gaze from the sight of England—solid, home ground after days of fire and fury.

Around him, the men stirred. Those who were too weak to stand were helped to their feet by mates or naval ratings. A few whispered to each other, but most just stood silently with pale faces and hollow eyes. Their bodies swayed with the subtle motion of the ship. Jacks tilted his helmet back and glanced at Archer.

"Bloody hell, Sir. We're here. Good old Blighty."

Archer didn't reply. He could feel the weight in his chest easing, the tension bleeding away with each yard closer to the pier. The faint murmur of the shore grew louder; voices shouted orders, engines rumbled and the distant clatter of stretchers on cobbles.

The Sabre slowed, and her engines dropped to an idle as she nosed up to the quayside. A gangplank was swiftly lowered, clanging onto the stone dock, and the men crowded forwards, eager to be off. Nurses in crisp white uniforms moved through the throng, followed by orderlies and St John Ambulance men.

"Right, lads!" bellowed a petty officer, his voice rough and commanding. "Stay steady. No rush now. We'll get you all ashore. The wounded will go first."

Ambulances lined the quay with their rear doors open, waiting for the worst of the wounded. A medical officer strode forwards with his clipboard in hand, calmly issuing orders to his staff. Archer watched. and an eerie silence fell over the ship and the dock as the first of the wounded were carefully guided down the gangplank—some so swathed in bandages, they barely looked human. A naval rating moved briskly to help, murmuring quiet reassurances that barely reached the men's ears.

As the crew began guiding the walking wounded off the deck, Jacks nudged Archer, pointing at a line of vehicles. "Looks like they've got half the bloody county here to see us in."

Archer gave a faint nod. Trucks and ambulances stretched down the quay as far as he could see. Soldiers and civilians alike were lending a hand, unloading supplies and preparing to move the rescued troops. The unmistakable smell of disinfectant and petrol hung thick in the air, but there was no lingering stench hiding behind it anymore.

The padre came over to where Archer was watching the walking wounded was followed by rescued soldiers who stepped onto solid ground at last. An officer came down with the first group and immediately started organising the men across the quayside, lining them up along the front of a warehouse. More and more men filtered their way towards him, drawn by his steady, commanding presence.

The padre stood beside Archer, and his gaze fixed on the men filing past. He gave a weary, bittersweet smile.

"They've been beaten," he said quietly, almost to himself. "But look at them...still proud. Still soldiers. Whatever's next, they've earnt the right to hold their heads high."

Archer glanced at him, taking in the padre's haunted expression. Before he could think of a reply, an NCO with the officer called out.

"2nd Battalion, Royal Fusiliers, fall in over here!"

The men started to fall in straight from the gangplank, their movements stiff and weary but driven by a sense of relief and duty.

Archer had observed another officer, red-banded and clearly a staff officer.

Archer turning to Jacks, "Get the lads together. It'll be our turn soon. I'm going down there to find out what's happening."

With that, Archer—followed by the padre—made his way to the gangplank. Both men made their excuses as they pushed through the waiting soldiers. They finally reached the bottom of the gangplank and spotted the staff officer, a captain, standing with a clipboard.

Archer approached the captain. "Sir, I'm Second Lieutenant Archer of the 9th Greenmoors, and this is Captain Cartwright, our padre."

"Good evening, Lieutenant. Captain." The officer, smart and elegant in his uniform, could have been at a cocktail party for all the fuss he made. His response was polite, almost too polite, for what was going on around them.

"Sir, we've collected a bit of a mixed bag along the way. What do we need to do once we're off the ship?"

The staff officer consulted his clipboard briefly before addressing Archer.

"Lieutenant Archer, upon disembarkation, you'll lead your men to the reception area designated for the 48th Infantry Division. There, you will receive food, medical attention, and further instructions. For the attached personnel from other units, direct them to the reassembly point over there," he said, pointing towards a large tent marked 'Reception Centre'. "They'll be processed and reassigned accordingly."

Archer nodded, appreciating the clarity amidst the confusion.

"Understood, Sir. We'll proceed as directed."

The officer offered a brief, encouraging smile.

"Welcome home, gentlemen." He held out his hand, Archer took it with a tired grip, but the captain held him firmly. "Lieutenant, you've done your country proud."

Archer turned and looked at the padre with a small smile of

bemusement before glancing back up at the ship. He signalled for Jacks to bring the men down. As they came down the gangplank, Archer met each one, directing the men of the Greenmoors to one side and the others to the opposite side.

Finally, RSM Jennings appeared, and Archer stepped forwards to meet him.

"Mr Jennings," Archer's tone was steady and serious. "This, I'm afraid, is where we part company." He pointed towards the reception area at the end of the dock. "If you can take this group over there, they'll get you sorted—food, medical treatment, and get you all on your way."

Jennings said nothing at first, but turned, stepped in front of the small group, and called the men to attention. Then he turned back and marched towards Archer.

"Troop ready for inspection, Sir!" He held a firm salute over his right eye, his body rigid and unyielding despite its weariness.

Archer responded immediately. Standing tall, shoulders upright, he returned a sharp salute. "Thank you, Mr Jennings."

Archer approached the eleven men standing at attention in front of him. He hesitated. Suddenly, he felt at a loss for words when he noticed that the wounded men who had travelled with them hadn't gone to the medical teams with the casualties, but they'd remained with their comrades. Archer hesitated for a moment longer, his throat tightening as he locked eyes with each one of them: the survivors, the men who had made it through the fire.

He took a breath and immediately told them to stand at ease, his voice rougher than he intended.

He took a deep breath and forced his voice to stay steady.

"I'm grateful to each and every one of you," he began, his gaze moving from face to face. "You've carried out your duty to the best traditions of the British Army—through hell and high water. You never faltered, not once. You made it here because you stood together, and that's something no one can ever take from you."

A silence hung over the group. The men barely dared to breathe. RSM Jennings stepped forwards. His movements were still precise despite his worn frame. He reached up to his shoulder and carefully unfastened the cloth insignia from his epaulette, holding it in his hand for a moment before offering it to Archer.

"Sir," Jennings said, his voice rough but firm. "Take this— our way of saying thank you. You led us through, and that's something we won't forget."

Archer hesitated, looking down at the insignia. Then he reached out and took it with a nod of respect. One by one, the men followed Jennings' example—each man stepping forwards to remove his own regimental insignia and press it into Archer's hand as they shook his. Some muttered quiet words of gratitude or pride. Others simply nodded, eyes glistening despite their efforts to maintain composure.

By the time the last man had handed over his insignia, Archer was holding a small pile of cloth in his hand. He looked at the collection of insignia. His jaw tightened as he swallowed down the emotion that threatened to rise.

Then Matthews stepped forwards: the last man. He hesitated, and his gaze fixed on Archer's face before slowly unfastening his own insignia from his epaulette. Holding it in his hand, he glanced at it briefly, almost as if weighing the memory that it carried. Then he reached out and pressed it into Archer's palm.

For a moment, neither man spoke. The unspoken bond between them was stronger than words could ever express. Matthews gave a faint, weary smile, and kept his voice low and steady. "It's been a hell of a ride, and my honour to serve you,

Sir."

Archer managed a nod, gripping the insignia tightly. "It has," he replied, the words thick in his throat. "Thank you, Matthews. I'll hold onto these—and I'll remember."

With that, the men dismissed themselves and began walking towards the designated area.

Archer, still with a lump in his throat and almost a tear in his eye, gave a grunt and called out, trying to hide the emotion he felt.

"Corporal Jacks, get the men ready—we're moving!"

"Yes, Sir!" Jacks' response was, as always, immediate and firm. "Lads, fall in!"

The scuffle of tired feet scraped along the stone and concrete quay as the men moved around. Then Jacks, with the voice of a barrack room corporal, called out.

"Battalion! Battalion—shun!"

The staff officer Archer had been speaking to a few moments earlier raised his head and stared at the group—all seven of them. He turned to the lance corporal acting as his clerk, his expression incredulous.

"Did he just say battalion?"

With Jacks' command still hanging in the air, the men straightened as best they could, shifting into a loose semblance of order. Jacks glanced over his shoulder at Archer, then bellowed out with surprising force, given how exhausted he looked. "Right turn!"

The men pivoted awkwardly, some struggling with stiff joints and bruised muscles, but they all managed the manoeuvre.

Jacks gave a wink of approval before taking a breath and calling out, "By the right—quick march!"

The smart line stepped off, their boots scuffing on the stone quay. Their movements were less than perfect but resolute. As they passed the captain, Jacks called out, "Eyes—right!"

The men's heads snapped to the right, and they fixed their eyes on the officer as they marched past. Archer moved his rifle across his chest, touching it with his arm in a crisp, formal salute. The captain, catching the salute and the unwavering determination on their faces, smartly returned it with a faint, approving smile breaking through his stern demeanour.

"That's the stuff, boys!"

Archer fell in with his men. His steps matched theirs, and the steady rhythm of boots on stone almost hypnotic. As they moved along the quay, his mind wandered through the faces of the men they'd left behind: Richards at the bridge, Chambers and Bell at the farmhouse, Harding, Dixon, and Carter somewhere in the chaos of Cassel. Too many to name, too many to remember all at once.

His jaw tightened, the hard, raw ache of survival pressing into his chest. They had come through it, scraped and battered, but they had come through.

Yet there was still no word of Pembroke or Mallory. That knowledge grated at him more than he cared to admit. These men he'd come to trust and work with...there was a small hope they had seen it through together. The thought they might not have made it was like a knife twisting deeper with every step.

He glanced to his right, catching Jacks' eye for a moment, and managed a nod. They kept marching. Every step carried them farther from the fire and smoke of France.

For now, they were home.

That would have to be enough.

Authors Note

In *Fire and Fury*, I've tried to shine a light on some of the remarkable acts of sacrifice that took place during the dark days of World War II, many of them overlooked or forgotten. The story is grounded in the perspective of the ordinary soldier, aiming to capture the visceral, human experience of those caught in the chaos of battle.

Rather than focusing on the precise details of any one real life battalion in France in 1940, a task that would demand a level of historical specificity beyond my reach, I created the fictional 9th Greenmoor Light Infantry (GLI). This gave me the freedom to tell a good story, one that I hope is engaging, dramatic, and accessible, while still honouring the spirit of those times. My aim was to explore those desperate days through an authentic soldier's perspective, drawing inspiration from the real courage and sacrifice of men who fought to hold the line at places like Cassel, ordinary men facing impossible odds, whose actions deserve to be remembered.

In my first book, *Under Fire, Under Command*, I introduced the Greenmoor Light Infantry and its characters, from the scared young private to the well-educated commander, so I could send them off to do the brave deeds that a real "boys' own" story deserves. While researching that book, I discovered the incredible, and perhaps overlooked, fight for Cassel. Like many World War II enthusiasts, I'd always known that the battles for the BEF went beyond the beaches at Dunkirk, but learning about Cassel's desperate stand convinced me it had to be the heart of this second book.

Cassel, perched atop Mont Cassel in northern France, was more than just a picturesque town in May 1940, it became a natural fortress and a place of sacrifice. Its steep hilltop position commanded views over the surrounding plains, and its cobbled streets, thick stone buildings, and narrow approaches gave defenders a rare advantage in close-quarters combat, especially against tanks and mechanised infantry.

The decision to defend Cassel was made by General Alan Brooke, commander of II Corps, who would later become Commander-in-Chief, Home Forces, and ultimately Chief of the Imperial General Staff. Recognising the strategic importance of the high ground, Brooke ordered the 145th Infantry Brigade to hold the town as part of a defensive screen protecting the Dunkirk perimeter. Cassel, alongside strongpoints like Wormhoudt, Hazebrouck, and Bergues, formed a vital chain of resistance, holding back the German advance while the evacuation at Dunkirk, Operation Dynamo, was underway.

The stand at Cassel and other places achieved their purpose. It delayed the German timetable, forcing the enemy to fight for days over ground they had expected to bypass. In doing so, the defenders bought precious time for the Dunkirk evacuation, ultimately allowing more than 300,000 Allied troops to escape to Britain. The defence of Cassel was led by the 145th Infantry Brigade, the core of an ad hoc force known as "Somerforce," commanded by Brigadier Nigel Somerset. Cassel, along with other key strongpoints like Wormhoudt and Bergues, formed a vital part of the defensive screen designed to delay the German advance and protect the Dunkirk evacuation. The men sent to hold Cassel came from a mix of units, reflecting the composite nature of the British forces during this critical phase of the campaign. The backbone of the defence was the 2nd Battalion, Gloucestershire Regiment, and the 4th Battalion, Oxfordshire and Buckinghamshire Light Infantry. They were supported by artillery from the 140th (5th London) Field Regiment, Royal Artillery, sappers from the Royal Engineers, and elements of the East Riding Yeomanry, the Royal Army Service Corps, and the Royal Army Medical Corps.

In this novel, the Greenmoor Light Infantry is an amalgam inspired by these real men. Though they lacked heavy weapons and armour, their orders were clear, hold Cassel at all costs.

And that's exactly what they did—both in the story, and in the real battle.

From 25 to 29 May 1940, the defenders of Cassel withstood relentless assaults from elements of the SS Totenkopf Division—one of the Waffen-SS's most brutal and fanatical formations, supported by infantry and armour from other German units. Day and night, artillery and mortar fire pounded the hilltop town, reducing many of its stone buildings to rubble. Yet the British troops held firm, fighting street by street, house by house, often reduced to brutal close quarters combat amid the ruins. By the fourth day, Cassel was fully encircled. Communications were severed. Ammunition was running low. And still, they refused to surrender. With no prospect of relief and no route of retreat, their final actions were marked by grim determination and extraordinary courage. Only a handful managed to escape under cover of darkness. The majority were either killed in action or captured—many of them exhausted, wounded, and out of food and water.

One of the more astonishing accounts tells of Regimental Sergeant Major Albert Hawtin, who on 28 May 1940 leapt from the first floor of a building and dropped a Mills bomb through the hatch of a German tank. This act of fearless improvisation inspired the character of CSM Dixon in my story. Unlike my fictional version, the real RSM survived the war as a prisoner of war.

For the sake of the story, I have embellished or reimagined some details—such as Archer and his men being left to defend the retreating battalion by holding the Rue de Bergues, a real street lined with townhouses, shops, and the other buildings you'd expect in a town of the period. Whether the Germans were truly forced up that particular street is, I must admit, a little author's licence. There was indeed serious and hard fighting in the streets and between buildings, but the specifics are hard to pin down. As I've said before, this is not a strict historical account, but a story inspired by the events between 25 and 29 May 1940.

While the defence of Cassel forms a large part of this novel, *Fire and Fury* also follows what came after. For the surviving men of the Greenmoor Light Infantry, the battle did not end with the fall of the town. Their desperate breakout, through villages and shattered countryside, is fictional but inspired by the real attempts made by scattered groups of British soldiers to reach the coast. Some made it to Dunkirk. Others did not. In writing their journey, I wanted to explore not just the fight itself, but also the fear, exhaustion, and quiet determination that defined so many men's experiences in those final days of the campaign in France.

The Greenmoor Light Infantry, my fictional creation, stands in for the many real units that fought with quiet bravery and grim determination in those desperate final days in northern France. Writing the GLI gave me the freedom to explore the soldier's experience with emotional depth while staying rooted in historical truth. Though their names are imagined, their courage is drawn directly from the men who stood fast at Cassel—knowing the odds and holding the line anyway.

The defence of Cassel came at a terrible cost. The British 145th Infantry Brigade, Somerforce, at the heart of the stand, endured devastating losses in the face of overwhelming odds. The 2nd Battalion, Gloucestershire Regiment, suffered 5 officers and 132 men killed, with 472 taken prisoner. The 4th Battalion, Oxfordshire and Buckinghamshire Light Infantry, faced similar devastation, over half the battalion was lost, with 21 officers and more than 180 men captured, 20 of whom later died in captivity. The gunners of the 367 Battery of the 140th (5th London) Army Field Regiment were almost entirely wiped out, of their number, only three men reached Dunkirk. 102 were killed or wounded, and 216 were taken prisoner.

Few escaped the German encirclement. Brigadier Nigel Somerset, commander of Somerforce, was himself captured, an extraordinary testament to the determination and sacrifice of those who held the line until the very end.

These figures underscore the brutal nature of the fighting and the staggering price paid by the defenders of Cassel and other strongpoints. Their stand bought precious time for the Dunkirk evacuation and helped shape the course of history. It is their spirit I have tried to honour in the story of the Greenmoor Light Infantry.

In a small way, I hope that my story—set around these events— pays tribute to those brave, brave men who stood against impossible odds. It was their knowledge of the likely outcome, yet their determination to fight on regardless, that makes their sacrifice all the more remarkable.

Thank You for Reading

If Under Fire and Fury kept you turning pages, please consider leaving a review on Amazon. Even a brief review helps other readers discover the book and supports independent authors like me to keep writing.

Want to know more?

Visit **www.richardabasquill.com** to explore the history behind the Greenmoor Light Infantry, get updates on upcoming books, and access exclusive content.

Your support means everything.

Richard A. Basquill

Printed in Dunstable, United Kingdom